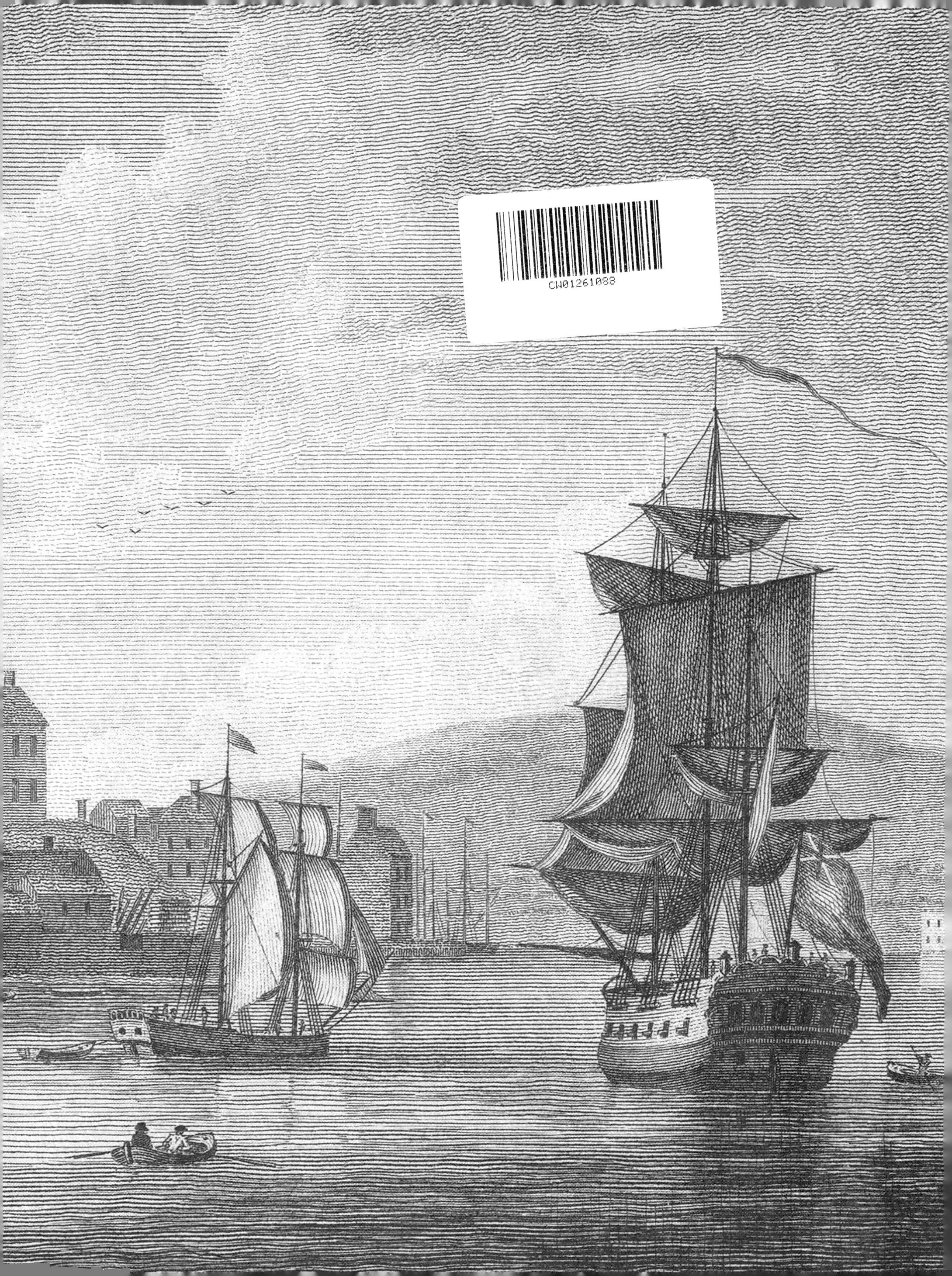

CW01261088

ISLAND CITY
The Archaeology of Derry~Londonderry

ISLAND CITY

The Archaeology of Derry~Londonderry

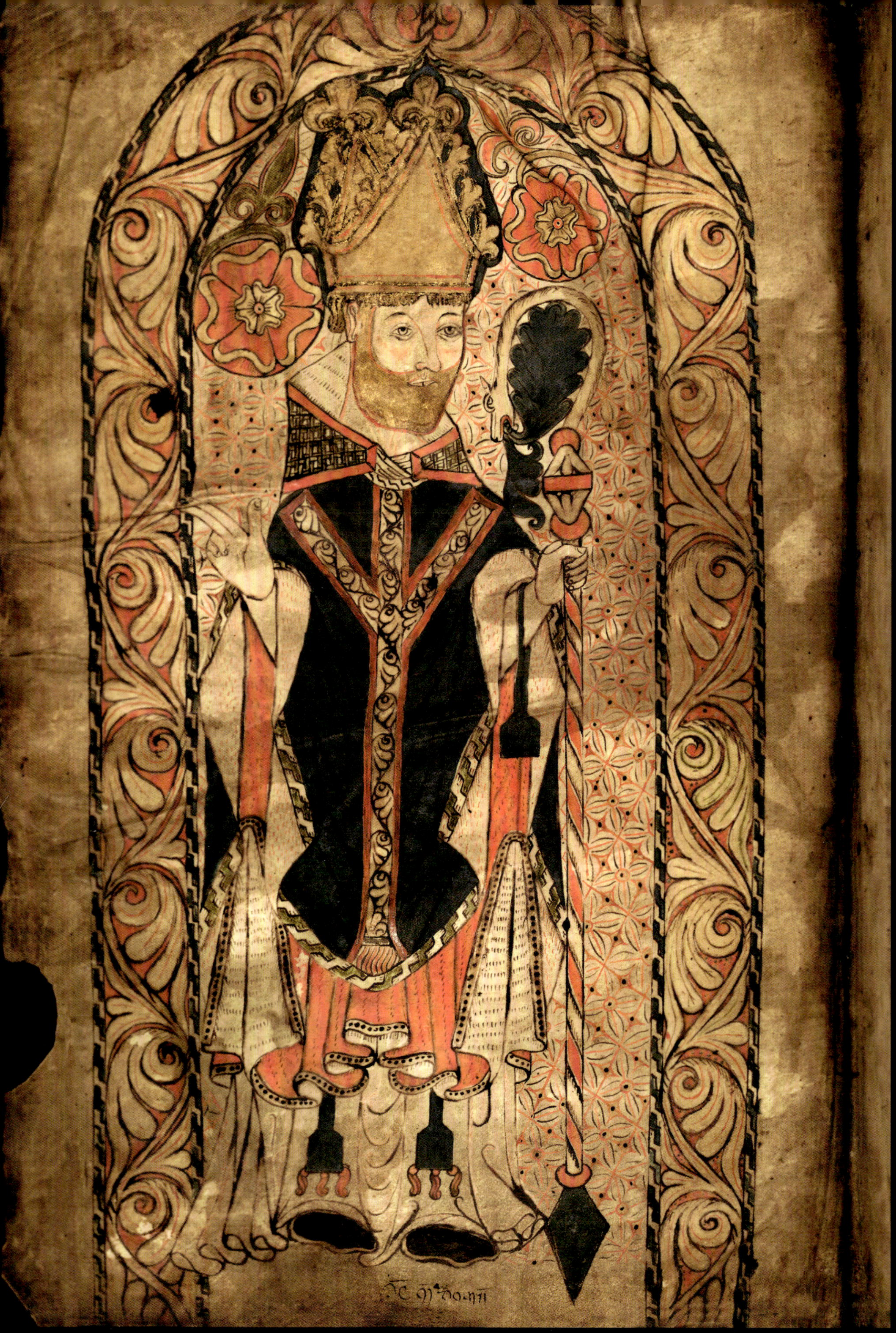

ISLAND CITY
The Archaeology of Derry~Londonderry

Ruairí Ó Baoill
Photography by Tony Corey

Northern Ireland Environment Agency & Derry City Council

BUILT HERITAGE
NORTHERN IRELAND ENVIRONMENT AGENCY
Waterman House, 5-33 Hill Street, Belfast BT12LA
www.doeni.gov.uk/niea/built-home

&

DERRY CITY COUNCIL
HERITAGE & MUSEUM SERVICE
Foyle Valley Railway Museum, Foyle Road, Derry, BT486SQ
www.derrycity.gov.uk/Museums/Heritage-and-Museum-Service

Published by the Northern Ireland Environment Agency (Built Heritage)
and Derry City Council 2013

ISBN 978-1-907053-67-2

Design, layout and maps copyright © NIEA, 2013
All images copyright © NIEA, 2013, except pages vii; ix; x; xiv; 2; 40;
59; 60t; 60b; 61t; 72t; 77; 88; 89; 91t; 93t; 94; 95; 96t; 98; 99; 109; 114;
118; 119; 124t; 124b; 125; 126; 128t; 128b; 136-137; 140.

Text: Ruairi Ó Baoill
Photography by Tony Corey (except where otherwise stated)

General Editors: Terence Reeves-Smyth (NIEA) & Paul Logue (NIEA)

Designed by April Sky Design (Colourpoint), Newtownards

All rights reserved. No part of this publication may be reproduced, stored in a
retrieval system, or transmitted in any form or by any means, electronic, mechanical,
photocopying, recording or otherwise without the permission of the publisher.

Applications for reproduction should be made in writing to Built Heritage, NIEA,
Waterman House, 5-33 Hill Street, Belfast BT12LA

Front Cover: Detail from hand-coloured etching 'Londonderry' attributed to Henry Brocas senior, c1800
Rere Cover: Staffordshire ware found on excavation in Londonderry
Page i: View of the Royal Bastion and city walls with former bishop's palace and cathedral in background.
Page ii: Image from the 'Life of Colum Cille' by Maghnus Ó Domhnaill, the Bardic poet, composed in 1532.
Copy on seal skin parchment c.1540-50 (Bodleian Library, Oxford)
Page xi: Detail from 'View of Londonderry', by Jacob Henry Connop, 1863 (Private Collection)
Page x: Aerial view of Londonderry taken by Professor St. Joseph in 1952 (Cambridge University Collection)
Page xii: The Nave of St. Columb's Cathedral

*Dedicated to the Memory of
Annie Barnes
(1935-2012)
&
Tom Robinson
(1957-2009)*

Acknowledgements

This book was commissioned by the Built Heritage Division of the Northern Ireland Environment Agency (NIEA) and by Derry City Council. The author is grateful to the staff of the NIEA: Built Heritage, notably Paul Logue, for final editing of the book and much other assistance during the project; Terence Reeves-Smyth, for final editing, assembling images and laying out the book's design; Tony Corey and Gail Pollock for most of the photographs in the book, many of them specially undertaken by NIEA; Rosemary McConkey, Christina O'Regan, Rhonda Robinson, Emma Mc Bride and Kim Rooney. At Derry City Council I am grateful to Roisín Doherty, Head of Heritage and Museum Service; Margaret Edwards, Education Officer and Tony Boyle, Collections Assistant. Thanks also to the Centre for Archaeological Fieldwork, School of Geography, Archaeology and Palaeoecology, Queen's University Belfast, particularly Dr. Colm Donnelly, Ruth Logue, Cormac McSparron, Dr. Philip Macdonald, Naomi Carver, Dr. Emily Murray, Sarah Gormley and Lorraine Barry of the School of Geography.

Others I would like to thank include Brian Scott, for the initial editing of the book; Philip Armstrong, for providing inspired reconstruction drawings that bring the life the important periods in the story of the city; Brian Lacey, for all the information about his excavations in the city, for pre-publication access to his forthcoming book on Medieval and Monastic Derry and for generously sharing his vast knowledge of Derry. The Dean St Columb's Cathedral, William Morton and Ian Bartlett kindly allowed access to the important objects on display in the Chapter House of the Cathedral; NAC Ltd, Farrimond MacManus Ltd, Gahan & Long Ltd and ADS Ltd for supplying information about their excavations in and around the city. Thanks also to Isabel Bennett, Professor Audrey Horning, Eoin Lennon, Nick Brannon, Cormac Bourke, Robert Heslip, Philip Gililand, Michael Boyle, Roy Hamilton, Patricia and Conal Óg.

Contents

Acknowledgements vi
Foreword xi
Preface xiii
Introduction 1

Prehistory 5
    Mesolithic Settlers 6
    The Neolithic Period 10
    Thornhill 19
    The Bronze Age 25
    The Iron Age 34

The Early Christian Period 37
    Early Christian Derry 39
    The Grianán of Aileach 41
    Raths, Cashels and Crannogs 44
    Ecclesiastical Monuments 48
        St Colum Cille's (Columba's) Church in Derry 54

The Medieval Period 57
The Development of Medieval Derry 58
        The Knight's Effigy 64
        Bishop Street Excavations of 2013 - the Medieval Deposits 66

Island City. The Archaeology of Derry~Londonderry

    St. Colum Cille (St. Columba) and his Churches Derry 71
    Medieval Sites in the Vicinity of Derry 77
    Derry from the Sixteenth to Early Seventeenth Centuries 81
        The Many Faces of a Cardinal 84
    Late 16th and Early 17th-Century Sites in the Vicinity of Derry 90
        The Glengalliagh Bell 97
        Foldouts: *Derry in the Medieval Period*
                Sir Henry Docwra's Town

The Plantation City of Londonderry 101
    The Walls of Derry~Londonderry 102
    Gates and Bastions 105
    Archaeological Investigations Around the Walls 121
    The Layout of the New City 123
    St Columb's Cathedral 127
    The Houses within the Walled City 135
    Life in the Walled City 140
        Bishop Street Excavations of 2013: The Skeletons 152
    The 'Great Siege' of Londonderry 156
    Seventeenth-century Sites in the Vicinity of Londonderry 163
        Foldout: *The Siege of Londonderry 1698*

Epilogue
    Epilogue 167
Bibliography 173
Notes 187
Illustration Credits 189
Appendix 190
Index of People and Places 192

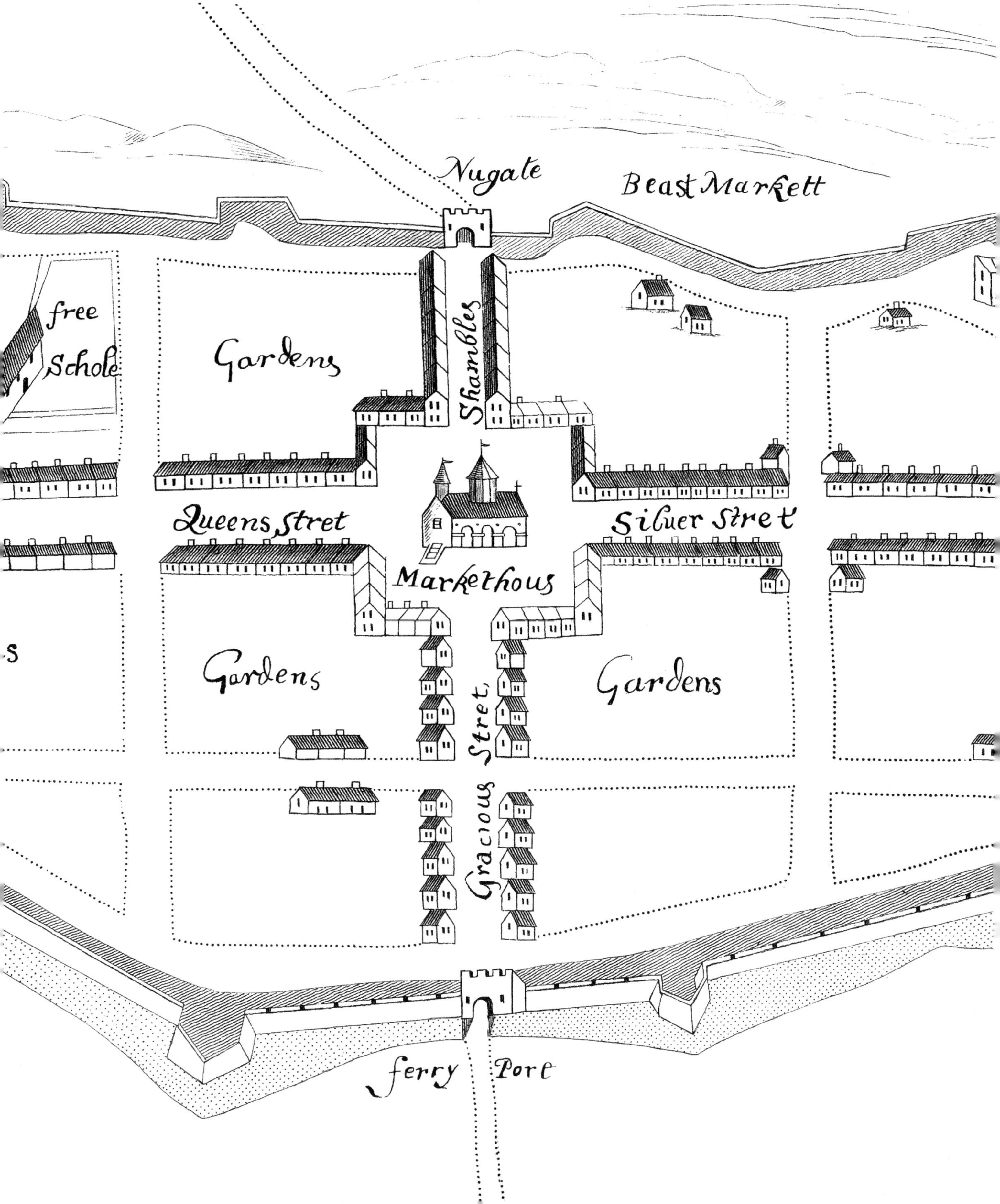
Nugate
Beast Markett
free Schole
Gardens
Shambles
Queens Stret
Siluer Stret
Markethous
Gardens
Gardens
Gracious Stret,
ferry Port

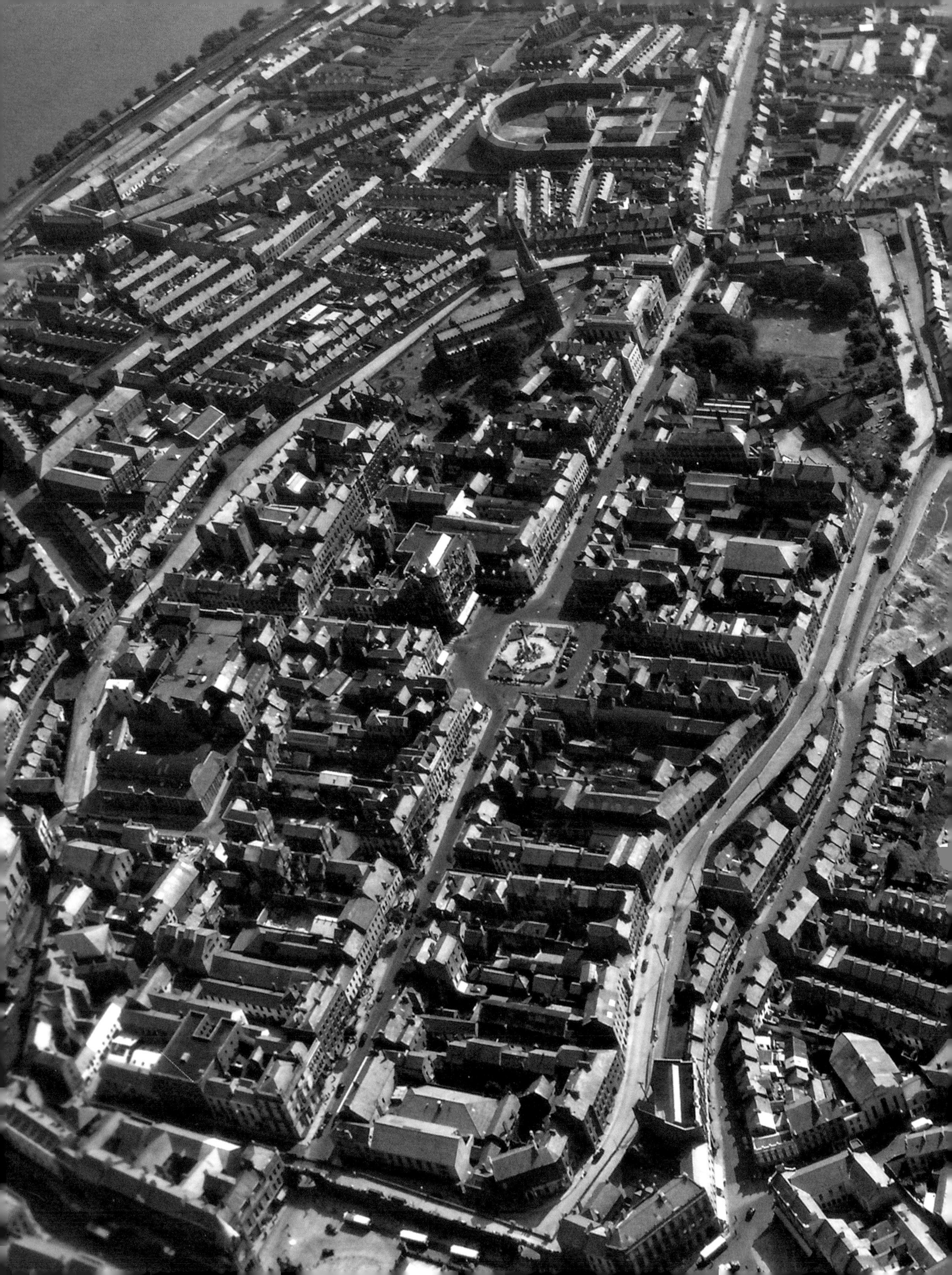

Opposite: Londonderry aerial view 1950s

Foreword

Derry is a modern city with a deeply rooted past. Visitors often remark that it has a 'sense of place' - somewhere where you can literally reach out and touch history. The famous seventeenth-century walls are perhaps the city's most prized historic asset. These walls are both an artefact and a living part of the city; part of its past, present and future. This book gives the modern reader a real 'vantage point' over the city, from which we can look back to the distant past and the stories of ordinary people.

This human story starts some 9,000 years ago, with our earliest ancestors moving 'Twixt Foyle and Swilly' as they fished and gathered for their livelihood. Their world was very different to the one in which we live, but we can still trace its geography. During the next part of the story, we see a much older 'Walled City', a community of farmers some 6,000 years ago who lived within the wooden walls of Thornhill.

An important chapter of this book focuses on the coming of Christianity. In it we learn of Colum Cille, one of our most famous citizens, a man with connections far and wide. And these connections, the relationship of the city to the wider world, is theme that occurs many times in our history, from Colum Cille's links to Donegal through to the landholdings of Peter Benson, the builder of our famous Walls, who also held lands in Donegal.

Understanding our rich archaeological heritage, through the stories of people, places and the artefacts they left behind, from distant ancestors and to our living city, enriches us all. In this book there is an insight into over 9,000 years of cultural diversity. In this City of Culture year, it is a timely insight, as we look forward to the continuing heritage and cultural vibrancy in Derry.

Mark H Durkan MLA
Minister for the Environment

Island City. The Archaeology of Derry~Londonderry

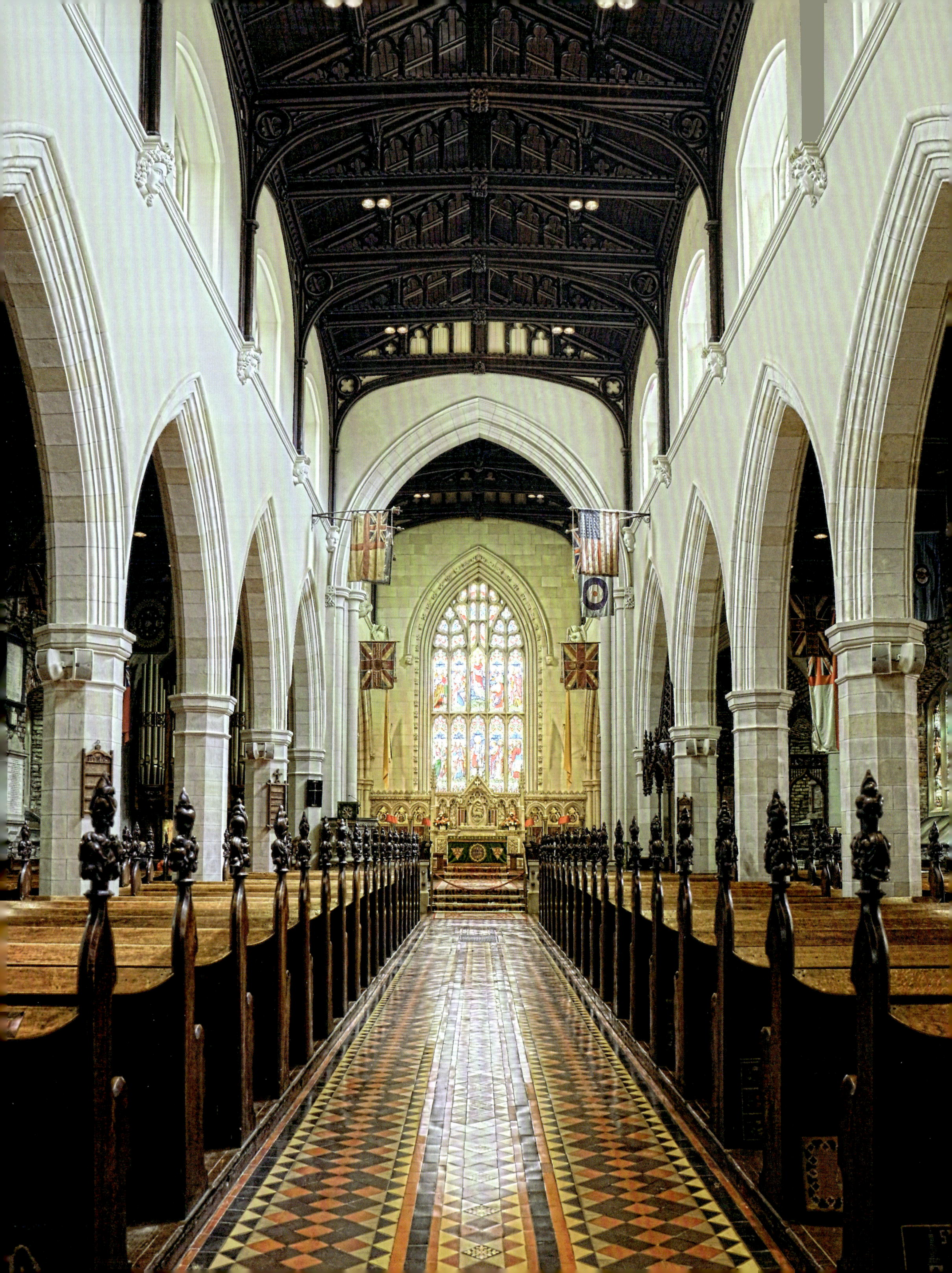

Opposite: The Cathedral Nave

Preface

Archaeology is about discovering our past. The very act of digging reveals new finds which provide information about our ancestors and past societies. Archaeology continues to challenge our perceptions of who we are and where we have come from.

Over the past number of years, there has been a wealth of funding provided for archaeological excavations . However, funding and resources are still needed to complete post-excavation work and publish the results. Without reports and publication the information is not available to the public. The primary aim of this book has been to gather together information regarding the archaeological excavations which have taken place in the city and collate this information into one volume. It is not meant to be an 'academic' publication but one which is easily accessible to all. This book is the result of a partnership project between the Northern Ireland Environment Agency (NIEA) and Derry City Council Heritage and Museum Service.

This year we – NIEA and Derry City Council – have jointly undertaken three archaeological excavations with archaeologists from the Centre for Archaeological Fieldwork, Queen's University of Belfast. These were at Prehen House, Elagh Castle and Bishop Street Within. They have captured the attention of locals and the media, putting archaeology firmly at centre of attention within the city and region. Local community, schools and volunteers have been inspired to discover their heritage and have become actively involved.

It is a fitting time to launch this publication during the year of City of Culture 2013. We can truly say that this city is undergoing a 'cultural renaissance' and it is 'telling its own story'. I would like to encourage you to be part of that story, as we, through archaeology, uncover our past and continue to write new chapters in our city's history.

Cllr Martin Reilly,
Mayor, Derry City Council

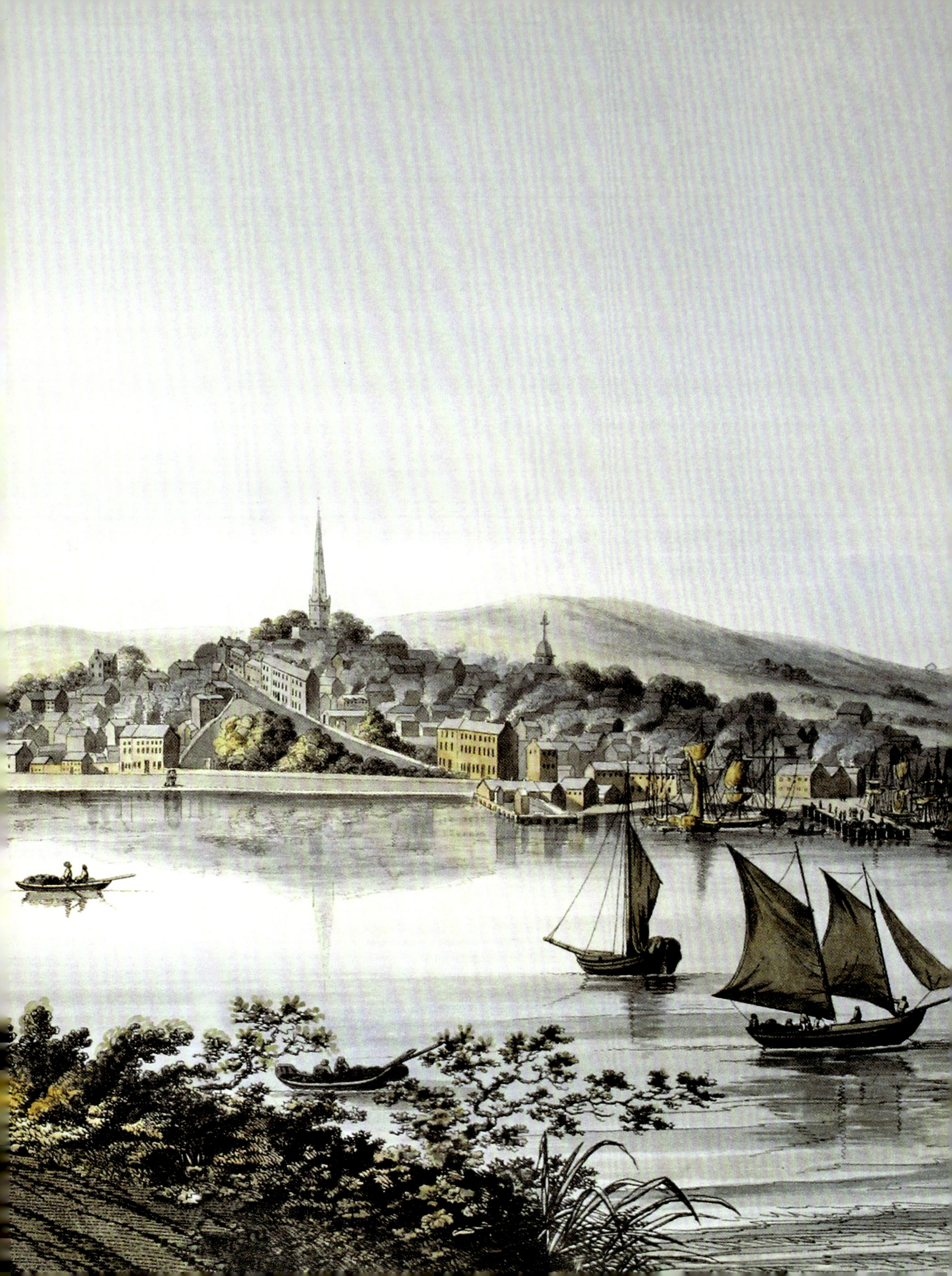

Opposite: Detail of a hand coloured print etching 'Londonderry' attributed to Henry Brocas senior and dated to around 1800.

Introduction

The city of Derry~Londonderry stands on the banks of the River Foyle close to where it winds its way into Lough Foyle and, ultimately, the north Atlantic. It is only 32km (20 miles) from the open sea off the northern Irish coast, and only 8km (5 miles) from the narrow Foyle estuary. Thus, the location of the settlement means that it is easily accessible by water, sitting on a route linking seafarers with the interior of Ulster through the River Foyle and its tributaries. The modern City centre area was once a roughly oval-shaped drumlin-like island in the River Foyle but over time the river channel around the western side of that island gradually silted up to form a bog. This is still reflected today in the modern name for that area of the City, the 'Bogside'. Today the 'island' encompasses an area of about 80ha and at its highest point, close to St Columb's Cathedral, is almost 40m above sea level. Most of the historic core of the City sits on glacial deposits of boulder clay overlying the local rock, Pre-Cambrian schist which has been exposed at the surface in some places throughout the island.[1]

The name 'Derry' comes from the regional pronunciation 'Dirrah' of the Irish word 'Doire' meaning 'oak grove'. The name suggests that an ancient pre-Christian religious or sacred centre once existed here. Around AD 500, Derry was known as 'Doire Calgach' meaning the 'oak grove of Calgach'. We do not know who Calgach was, though most likely he was a pre-Christian warrior chief or religious leader. Later, the Christianised settlement was called 'Doire Colmcille' meaning the 'oak grove of St Colum Cille', after the celebrated Irish saint who is said to have founded a church here.

During the 1500s, Tudor sources referred to 'the Derrie', and the prefix 'London' was added in 1613 when the new London Plantation settlement was granted its charter by James I. The name 'Londonderry' was intended to emphasise the connection with and funding by the City of London. It is common practice now to refer to Derry~Londonderry, reflecting both traditions that exist in the city. Whichever version we use, 'Derry', 'Londonderry' and 'Derry~Londonderry' are just the latest in a series of names to be given to the settled place that has existed here for over a thousand years.

The area covered by this book comprises archaeological sites within the modern parish of Templemore (which also includes the Donegal divisions of Muff, Burt and Inch) and the parish of Clondermot. These parishes surround the City, Templemore on the western bank of the River Foyle, Clondermot on the east. This is an archaeological story and while we must by necessity set archaeological finds in context using historical sources, the book is not intended as another history of the city. Indeed, written history only began at Derry with the early Christian monks

Griffin Cocket's Map of north-west Ireland c. 1602.

and archaeology alone can tell the story of our place before that time. One name looms large when writing on the story of Derry – that of Brian Lacey. His publications, both popular and academic, on the history of the city as well as on the histories of both Counties Donegal and Londonderry are well-known and run into double figures. Anyone writing about Derry's past is indebted to him for the ground that he has already covered.

This book is a general overview of work, both archaeological and historical, undertaken by many people and some of the important previous publications are listed in the Bibliography. Much of the information comes from published archaeological reports, some from unpublished archaeological reports lodged in the Monuments and Buildings Record (MBR) in Waterman House, Hill Street, Belfast. Another invaluable source for anyone studying the archaeology of Ireland are the summaries of unpublished excavations collated in the annual *Excavations Bulletin* (edited by Isabel Bennett). All of these help to shed light on the character of the evolution and development of the settlement and of its hinterland.

The four main chapters deal with important milestones in the development of the city, and include sections that focus on particular aspects. The first two chapters describe prehistoric and Early Christian archaeological remains in and around the city along with the legacy of St Colm Cille; the third chapter covers the Medieval settlement and the various ecclesiastical foundations that made Derry so famous in the Middle Ages. That era came to a close with the Nine Year's War at the end of the 16th-century and the foundation of a new English garrison town by Sir Henry Docwra. The archaeology and architecture of the early 17th-century walled town, developed as a result of the Plantation of Ulster, and of the dramatic sieges of 1649 and 1688–89 are considered in the fourth chapter. In the short final chapter, the Epilogue, there is a brief overview of the town's massive growth in the 18th and 19th centuries, when the city emerges as an important manufacturing centre with a significant Atlantic port.

Not every archaeological site is included – it would not be possible, or desirable, as there are a large number of sites. However, efforts have been made to include all the important locations and those readers who wish to investigate further can consult the database of all of the known archaeological sites in both the city and county held in the Monuments and Buildings Record (MBR) in Hill Street, Belfast. A shortened version is also accessible on the Northern Ireland Environment Agency's website.

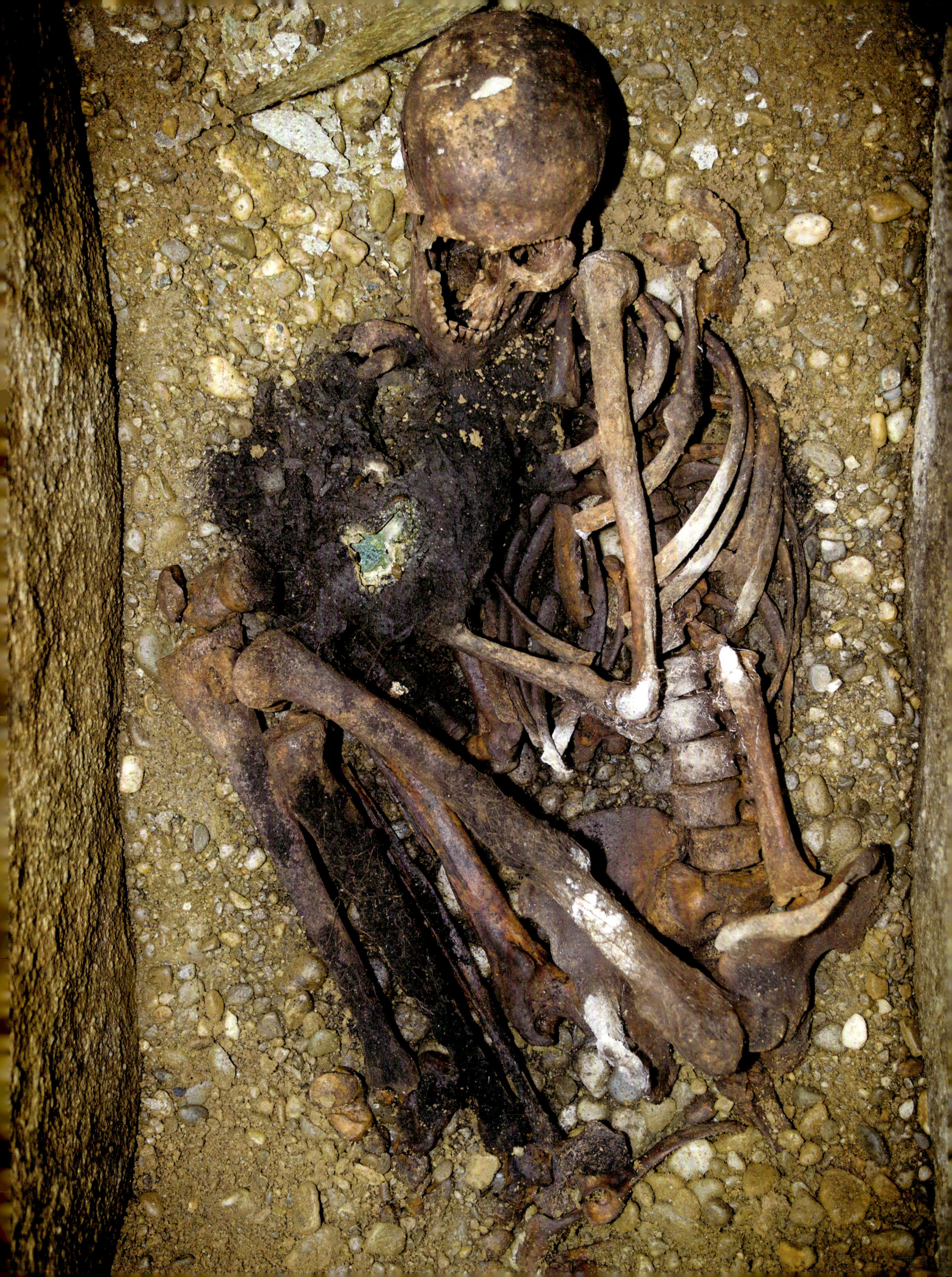

Opposite: Early Bronze Age cist burial containing a skeleton with a bronze dagger uncovered during excavations at Ballyoan in 2006

The Prehistoric Period

At the end of the last Ice Age around 12,000-14,000 BC, the large ice sheets that covered much of northern Europe were retreating and temperatures were beginning to slowly rise.[1] Ireland had become habitable for hardy trees such as willow and juniper, but it was to take another few thousand years for sufficient soils to form above the Ice Age gravels and allow a wider range of trees and plants to follow. With so much water still locked up in ice sheets, the sea levels were at least 130 metres below today's levels, thus exposing enough land to form a 'land bridge' with Great Britain. It is now generally accepted by quaternary specialists that in these conditions both flora and fauna were able to migrate dry-shot across to Ireland. As time progressed the ice melted and retreated further northwards, the sea finally rose to envelope and submerge the land bridge, separating Ireland from Britain. The range of native Irish fauna and flora in Ireland was now fixed to what had already crossed the bridge to become stranded on the newly-created island. Our earliest land animals then included the familiar types such as foxes, badgers, mountain hares and stoats, but also wild pigs, wolves and brown bears. Our rivers and lakes contain trout and eels, but many fish were absent, such as the trench, roach, minnow and rudd. The waters of the Irish Sea evidently rose too fast for many species to cross the land bridge, for compared to the British and European mainland we have a noted paucity of native flora and flora. Consequently, prehistoric Ireland was without many of the trees and shrubs so familiar to Britain, such as beeches, hornbeams, limes and field maples, while many animal species were also absent, famously snakes, all of which contributed to the distinctive ecology of the prehistoric Irish landscape and its available resources.

Map of Prehistoric sites in the Derry area.

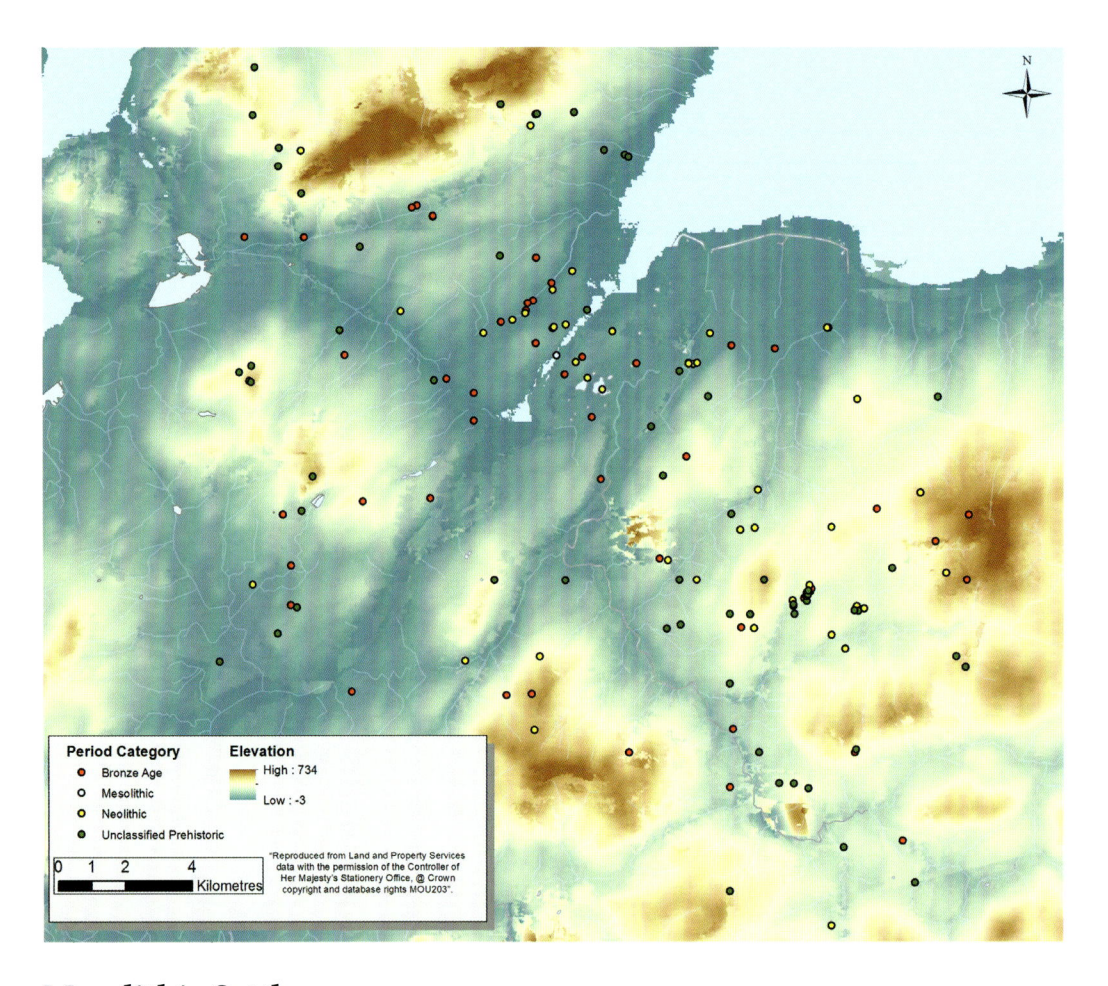

Mesolithic Settlers

The first archaeological evidence of people settling in Ireland dates to the Mesolithic period (*c.* 8000–5500 BC). During this time the landscape of Ireland was heavily wooded. The new settlers lived a semi-nomadic lifestyle, exploiting whatever resources were available to them, and had to be hunters, fishers and gatherers in order to survive. Our most complete evidence for these earliest peoples in Ireland was found at an archaeological excavation at Mount Sandel beside the River Bann near Coleraine, around 40 km (25 miles) northeast of Derry.[2] Excavations there showed that the Mesolithic settlers lived in a series of huts that have been scientifically dated to around 7500-7000 BC. The huts were roughly circular and measured around six metres across. Archaeologists found that their outline was marked by the holes where wooden poles had been driven into the ground and then bent over and tied all together in the centre to make a domed frame. Other poles or branches were probably then woven through the framework to make it more solid. Hides, strips of birch bark and sods could then have been used as a final waterproof and insulating covering for the little houses. Heat was provided from a central hearth around which people would have gathered. Bone and seed remains from storage pits, which later became filled with rubbish and were covered over to keep vermin away, revealed that the Mesolithic settlers were catching and eating wild pig, hare, birds, eels, salmon and trout. In addition to mammals, birds and fish, the remains of hazel nut shells and, possibly, wild apples were also found in the pits showing that the Mesolithic diet was varied. The evidence suggests that the Mesolithic settlers living at Mount Sandel moved around the landscape from season to season, gathering and storing fruit when it was available, as well as fishing and hunting animals that also followed a migrational pattern.

The country around the modern city of Derry~Londonderry would have provided abundant resources for the first peoples who came to live there, the River Foyle and all of the tributaries and lakes, as well as Lough Foyle, providing fish and shellfish. The forests and vegetation that covered much of the surrounding hills and countryside would have supplied Mesolithic families with wood for fuel, houses and tools, as well as nuts, fruit and berries for food. Mammals such as wild boar and hare could be hunted for food and hides. Birds too would have played an important part of the diet and feathers used as insulation in clothing, ornamentation and to fletch arrows. In the Early Mesolithic, the population of the Derry area would have been very small and may only have amounted to a few extended families. The Mesolithic settlers at Derry could exploit a variety of resources from the nearby hills, rivers, lakes and coasts. For example,

The outline of a sub-circular Mesolithic hut uncovered during the Mount Sandel excavations, 1973-1977.

during the summer they could catch fish in the River Foyle, later in the year they could move up to the shores of Lough Foyle and catch birds such as geese; shells and seaweed could be gathered along the coastline and animals, such as pig, hunted in the woods of Inishowen. Their lives must have been governed by whatever plants, animals and seafood were available during the various seasons of the year and they would have moved around to ensure that they had access to enough food to survive. As a result, some settlements may only have been temporary and left very little evidence for archaeologists to investigate. However, as we have seen, some traces of Mesolithic meals survive along with flint tools and have allowed archaeologists to start piecing together the story of these earliest settlers. There is very little evidence in Ireland of how Mesolithic people treated their dead. However, an excavation in Co. Limerick has shown that some at least were cremated and then the cremated remains placed in pits with stone tools.[3]

The Mesolithic period in Ireland is divided by archaeologists into two periods, based on the different type of flint tools being produced in either. From around 8000 BC – c.5500 BC, the Early Mesolithic people generally created small flint blades known as microliths (Greek for 'small stones'). Several of these would then be used together to make a variety of tools, such as harpoons for fishing and arrowheads for hunting or for use as weapons. Other flints were fashioned into scrapers to clean the insides of animal hides so they could be made into clothes, coverings for huts or pouches and bags. Flint tools known as burins may have been used for working animal bone and also antler, although we are not sure if red deer existed in Ireland at this time. Axes were also being produced for woodworking and possibly for defence. In the Later Mesolithic period (c. 5500 BC – c. 4000 BC), it would appear that microliths went out of fashion and larger bladed tools made from single pieces of flint were the norm. The most common of these larger flint tools are known as 'Butt-trimmed Flakes', leaf-shaped flints that were chipped down at their base presumably to help with attaching a shaft or handle.

We are uncertain as to where the first settlers to Ireland came from and how many waves of settlers there were during the Mesolithic period. But recent scientific research, based on the study of the DNA of a certain type of snail, has thrown up an intriguing possibility for the origins of at least some of our earliest ancestors. The particular strain of snail in question is found only in Ireland and the eastern Pyrenees area of southern France and northern Spain. It is not found anywhere in between so natural migration of the snails by land, when sea levels were lower and the land bridge existed, can be ruled out. The snails, a known source of food in Mesolithic Europe, must have crossed the seas. The eastern Pyrenean region is linked to the Atlantic by the Garonne River in southern France. Consequently, the new theory suggests that at least one wave of eastern Pyrenean Mesolithic colonists migrated by sea to Ireland via the Garonne river valley during the Mesolithic period, bringing the snails with them as a source of food.[4]

As mentioned above the evidence for the houses where ancient peoples lived or died often does not survive to be found by archaeologists. Sometimes archaeologists only find evidence of the tools that prehistoric peoples discarded or hid, implying that a settlement may have been close by.

A flint knife of Mesolithic date was found in one of the external post-holes in the early Neolithic structure uncovered close to Enagh Lough in 1998 and described later in this chapter[5]. Butt-trimmed flakes were reportedly found in the lowest levels on the excavations at Rough Island in

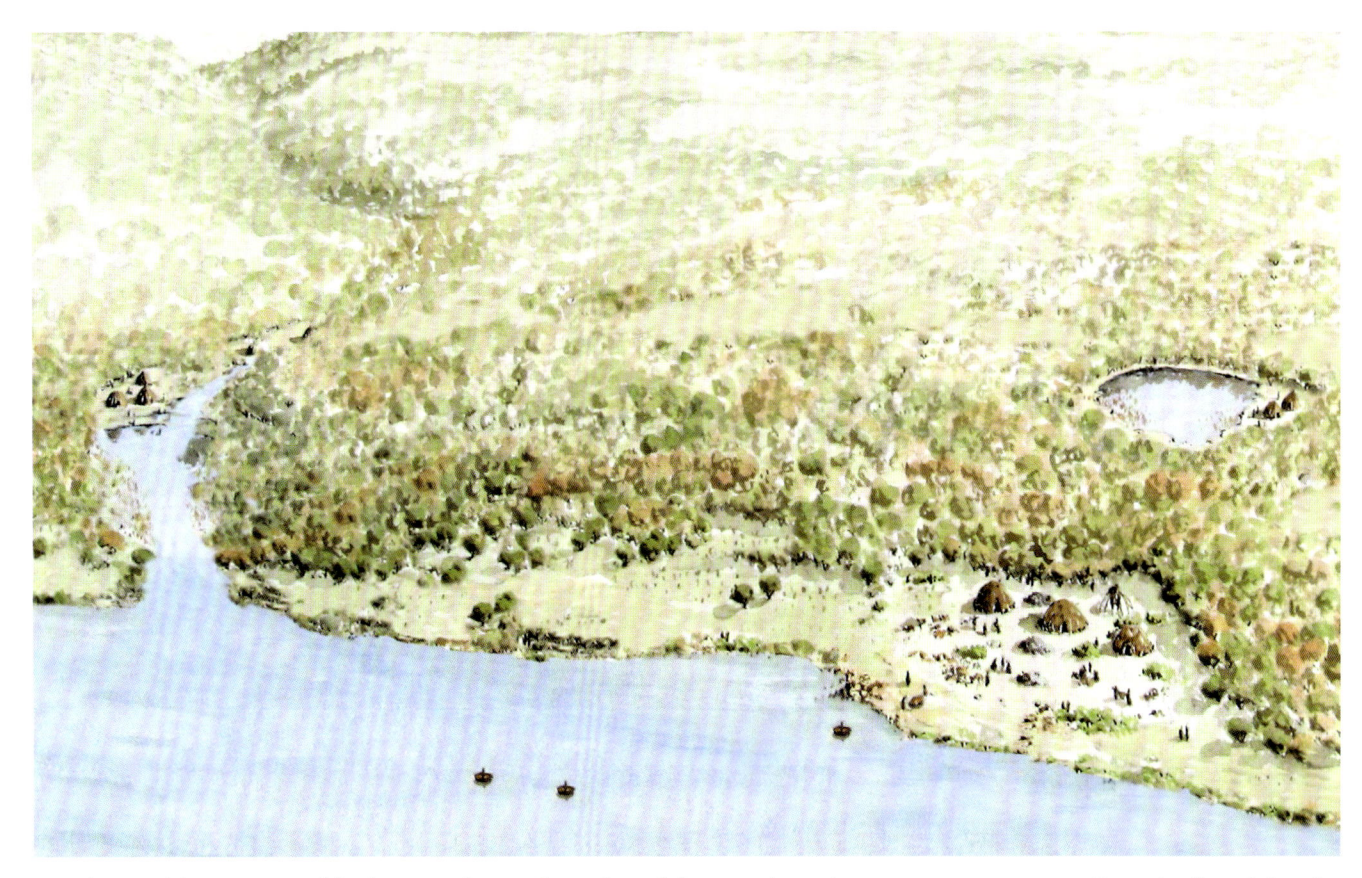

Reconstruction painting of how Mesolithic settlements along the Foyle might have looked.

Enagh Lough[6] so it is possible that Enagh Lough, with its fishing and nearby rivers, was an area Mesolithic settlement. In what is now Co. Donegal, Early Mesolithic flint axes, cores, blades and other artefacts were found on the beach at Greencastle, Inishowen[7], some 36km to the north-east of the city. Later Mesolithic material was excavated at a site of an ancient beach around 50km to the north-west, at Urrismenagh, Dunaff Head, in Inishowen in 1966.[8] In the succeeding decades, as a result of erosion and turf cutting, further material has been uncovered at Urrismenagh, including two stone axes. Later Mesolithic material has also been found in more recent times on Inch Island in Lough Swilly, about 1.6km from Burt.[9] All these finds attest the presence of our Mesolithic ancestors who moved throughout the Derry area in search of food and resources but we must await further discoveries if we are to locate another definite camp site such as that from Mount Sandel. Archaeologists believe that fish made up a great degree of the Mesolithic diet so the finds of artefacts at the above locations may well point to important future discoveries on the banks of the Foyle and Swilly.

Neolithic period (c. 4000 BC–2500 BC)

During the Neolithic (from the Greek for 'New Stone') in Ireland there were further colonisations of the island. The new settlers did not live a nomadic lifestyle, creating instead permanent farming settlements. They grew cereal crops such as wheat and barley and kept domesticated animals such as cattle, sheep, goats and pigs, all animals new to Ireland at this time. We also have archaeological evidence of trading between settlements being carried out at this time.

These new arrivals had stone axes for clearing the forests to make way for their settlements and cultivation, flint arrowheads, javelins for hunting and grinding stones for processing cereals into flour. In Ulster they often used axes made from a high-quality stone called porcellanite. Its two main sources are at Tievebulliagh near Cushendall and at Brockley on Rathlin Island, both in Co. Antrim, but artefacts made from porcellanite are found all over Ireland and Britain indicating trade links. As part of a radical change in lifestyle and technology, the Neolithic was the first period when people in Ireland began to use clay pots for storage, cooking and burial rituals. With agriculture and domestication of animals providing a more secure source of food the Neolithic peoples in the Derry area, as elsewhere, were able to live in permanent settlements. As a result of this greater ability to control the landscape the population numbers rose considerably. Most dramatically of all, the Neolithic people of Ireland started erecting large stone funerary monuments, known as 'megaliths' (from the Greek for 'large stones') to commemorate and house some of their dead and possibly also to mark out territory. These burial monuments indicate that Neolithic people had complex religious beliefs and a well-organised society. It must have taken concerted communal effort to clear forests and vegetation and to erect the massive stone monuments that still dot the Irish countryside.

Neolithic Court Tomb at Ervey, Co. Londonderry

Neolithic leaf-shaped and lozenge-shaped flint arrowheads found on the Thornhill excavation in 2000

The number of people around Derry during the Neolithic period may have run into the hundreds, and archaeological evidence for where they lived is found in a variety of locations – on ridges, beside lakes and even on islands. It takes the form of settlement activity, houses, religious sites and tombs, as well as isolated finds of Neolithic pottery, flint and stone tools.

Considering the substantial settlement that later evolved on the 'island of the Derry', it is perhaps surprising that we have more archaeological information about the lives of the people, their houses, burial sites and religious monuments in the Neolithic and Bronze Age in the area around the modern city than we have for the Early Christian or Medieval periods. Much of this information has been derived from archaeological excavation. Neolithic flint scatters have been found at Ballyarnett[10] and also at Curryneirin[11], showing human activity at these sites. An excavation in Ballynashallog in 2002[12], revealed Neolithic flint working activity, and tools recovered included part of a leaf-shaped arrowhead and some hollow scrapers. Hollow scrapers are flint tools believed by some archaeologists to have been used in the production of arrow shafts. The site was *c.* 200m from the Thornhill excavation discussed below, as well being close to the location of two possible circular enclosures[13], noted on an aerial photograph.

Evidence of Neolithic settlement has been found at several sites in the area around the city. At Ballynagard[14] evidence of occupation was uncovered during excavations there. At Campsey Upper[15], two areas of occupation were uncovered, consisting of a series of pits and stake holes. Finds included Neolithic pottery, a porcellanite axe head and a flint knife. The porcellanite axe must have come from Co. Antrim, the only source of this much-prized resource in prehistory. At Coolkeeragh[16], a series of pits and a spread of burnt stone were discovered. From amongst the stones of the burnt spread came sherds of Neolithic pottery, and evidence of small-scale tool making working in the form of a flint flake and a possible arrow head. At Shantallow, Neolithic pottery and flint, including an arrowhead, were found during construction work in 2001.[17] In 1996 and 1998, two other excavations at Shantallow uncovered the remains of a Neolithic track way, undoubtedly

Decorated Neolithic pottery found on the 1940 excavation of the crannog at Rough Island, Lough Enagh

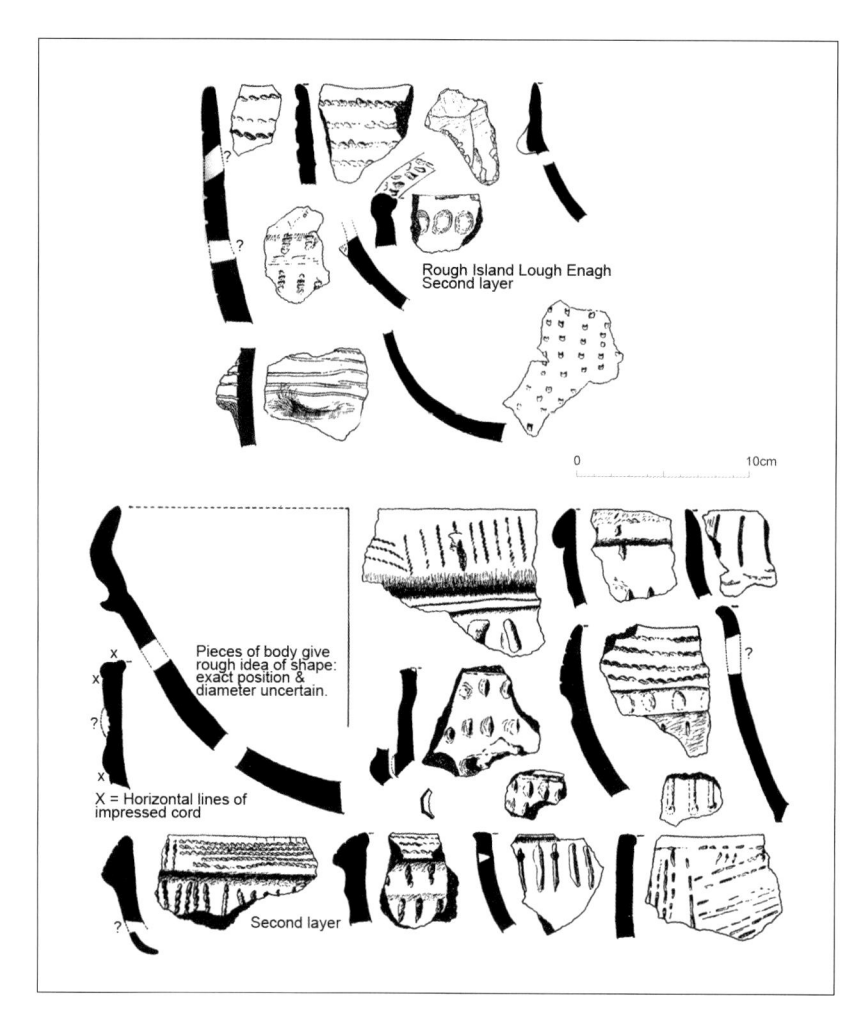

evidence of movement between places, presumably settlements, in the landscape. The first, at Ballyarnett Lake, was carried out in 1996.[18] During the machine cutting of a sewage pipe, a layer of peat overlying the subsoil was found to have groups of stakes driven down through it. These were discovered along with a platform which was around 15m long and 50cm thick, composed of compact sandy soils, stones and timbers. Associated with the platform was a small Neolithic bowl and part of another pot; also found in the trench were some crude flints and part of a porcellanite axe.

The second track way *c.* 270m to the south-west of Ballyarnett Lake took the form of a stone kerb and some timbers – planks and beams – with wooden stakes set in the ground at either end.[19] Flints, a polished stone axe and most of a Neolithic pot were uncovered with the platform. Finally, an excavation in 1940 investigated the crannog, or man-made island, in Lough Enagh East, Stradreagh Beg townland where the lowest layers of the crannog contained worked flints and sherds of Neolithic pottery.[20]

The most common and impressive Neolithic domestic structure found in Ireland is the early Neolithic house. More than 80 of these have now been investigated on 50 different excavations across Ireland.[21] They were constructed of timber and usually rectangular or sub-rectangular in shape, though some were square and some also have annexes attached. They seem to average

Excavation of a Neolithic house at Cloghole Road in 2009

between 6-12m long and 4-8m wide, though larger examples have been uncovered. Usually the buildings have wall foundation trenches within which the house walls of split oak planks or posts are set and held in place with stone and soil packing. Some houses have internal load-bearing post holes to help support the roof, which we presume to have been made of thatch or sod. Hearths for cooking and heat have been found both inside and located close to houses. Recent studies suggest that this type of building was commonly constructed across Ireland within the relatively short timeframe of perhaps 100 years, from 3700-3600 BC.[22] Why this is the case is uncertain, though one theory is that it reflects a group of colonists making landfall at different locations around Ireland.[23] The scientific study of pollen samples from bogs across Ireland seems to show that the rectangular Neolithic houses were being erected in the Irish landscape around the same time as the practice of farming became common.

During the Middle and Later Neolithic, the shapes of houses change to become predominantly oval or circular. Both rectangular and circular forms were uncovered during the 2000 excavation at Thornhill, one of the biggest clusters of Neolithic houses found to date at any site in Ireland.[24] The site was a Neolithic settlement located on a low ridge overlooking the mouth of the River Foyle, 6.5km north-north-east of the City centre. Within the site were uncovered the remains of five Neolithic houses – four rectangular (Structures A, B, D and E) and one circular (Structure C).

The Neolithic houses uncovered at Cloghole Road in 2009 after excavation.

Aerial view of Lough Enagh with Rough Island crannog

Extensive occupation debris was also uncovered. The cluster of buildings clearly represented part of a Neolithic village. The rectangular houses at Thornhill measured 9m by 4m on average, and had walls constructed of posts or planks set in linear foundation trenches. One house was divided into at least two rooms and the entrance, located in the north wall, had a large flat stone placed centrally in the doorway. To the inside of this threshold stone, a shallow curvilinear bedding trench was uncovered representing an internal porch. The circular house consisted of two concentric circles of post- and stake-holes that marked out the line of the walls. It was approximately 6m in diameter and had an external porch-like entrance on the south-east.

In 1998, three archaeological sites were identified and excavated close to Lough Enagh[25], on the eastern side of the Foyle some 1km to the north-east of the city centre. While Site 1 was of Bronze Age date (see below), Sites 2 and 3 were Neolithic buildings.[26] The structure at Site 2 was a rectangular house with one rounded end, measuring roughly 3m by 4m and oriented north-west/south-east. It had wall foundation slots that were 20-40cms wide by up to 15cms deep and roughly U-shaped in profile. It was built with a partly stone-packed foundation trench, postholes at the northern and eastern corners, and a single posthole close to the centre.[27] Finds associated with it included fragments of pottery bowls dating to the early Neolithic and a single butt-trimmed flint blade. Calibrated radiocarbon dates were retrieved and one from charcoal within the construction trench gave a date range of 4230–3790 BC, the second, from hazelnut shells yielded a range of 3770–3530 BC.

The second Enagh Neolithic structure was uncovered at Site 3, some 300m to the east of Site 2. The evidence was more ephemeral, and consisted of a roughly circular pit, 3m by 2.6m and 30cm deep. There were two postholes outside the pit and a patch of charcoal. It was

Island City. The Archaeology of Derry~Londonderry

interpreted by the excavator as perhaps 'the site of a light hut, possibly originally covered by hides'.[28] Associated finds included a single piece of struck flint, sherds of coarse pottery and a single grain of barley, suggesting that it was an occupation site. A calibrated radiocarbon date of 3950–3530 BC was obtained from the charcoal fill of the pit. The structures uncovered at Enagh lay approximately 1 km to the south-east of the major settlement at Thornhill, across the river and close to its eastern shore. Site 2 was located on the west-facing slope of a ridge, approximately 200m to the east of the river bank, while Site 3 was approximately 200m further east again. The significance of the sites is that although they were on the other side of the river, there was a clear line of sight between Enagh and Thornhill. The rectangular structure at Site 2 was of similar size to Structure A at Thornhill, but smaller than the other three uncovered there. The excavated archaeological evidence suggests that settlement at Enagh was smaller and less complex than at Thornhill, and thus it is tempting to see this Early Neolithic site, a short boat ride across the river, as a satellite of the much larger Thornhill settlement. It is very possible that the community who lived at Enagh may have been some of those who took part in rituals and also domestic activities at Thornhill.

At Caw, approximately 3km to the south of Thornhill, another rectangular Neolithic house was discovered during excavations that turned up multi-period archaeological remains.[29] The house measured roughly 7m by 5m internally and was oriented north-west/south-east. This is similar in size to Structure E at Thornhill, though larger than Structure A and smaller than Structures B and D. The eastern and western walls of the Caw structure had been badly truncated by later boundaries, and the wall slot was observed to be 'intermittent with several clear gaps'.[30] There were large packing stones and postholes in the surviving wall slots and a possible doorway was located approximately halfway along the east wall. Like the rectangular structure at Enagh, that at Caw had a shallow pit in the centre, which was interpreted as a structural posthole. Another pit, 80cm to the north of it, contained a layer of burnt sand at the base and was probably an internal hearth. Finds associated with the structure at Caw included sherds of Neolithic pottery. A calibrated radiocarbon date of 3905–3705 BC, obtained from a charcoal sample in its north wall, places the building in the Early Neolithic period. The discontinuous method of construction, with both wall slots and postholes, was the same as was used in the construction of Structure B at Thornhill, though the Caw building was smaller than the structures there. Like the settlement at Enagh, it is tempting to see Caw as another satellite of the bigger Thornhill settlement, and to envisage the community at Caw possibly also being involved with activities at Thornhill.

In 2009, the number of excavated Neolithic houses from around the city reached double figures when three more definite examples were uncovered during archaeological investigations on the new Maydown to City of Derry Airport dual carriageway scheme.[31] All three were found at a site in Upper Campsey, close to the Cloghole Road opposite the Whitehorse Hotel. The first two uncovered were in close proximity to one another. It is uncertain at this stage whether they were contemporary, or if one replaced the other. House 1 was *c.* 13m long and 6m wide internally, with internal divisions marking distinct areas of activity. Within an external posthole was found a complete, but smashed, Neolithic pot. House 2 was *c.* 10m long and 6.5m wide internally, only

Early Neolithic carinated pottery vessel as it was being excavated at Cloghole Road in 2009.

marginally bigger than House 1. Again, an internal division and a small number of internal, non-structural features suggested areas of activities within the house. House 3 was larger than the other two and measured 15m long and 8m wide internally. A number of internal and external features were uncovered, including structural postholes, hearths and pits.

A semi-circle of posts enclosing a pit and a hearth feature in Area C of Site 1 indicated the remains of half of a round house. Pottery sherds and stone tools were recovered but the dating of the round house remains uncertain, although it is presumably a later Neolithic or Bronze Age structure. Amongst the very many pits, post holes, spreads of occupation material and other smaller archaeological features uncovered along the route of the road development were finds of early Neolithic pottery, and an assortment of stone and flint tools including a porcellanite axe. All suggest a substantial domestic settlement existed at the site during the Neolithic.

During the Neolithic period communities began to build what we can regard as stone tombs. The dominant type of Neolithic stone tomb in the northern half of Ireland is the court tomb. These usually take the form of a chambered gallery containing the burials, covered by a long cairn that opened at one end onto a semi-circular forecourt. Such prehistoric monuments were frequently erected in prominent places in the landscape, possibly as territorial markers by the various settled groups, while contemporary settlements are rarely found nearby.

The remains of a possible court tomb are to be found at Lisdillon[32], while a single upright stone at Glenderowen[33] may also signify the site of another megalithic tomb, of unknown type. At Edenreagh Beg[34] and at Elagh More[35] are the traces of two megalithic tombs in the form of isolated stones. The sites of two other megalithic tombs, now destroyed, are known from Gortica[36] and Gortgranagh[37], and were listed in early Ordnance Survey records. Given the abundance of settlement evidence it is surprising that there are so few tombs surviving in the region. It is possible that many were destroyed in the succeeding millennia as the landscape was extensively used for crops, cattle and settlement but this seems an easy and unsatisfactory explanation, which archaeologists must explore in the future.

Plan of a Neolithic house (E) uncovered at Thornhill in 2000. The outlines of the wall foundations are shown in darker blue, with other possible structures nearby highlighted lighter blue.

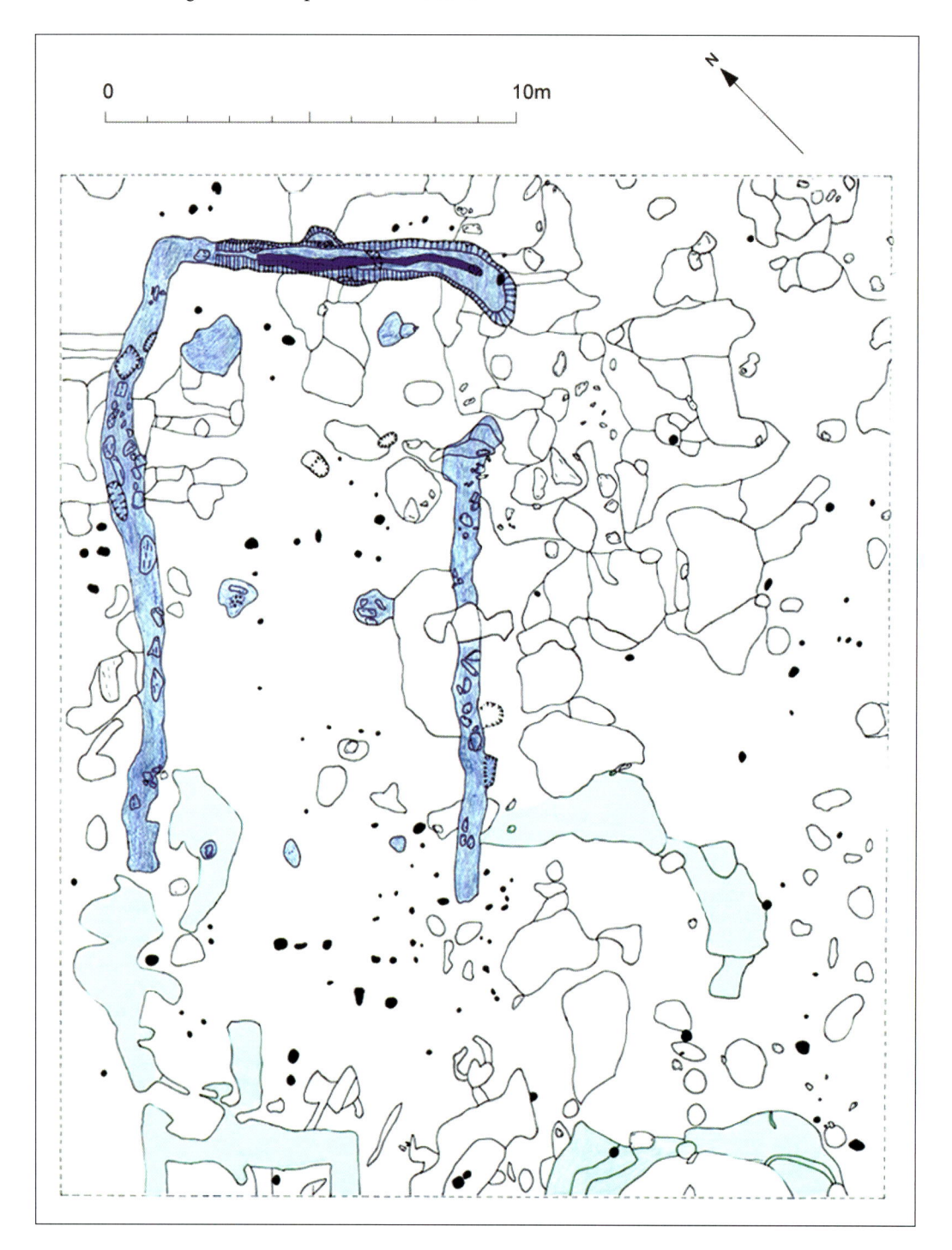

Thornhill

The remains of a substantial Early Neolithic settlement, on a low ridge close to the mouth of the River Foyle, were uncovered and excavated in 2000 in advance of the construction of the new Thornhill College, some 6km (4.5 miles) to the north-east of the city centre.[38] Prehistoric activity had been first recognised in 1995 as an extensive flint scatter, but the true scale of settlement did not become clear until the topsoil was stripped back, revealing the extensive structural remains five years later.

Excavation of Neolithic house (E) at Thornhill in 2000. Clearly visible are the outlines of the wall foundations, which had been filled with dark clay after the timber had rotted away.

Archaeological remains were recorded over an area measuring approximately 4000m² and these included the foundation trenches for at least seven separate, concentric wooden palisaded enclosures. These represented several phases of occupation and surrounded an area containing a minimum of five timber buildings, both round and rectangular in plan. More timber buildings would have existed at the site but were not identified as only a small percentage of the site was excavated in 2000, the majority being preserved for future generations. The enclosures and buildings have been dated to the Early Neolithic period (c. 4000–3500 BC) based on the artefact assemblage, along with direct evidence for human conflict on the site. What makes Thornhill special is that it is currently one of very few discoveries of an enclosed community from this early period in Ireland. We have evidence of communities from other excavations of Neolithic sites in Ireland, and we also have evidence for enclosures, but it is only above the mouth of the River Foyle at Thornhill that we have the two functioning as part of one unit. The nearest excavated parallel to Thornhill is at Knowth, Co. Meath, where concentric palisade trenches enclosed a possible Early Neolithic settlement.[39]

Coloured plan of main features uncovered in Area 2 of the Thornhill excavation in 2000.

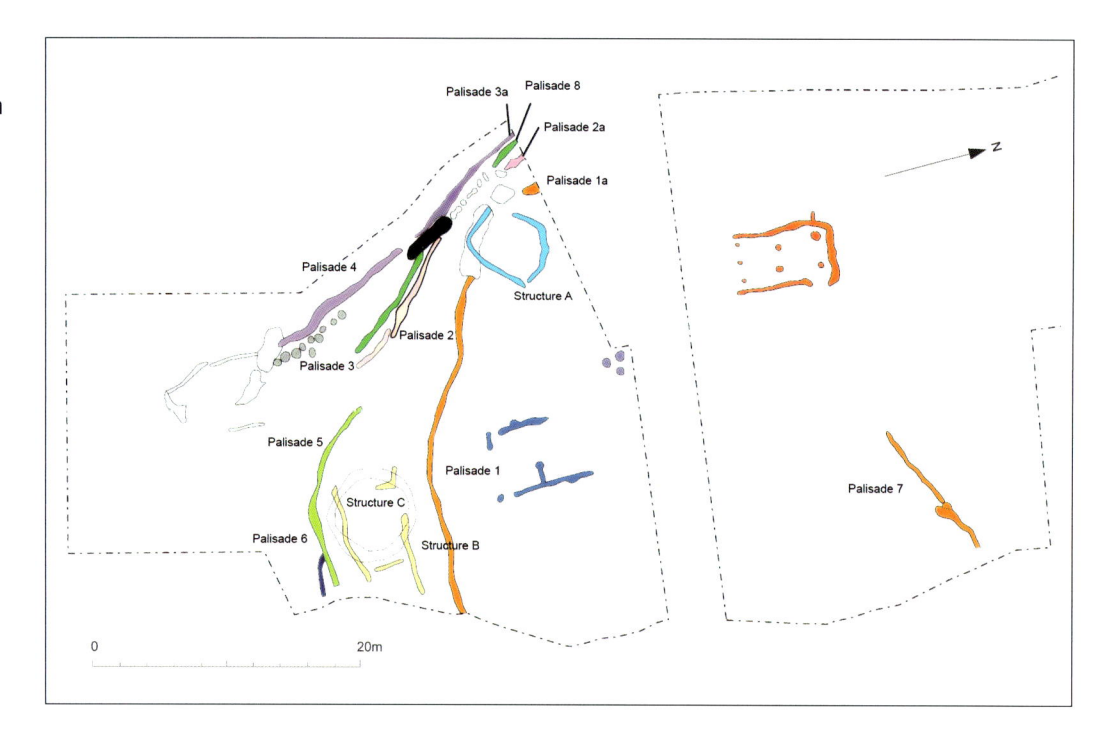

The area uncovered at Thornhill contained hundreds of stake-holes, post-holes, pits and spreads of occupation debris, indicating a wide range of activities. Excavation quickly identified that a number of the features represented the linear foundation trenches of timber palisades. Seven gently curving palisade trenches, surviving up to 25m in length, were on average between 30cm and 50cm both in depth and width and, in places, contained the charred or waterlogged remains of timber posts and planks. The posts and planks had originally been held in place by means of stone and soil packing. There were two main breaks, or entrances, through the palisades, which would have given access into the settlement from the west. One of the timber palisades surrounding the site had been partially burnt down, and mixed in with the burnt debris seven flint arrowheads (a third of the total found during the excavation) were discovered, presenting explicit evidence that the site had been attacked. Although part of the palisade had been set on fire, none of the excavated buildings showed signs of having been burnt, suggesting that the assault was not wholly successful. Repairs made to the burnt palisade after the attack, in the form of a line of 13 posts, further indicate that the assault did not cause the abandonment of the settlement. Stretches of some of the other palisades also showed signs of having been replaced, but most likely as routine repair of rotten posts and planks, not conflict.

A vast range of artefacts, numbering in the thousands, was uncovered, including stone and flint axe fragments, quartz, flint and stone tools, beads and saddle querns. Two of the stone axes had been broken during the Neolithic period and their pieces separated to be found later by the archaeologists on different parts of the site. The pottery assemblage consisted predominantly of undecorated Neolithic bowls, common during the period 3800–3600 BC, with decorated types amounting to less than 5% of the sherds recovered. Non-local material provided evidence of trade and exchange, and included fragments of porcellanite axes from Co. Antrim and at least one greenstone axe. There seemed to be little evidence for the primary working of flint on site. Only a few flint cores or rough-

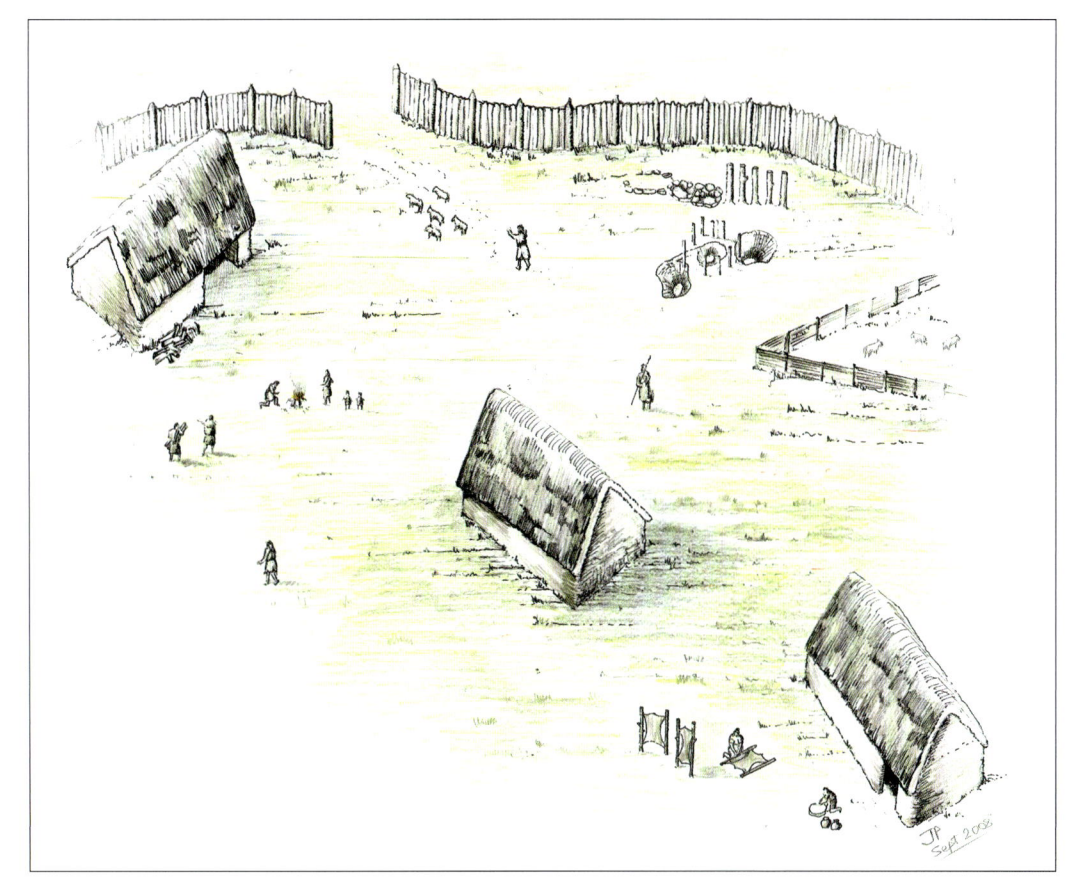

Reconstruction drawing by James Patience (NIEA) of how part of the Neolithic settlement at Thornhill might have looked.

outs were found and flint chippings from the making of tools were also uncommon, with the vast majority of flint work being finished items. There appears to be little or no flint in the local geology and much of the flint may have been imported from the nearest source some 24km away to the east across Lough Foyle in the Downhill area. The excavation showed that the cereal crops were threshed and winnowed at Thornhill and then processed into flour using saddle querns. The small Structure A had much evidence for grain processing in and around it. This suggests that cereal was being grown locally for the community at Thornhill.

Clearly the amount of effort and the numbers of people needed to construct a settlement like Thornhill was considerable and the wealth of material and archaeological remains found would seem to represent a lengthy period of activity. Positioned as it was, at the mouth of the Foyle and its tributary systems, the site and its immediate neighbours would have lain prominently on routes offering easy access into what are now Counties Donegal, Londonderry and Tyrone, and all must have been part of the trade and exchange network between western Ulster and modern Counties Antrim and Down.

The archaeological evidence of burning and repair along a stretch of one of the palisades suggests that the dangers to the settlement were real rather than imaginary, and it is one of the few excavated examples of conflict archaeology from an Irish prehistoric site. This evidence of aggressive behaviour in the Neolithic in Ireland is not however unique to Thornhill and shows that even 6000 years ago humankind had its darker side. For example, at Poulnabrone, County Clare, two skeletons were

Drawing of some of the Neolithic flint, stone and pottery artefacts found on the Thornhill excavation in 2000.

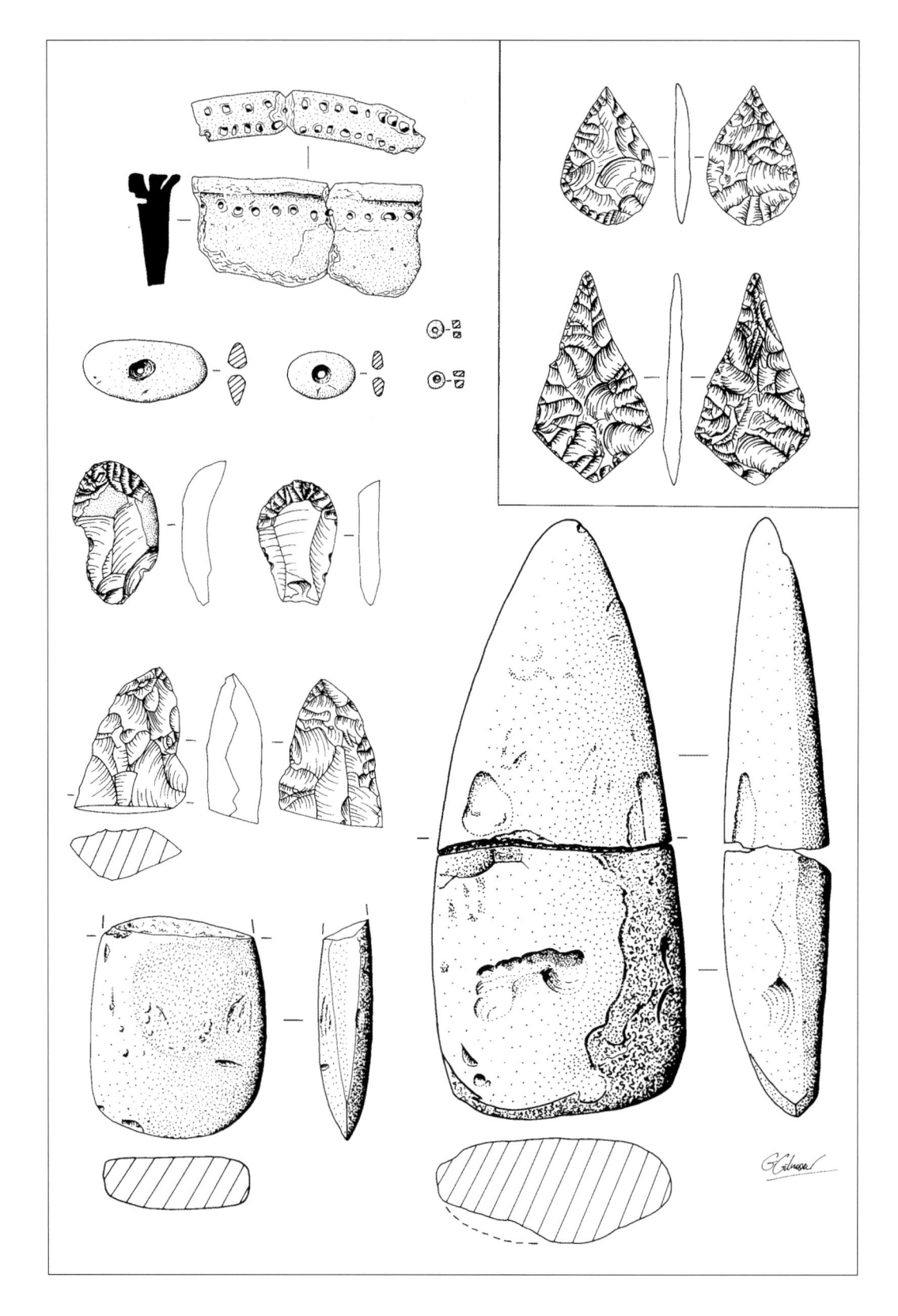

Flint arrowheads from the Thornhill excavation.

Polished and unpolished stone axes from the Thornhill excavation, including porcellanite

Drawings of an Early Neolithic carinated bowl from Thornhill.

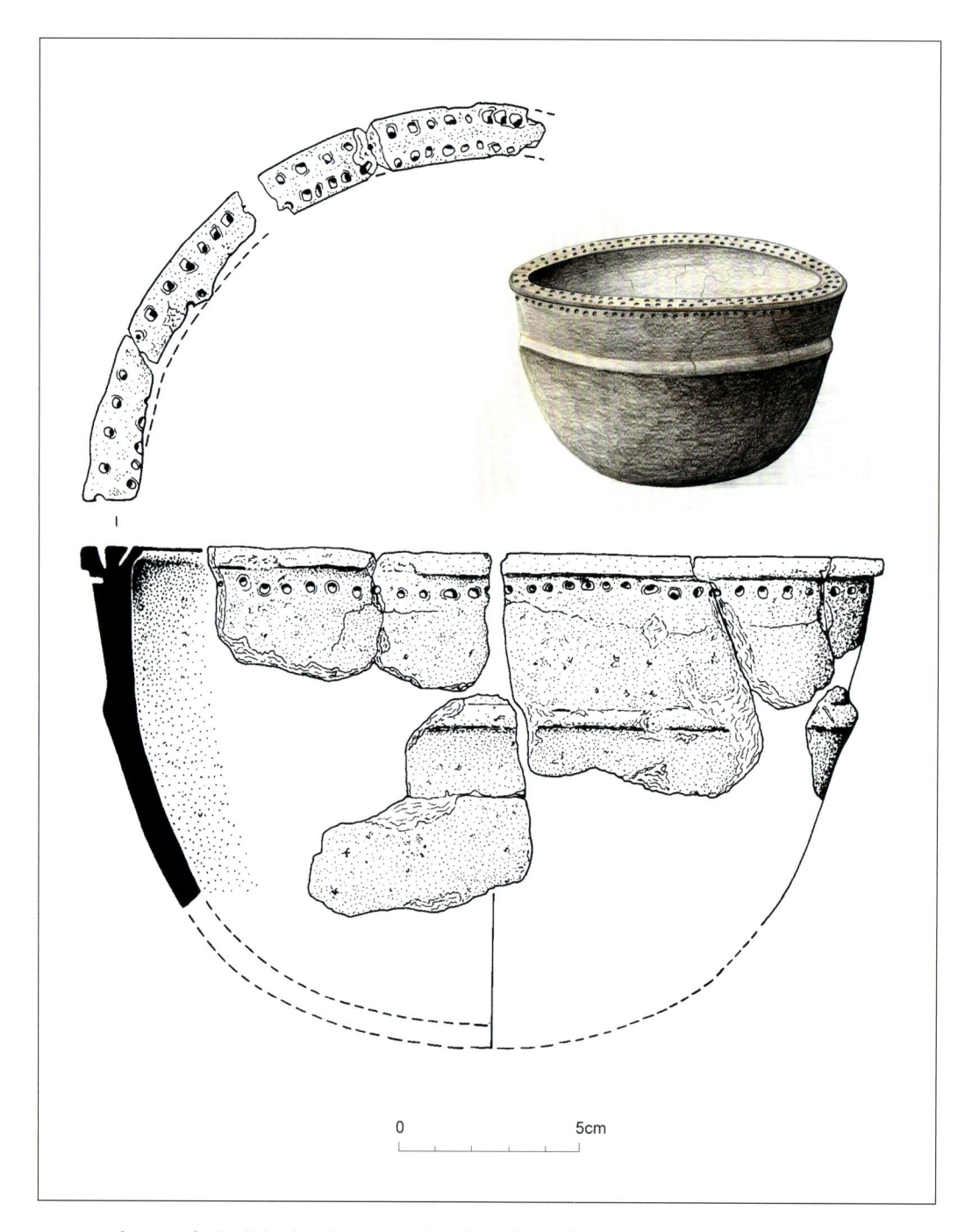

excavated, one of which had a chert arrowhead tip lodged in its pelvic bone, the other exhibiting evidence of a healed blunt-force trauma to the head. Even more dramatically, an Early Neolithic house excavated at Ballyharry on Islandmagee also showed evidence of having been attacked. Over 30 arrowheads were found in and around the excavated structure, which was also subjected to intense burning.

Back at Thornhill, two sets of conjoined pits, clearly of a ceremonial rather than everyday nature, were located at the entrances through the defensive palisades. One of these sets, made up of three

Reconstructed early Neolithic carinated bowl from Thornhill

large pits, cut through the slot trenches of a number of the enclosing palisades, demonstrating that it post-dates the palisades. The pits seemed to have originally contained upright timber or stone totems, and their fills yielded deliberately placed rubbing stones, a shattered carinated pottery bowl and burnt quartz.

There is no archaeological evidence of occupation or settlement activity at Thornhill beyond the Neolithic. Why it went out of use is puzzling, as we have seen that there is plenty of archaeological evidence for human activity continuing through the Neolithic and into the Bronze Age within the Thornhill catchment area. These include Neolithic structures and occupation, megalithic tombs, burnt mounds, standing stones, cist burials and individual finds of artefacts. Whether Thornhill went into decline as a result of environmental factors, disease, conflict or other changes such as a lack of children to take the community forward may never be known.

The Bronze Age (*c.* 2500–600 BC)

In the third millennium BC mining, smelting and the working first of copper, later of bronze (an alloy of copper and tin) began in Ireland, allowing the production of metal tools and weapons. New pottery forms appeared too, notably the type known as 'Beaker' because of its shape. Gold also started to be panned and worked at this time[40] and so many gold artefacts survive from the Bronze Age that it is sometimes referred to as 'Ireland's Golden Age'. The new metal technologies

Bocan Stone Circle, Co Donegal

produced artefacts that represented obvious wealth and status, such as weaponry or personal adornment which could be worn on clothes or as jewellery. We presume that this had the effect of allowing social divisions to become more apparent. There was probably a degree of segmentation in society with people having defined roles – those who mined the ores may not have been able to afford to wear or display the tools, weapons and jewellery made from them. Flint continued to be used, and barbed-and-tanged arrowheads and stone guards to protect archers' wrists are common finds of the Bronze Age in Ireland.

The earlier part of the Bronze Age in Ireland is typified by the erection of stone circles (although these may have begun in the Late Neolithic period), wedge tombs, cist burials and standing stones, perhaps a reflection of new ritual and burial rites. As the new metal technology increased wealth, the desire to acquire and to protect these assets almost certainly led to a more militaristic and warlike society, especially by the Late Bronze Age (*c*. 1200–600 BC). At that time we see the development of tribal or royal centres, such as the large defended settlements at Knockdhu, Co. Antrim[41] and Haughey's Fort, Co. Armagh.[42]

There is much archaeological evidence to show that there was extensive settlement on both sides of the River Foyle during the Bronze Age. In Ballyarnett townland[43] significant evidence of Bronze Age lake settlement was uncovered in 2002 and 2004. This included the creation of a palisaded timber platform consisting of a settlement built on timbers driven into water or boggy ground and surrounded by a defensive timber palisade. The site had four successive phases of activity, showing that the settlement there had lasted for a considerable time. One of the palisade posts was dated to between 1740–1520 BC. Amongst the finds retrieved from the excavations were sherds of Cordoned Urn pottery vessels, a tanged arrowhead made from basalt, everyday cooking pottery vessels and possible metal working debris. Further excavation in 2004 uncovered

Eskaheen Standing Stone near Muff, Co Donegal

more of the Bronze Age lake settlement, including a hearth and a furnace or oven. Amongst the many 2004 finds were the remains of at least twelve pottery vessels, metalworking debris, saddle querns for grinding corn, hammer stones, a fragment of polished stone axe, a possible anvil stone, a net weight, a fragment of a faience bead and a variety of flint projectiles and tools. All these artefacts give us a picture of life at Ballyarnett during the Bronze Age. Corn from nearby fields was being ground for food, some of which was being cooked and also stored in the pottery vessels. Fish were being caught in the Foyle by both line and net. Flint tools were being made and flint weapons produced to use for hunting animals and for defence of the settlement. Metalworking was also taking place on site possibly producing jewellery and bronze weapons and tools. The archaeological evidence also suggested that the site had been finally abandoned after becoming too waterlogged. It is tempting to see the Bronze Age activity at Ballyarnett Lake as having possibly been established by the descendants of some of those who had been involved at Thornhill in the preceding millennia

Between 2001 and 2004, a 16.2ha-site (40 acres) being developed as a new campus for Oakgrove Integrated College on the eastern bank of the River Foyle, some 4km (2½ miles) north-east of the City centre, was monitored by archaeologists.[44] The site was located close to the presumed location of *Dearg-Bruach*, an Early Christian monastic foundation[45], now covered by the Gransha Hospital complex. Amongst the various features uncovered were a burnt mound,

Standing stone at Dungiven

two groups of Neolithic pits, other pits and a hut circle. At one site (designated Site 19), flint and pottery from the Mid-to-Late Bronze Age (*c.* 1500 BC–600 BC) was uncovered. A series of sub-soil-cut features was interpreted as an enclosed late Bronze Age cemetery containing between eight and fifteen cist burials within a segmented palisaded enclosure. However, more recent publications have suggested an alternative interpretation of these features as the remains of an enclosed Bronze Age settlement containing a circular house and a smaller ancillary building.[46] Further excavation at the Oakgrove site, in 2004, uncovered Middle to Late Bronze Age pottery and a possible Early Christian structure, interpreted as a workshop. Bronze Age levels at Rough Island in nearby Lough Enagh yielded pottery and a socketed bronze spearhead[47], suggesting a similar type of lough side occupation to that at Ballyarnett. At Curryneirin[48], where Neolithic flints were also uncovered, Bronze Age flint scatters have been found suggesting continuity of human activity over several millennia in this area. In 2006, during the monitoring of topsoil-stripping in advance of the construction of the proposed Skeoge link road, two pits cut into the subsoil were investigated.[49] Radiocarbon dating of the charcoal within the basal deposit of one of the pits provided a probable date range of 2100–2040 BC, within the Early Bronze Age. So, even if no artefacts are recovered from an excavation the scientific examination of deposits collected can allow archaeologists the opportunity to date sites.

Bronze Age material was found at Site 1 of the three sites excavated in 1998 near Lough Enagh[50], the Neolithic evidence for which is described above. The site was situated some 250m to the east of Lough Enagh West. The excavation uncovered several post-holes and pits cut into subsoil that were interpreted as representing one or more buildings. Pottery of Early Bronze Age date was recovered from the pits, post-holes and overlying material. There were other archaeological features uncovered in the southern half of the site but as these were not under threat they were simply recorded and then covered in plastic and fine gravel to be preserved for the future. Aerial photographs suggest that the Early Bronze Age activity at Lough Enagh may have been close to an earthwork, now ploughed out and not visible above ground.

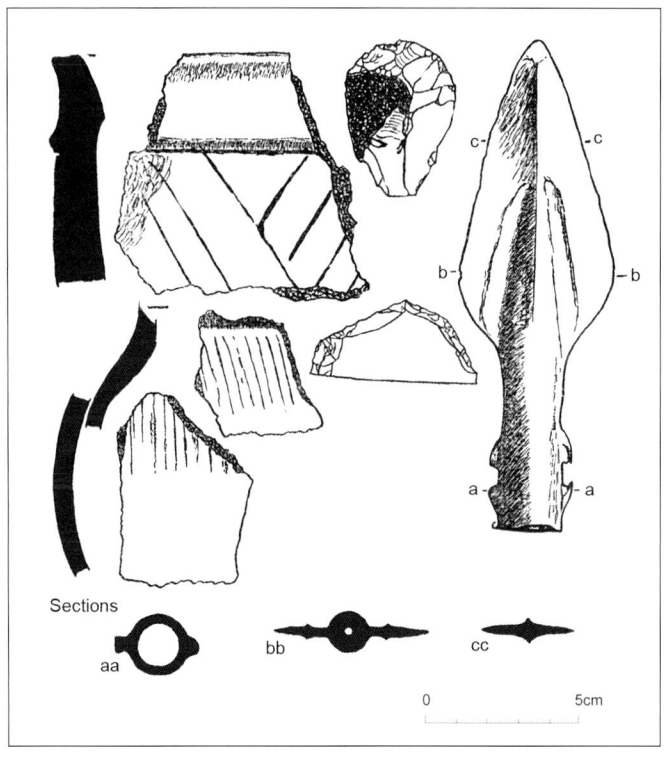

At Shantallow[51], where Neolithic pottery and flint was uncovered, Bronze Age pottery was also found supplying more evidence of continuous settlement in this part of Derry. At Maydown Industrial Estate nineteen pits and Bronze Age pottery were found in an excavation in 2002.[52] The pits were of irregular size and did not seem to have any direct relationship with one another. They were interpreted as perhaps serving a storage function. Also at Maydown, during excavations in 2009 which were carried out ahead of the new dual carriageway, a number of other Bronze Age discoveries were made[53], including features and occupation spreads, much Bronze Age pottery, flint and worked stone.

Bronze Age pottery, flint tools and a socketed bronze spearhead from Rough Island (O'Cahan's Garden) crannog on Lough Enagh, found in 1940

One of the most numerous Bronze Age sites found close to the modern city on both sides of the River Foyle (and one of the commonest monument types in Ireland) is the burnt mound, also known as a *fulacht fiadh,* meaning something like 'cooking place'. These are traditionally interpreted as communal cooking places and they normally consist of a large trough where water was boiled by throwing in heated stones and meat could thus be cooked. The troughs are associated with fires or pits for heating the stones and mounds of discarded heat shattered stones and fire rakings – hence the name 'burnt mound'. Although many archaeologists attribute these sites to cooking, burnt mounds almost certainly served other uses such as for brewing, dyeing cloth or bathing. By necessity they are often found close to sources of water such as rivers, lakes and small streams. At the Coolkeeragh site where Neolithic occupation was noted above, two Bronze Age burnt mounds were also discovered along with Bronze Age pottery.[54] In 2009, another burnt mound was found in an adjacent field during an excavation.[55] One was also uncovered at Ballynagard[56], and yet another at an excavation at Woodside Road, between Prehen and Gobnascale[57], along with linear gullies and pits. At Ballyarnett, 4km (2½ miles) to the north-west of the city centre, where Bronze Age lake side settlements have been found, three or possibly four burnt mounds are recorded.[58] Four burnt mounds were also investigated at Ballyoan in 2006.[59] Whatever their purpose burnt mounds are obviously an important and widespread feature from our past.

Island City. The Archaeology of Derry~Londonderry

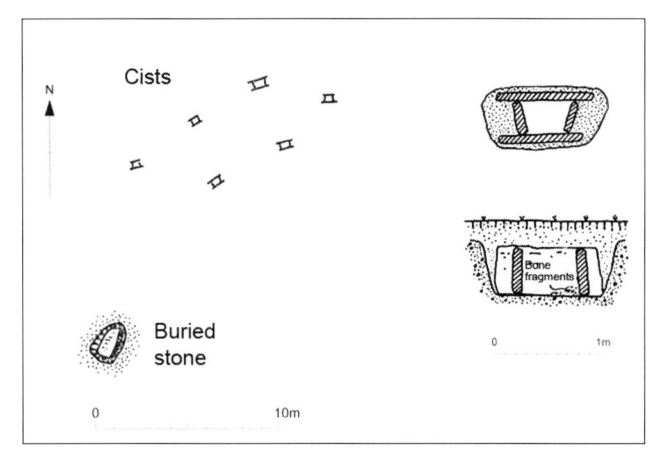

Plans and drawings of the Early Bronze Age cist graves at Shantallow, investigated by Professor Jope in 1951

From our evidence of Bronze Age tombs and burials in Ireland, it would appear that during this period there was a change in funerary practice from the selective, but communal, burial practices of the Neolithic to an equally selective, but individual, rite. This may represent the increasing segmentation of society, with the emergence of a ruling elite based on wealth and possibly military prowess.

In March 1988, members of the then Shantallow Historical Society out field walking in Shantallow townland, on the western side of the road from Derry to Muff in Co. Donegal, discovered the remains of a stone cist that had been disturbed by deep ploughing. NIEA archaeologists who excavated the burial[60] uncovered the skeletal remains of a man of some 25–30 years of age alongside a pottery vessel. The four slabs forming the walls of the grave were of local shale and set within a pit measuring 95cm long by 50cm wide and 45cm deep. The man had been laid tightly flexed on his right side in the cist, with his knees drawn up to his chest. His head lay at the northern end of the cist and behind it was the pot, still standing on its base. The pot is an Irish tripartite bowl decorated with horizontal rows of impressed triangles, and both horizontal and diagonal ornament made by pressing a comb into the damp clay before the pot was fired. Based on its style the bowl, and hence the burial, has been dated ate to around 1600 BC. The burial was subsequently removed and is on display in the Tower Museum.

A number of other cist burials are known within some 6.5 km (4 miles) from the 1988 Shantallow site. In 1952, in the same townland, a cemetery with six cist burials dating to the Late Bronze Age was investigated.[61] Roughly 10m to the west-south-west of the cists a stone, some 2m long and 1m wide, was observed lying flat in a pit specifically dug for it. It may have been a standing stone originally marking the location of the cemetery and later buried by farmers 'improving' the land. Another type of burial, a simple cremation within a collared urn set in a pit, was also discovered at Shantallow in 2004 and probably dates to the Early Bronze Age.[62] At least four cist burials have been recorded in Co. Donegal within a few kilometres of Shantallow.[63] In April 1994 a cist burial[64], 85cm long by 44cm wide and 53cm deep, was found and excavated in a large field at Clampernow, overlooking the Foyle. On the summit of Holywell Hill at Whitehouse and Ballymagrorty, is a large cairn with a cist[65], while at Creevagh Upper[66] the site of a cist burial was recorded, but this cannot now be located.

A major archaeological discovery was made during the monitoring of a pipeline corridor at Ballyoan in 2006, very close to the Gransha roundabout.[67] An Early Bronze Age cemetery was uncovered comprising of two inhumations and two cremations, each in a stone-lined cist, and at least two pit cremations in un-lined pits. One of the inhumations was of a child, the other an adult. The adult was buried with a bronze dagger in a leather sheath, and he was most likely someone of importance. Metal finds from Irish prehistoric graves are very rare and the survival of both the dagger and the sheath give us a glimpse at the types of perishable material put into such graves and further information on the burial rites being carried at Derry some 4,000 years ago.

Early Bronze Age cist burial at Straid, excavated in 1985

Another Bronze Age burial was found at Shantallow in 2004,[68] located at the junction of the Buncrana and Templemore Roads, on the north-eastern outskirts of the city. It took the form of a shallow circular pit, roughly 30cm in diameter and 12cm deep, into which a Vase Food Vessel containing cremated human remains had been placed.

During the excavations in 2009 along the new A2 Maydown City of Derry Airport dual carriageway scheme,[69] two ring-ditches, perhaps originally enclosing now ploughed away burial mounds were uncovered. The first at Site 4, Longfield More, was *c.* 30m in diameter, with the ditch measuring 1.6m wide and 50cm deep, and with an entrance 5m wide on the south-east into the interior. A large pit, close to the southernmost end of the ditch contained cremated bone, pottery and flint, and much pottery and flint was also recovered from the site. The second ring ditch was discovered at Site 8, Tully, and had an internal diameter of *c.* 25m. Among the other important Bronze Age features investigated along the road scheme were a cremation and cist and urn burials at Maydown and Upper Campsey.

During the Bronze Age, stone monuments were erected in prominent locations in the landscape that sometimes marked burials or perhaps tribal boundaries. At least five of these Bronze Age standing stones have been recorded in the environs of the City. Two still survive,

Early Bronze Age cist grave at Ballyoan during excavation in 2006

the other three having either been destroyed or their exact locations lost. At Avish[70] the stone is prominently positioned on the west-facing slope of Avish Hill, with excellent views to the west and north-east. It stands 1m high and is 60cm thick at the base. The other surviving standing stone is at Gortica. It is almost 2m long, 80cm broad and 35cm thick.[71] The three others were at Ballymagrorty,[72] Lismore or The Trench[73] and Lisglass.[74] Some of the stones may have been re-used and 'Christianised' in the Early Christian period (see reconstruction drawing of St Colum Cille's Derry).

In addition to the Middle Bronze Age spearhead found at the 1940 Lough Enagh excavations, a bronze axe head was found at Lisglass[75] in 1904. There are no surface indications of any site at the Lisglass find spot but the place of discovery was marked on 1907 and 1937 O.S. maps as 'Celt found (A.D. 1904)'. From time to time archaeologists are made aware of other metal finds made by metal detectorists in the Derry area. Not all are reported as it is illegal to excavate for archaeological objects both in Northern Ireland and the Republic of Ireland, without a licence from the government. The author would urge anyone who accidentally finds either Bronze Age metal or any other archaeological object to report it to the Museum curators in Derry~Londonderry or the NIEA in Belfast. They normally operate an appreciative and co-operative response in such circumstances and you may well also be entitled to a reward under the Treasure Act.

Early Bronze Age inhumation with bronze dagger at Ballyoan during excavation in 2006.

The bronze dagger found with the inhumation in the Ballyoan cist grave in 2006

Island City. The Archaeology of Derry~Londonderry

Early Bronze Age Food Vessel found at Straid near Londonderry

The Iron Age (*c.* 600 BC – AD 500)

The advent of what archaeologists call the Iron Age sees new art styles and high-status iron tools, weapons and jewellery, derived from the European 'Celtic' traditions appearing in Ireland. There is an increase in the construction of forts and fortified settlements in the landscape. However, the Iron Age is a very tricky period to study in Ireland, as the features found on many of its sites seems to be very similar to those of the preceding Late Bronze Age. The elite may have had new weaponry and wealth but the lifestyle of the people they ruled probably altered slowly during the centuries leaving few markers of change. The developed Irish Iron Age has been characterised as a time of great warrior-heroes such as Cú Chulainn (the 'Hound of Ulster'), of famed royal centres such as Emain Macha (Navan Fort) and epic military campaigns presented in literature such as *Táin Bó Cuailnge* ('The Cattle Raid of Cooley'). It may be that the Calgach of the early name of Derry, *Dóire Calgach*, was one such Iron Age mythological hero.

The stories and myths of the peoples of Iron Age Ireland were handed down orally for centuries before they were finally written down in the 7th and 8th centuries AD by Christian monks, so is hard to know how much these actually represent a true history of the period.[76] The Iron Age may have been a time of increased conflict in Ireland and it has been typified by some as marking the transformation of the island to what might be termed as a 'Celtic' identity. By the dawning of the early Christian period, in the 5th-century AD, Ireland was Gaelic speaking and the place-names were in Old Irish. The only excavation to date that has uncovered material dated to the Iron Age in the environs of the city was at Caw in 2003.[77] In Area 7 of the site, two bowl furnaces cut into the subsoil for iron working, were uncovered, and a charcoal sample from one (Context 161) yielded a date of AD 375–425, indicating that the ironworking on the site took place towards the end of the Iron Age.

Rivers in prehistoric Ireland were sometimes imbued with mythological powers, even being characterised as deities, such as the Rivers Boyne and Erne were. It is possible that the River Foyle was also regarded as a deity in prehistoric times. In the 1st century AD, the much larger island of Anglesey, off the coast of north Wales, was sacred to the Celtic tribes of the territory, as was the oak tree within the wider Celtic world. It is very possible that the 'Dóire' oak grove name signifies that such a sacred grove once existed on the Island of Derry.

Despite the wealth of excavated structures and settlement sites close to the 'Island', no prehistoric discoveries have been made to date in the core of the modern city. This may be due to destruction of early archaeological levels during the intensive phase of church building in the Medieval period, followed by the creation of the walled city in the 17th-century and the subsequent development into a thriving modern urban centre. As more excavations are carried out in the future, we may well start getting evidence for the first settlers to base themselves on the 'Island'.

Given the sheltered position of the 'Island', surrounded on all sides by the River Foyle during prehistoric times, it is possible that the place may have had religious significance, a place set apart from the 'secular' land on either side of the river. Certainly the oak grove connection would seem to bear this out. It could be that travelling to the 'Island' from either bank of the River Foyle during the prehistoric period meant travelling from a secular landscape over to a sacred one. What rituals were carried out by any priests on the island we may never know. However, given the presence of the oak grove trees and the nearby powerful river it might have been a combination of a celebration of the cycles of nature, the bounty that both plants and river provided and possibly even death and re-birth ceremonies similar to the Christian practice of baptism. These may have involved religious processions around the island, some of which may have been visible to people gathered on the 'secular' ground on either bank of the river.

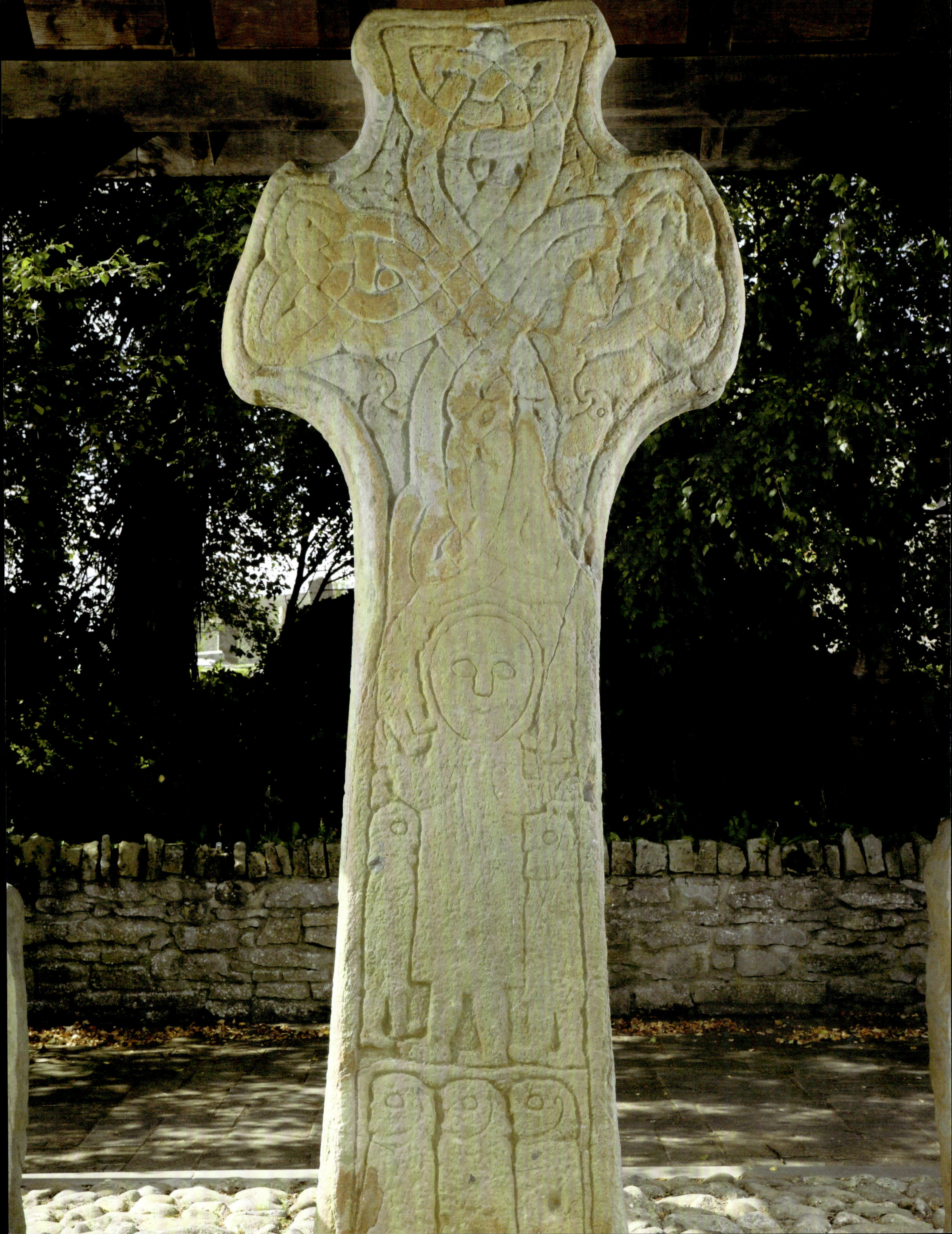

East face of the Donagh (St Patrick's) Cross, Carndonagh, Co Donegal. The cross dates to the 7th or 8th centuries.

The Early Christian Period

The coming of Christianity linked Ireland to the Western European Church and its network of contacts and ideas in the post-Roman world beyond our island. As missionaries and other church officials travelled throughout the country they connected Ireland with this wider world and introduced people to new ideas such as writing and books. Study of the Gospels was a central tenet of early Christianity, so literacy was a necessity and followed naturally in the wake of Christian missionaries. From this time we have various Irish Annals written down as chronicles, which listed notable events such as the births and deaths of important people, major battles, or harsh winters.

As Christianity became established in Ireland from the 6th-century onwards we see the foundations of major monasteries, such as at Derry and Armagh. The locations of these monasteries became proto-towns and the monastic communities included a mixture of religious people, craft workers and monastic farming tenants. The populations of these communities may not have been large by modern standards but they increasingly represented urban-like concentrations of wealth and resources in an overwhelmingly rural society. As a consequence, during the late 8th-11th centuries many were raided for their valuables. These raids were carried out by Irish lords as often as by the Vikings, although it is the Vikings who are more usually remembered for it today.

Ireland during this period was divided into hundreds of small kingdoms and sub-kingdoms known as *tuatha*. The economy was predominantly agricultural and rural. Towns had not yet developed. Clusters of more than a few dwellings were uncommon, except in the vicinity of the residences of important leaders and monastic centres. The rath or ringfort was the typical dwelling of Irish people during the 7th to 9th centuries (see below). Much of the landscape was still unenclosed and land was held in common ownership by the extended families whose people

Map of Early Christian sites in Derry's environs

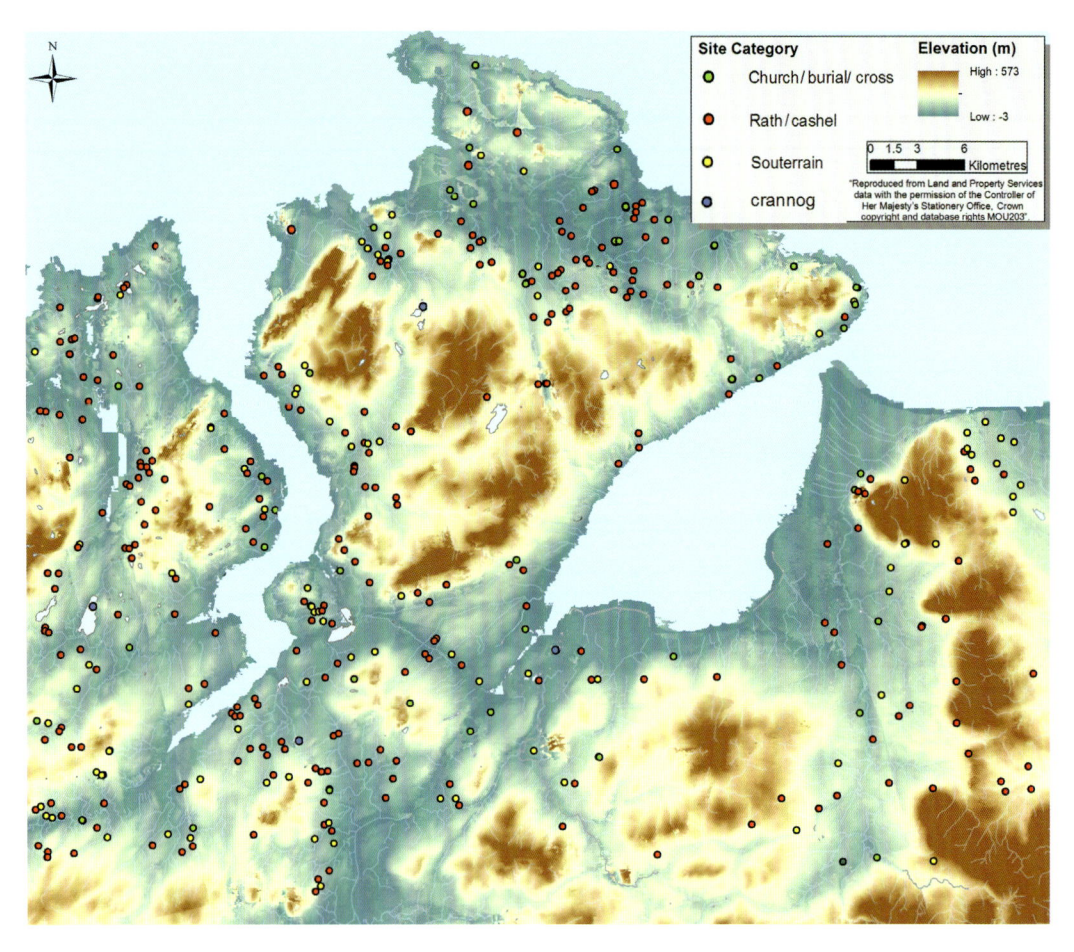

comprised most of the *tuatha*. From the Irish legal sources we know that cows were the basic unit of wealth and how many cows and calves you owned determined your status in society.[1] The importance of dairy products to Irish diet was central and it was these aspects of cattle owning that seem to have been most important in the early centuries of this period.[2]

In the northwest of Ireland a dynastic group of peoples formed which we know today as the Northern Uí Néill. They claimed descent from a single figure called Niall Noígíallach, or Niall of the Nine Hostages, and took control in Donegal and some adjacent parts of Derry and Tyrone around the same time as the adoption of Christianity. Two main branches of the Northern Uí Néill came to dominate the region and vie with each other for the Kingship of the Northern Uí Néill. The first claimed descent from Owen son of Niall and called themselves the Cenél nEógain meaning something like 'the people of Owen'. They were initially based in Inishowen (Inis nEógain – the island of Owen) and later took over what is now called Tyrone (Tír nEógain – the land of Owen). Their principal families in later times included the Mac Lochlainns and, most importantly, the O' Neills. The other main dynastic group of the Northern Uí Néill was the Cenél Conaill ('the people of Conaill') whose name is the main element of Tír Conaill, the old name for County Donegal, and whose principal family was later to become the O'Donnells.[3] The site of Derry was important because it was located at a strategic location on the River Foyle close to an important crossroads between the areas controlled by the Cenél nEógain and Cenél Conaill.

38 Island City. The Archaeology of Derry~Londonderry

Early Christian Derry

We have previously mentioned the warrior or leader figure *Calgach* represented in the name *Dóire Calgach* and that he may have been a mythological person. However, the one man who people most associate with Derry was most definitely real and it is with his life and works that the island in the Foyle first comes to international prominence. This man was St Colum Cille, also known as 'Columba' or 'Dove of the Church'. The foundation of his first church at Derry is recorded in the *Annals of Ulster* under the year AD 546 as simply *Daire Coluim Cille fundata est* ('Daire Coluim Cille was founded'). In the other great Gaelic annalistic compilation, which covers events in Ulster in detail, *The Annals of the Four Masters*, the event is described under the year AD 535 as 'The Church of Doire-Calgaigh was founded by Colum Cille, the place having been granted to him by his own tribe, i.e. the race of Conall Gulban, son of Niall'. Despite these early records it is not certain that Colum Cille was the original founder of the monastic settlement at Derry. It has been suggested that another cleric called Fiachrach mac Ciárain, a younger relative of Colum Cille's, established the original church at Derry either by himself or in conjunction with the saint.[4] In any case, because of the association with St Colum Cille, Derry became an important centre of Christianity until the end of the medieval period. The church that he is said to have founded there was called the *Dubh Regles*. Many archaeologists believe that it was prominently sited on high ground in the location where the subsequent Augustinian abbey stood and the current St Augustine's Church of Ireland church now stands. An alternative theory has it located further west on the Island, at the Long Tower (so-called because of the round tower that stood there). At present, neither siting can be said to be definitive and more research must be undertaken in order to move the question forward.

We know that by AD 720 the monastic buildings at Derry included a scriptorium – a room, which would have been dedicated, along with its staff of monks, to the production of manuscripts. In AD 720 a man called Caechscuile is recorded by the *Annals of the Four Masters* as having died. He was given the title 'scribe of Doire Chalgaigh' indicating that manuscripts were being created or copied at Derry and identifying the presence of a scriptorium. Early manuscripts were valuable and could be placed within covers made of metal and precious stones. Other buildings that a person would have seen at monasteries included a refectory, where the monks ate their communal meals, and craft workshops where metalworking was carried out. The monasteries would also have had extensive herb and vegetable gardens to provide the monks with fresh food.

Items like illuminated manuscripts, decorated crosses and chalices and altar plate used in the celebration of mass made meant that monasteries contained many beautiful and expensive objects. Such portable wealth eventually attracted the attention of raiders such as the Vikings. From the *Annals of Ulster*, we know that Cenél nEógain lords, based at Aileach, won a great victory over the Vikings at Derry in AD 833, the entry stating that 'Niall and Murchadh routed the foreigners in Daire Calgaig'. In AD 865 the *Annals of Ulster* describe how, 'Aed son of Niall plundered all the strongholds of the foreigners [the Vikings] in the territory of the North, both in Cenél nEógain and Dál Araidi, and took away their heads, their flocks and their herds from camp by battle. A victory was gained over them at Loch Febail [Lough Foyle] and twelve score heads taken thereby'. However, the Vikings returned, for in AD 893 the *Annals of the Four Masters*

Page from the Cathach, or the Psalter, of St Columba which is the oldest surviving Irish manuscript. Traditionally identified as the copy made by St Colum Cille from a book lent to him by St Finnian, which gave rise to the celebrated contention and judgement 'to every cow belongs her calf, therefore to every book belongs its copy'. The Cathach probably dates to the late 6th or early 7th centuries AD. It was later kept by the O' Donnells in Donegal

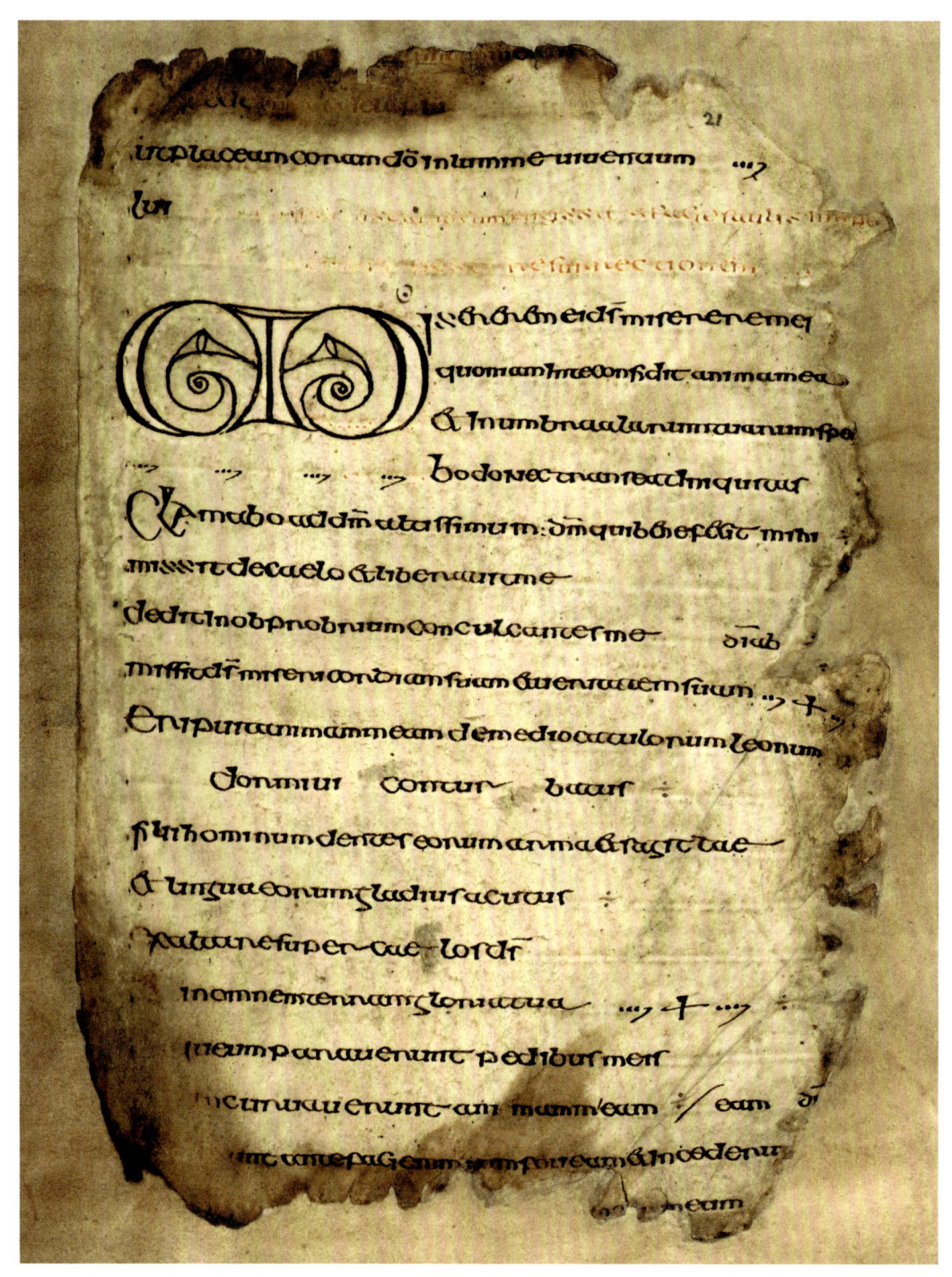

record how 'Ard-Macha [Armagh] was plundered by the foreigners of Loch Febail'. Towards the end of the 10th-century, the Vikings plundered the settlement at Derry again in the years AD 990 and AD 997.

It is unfortunate that archaeologists have not yet uncovered any churches or domestic buildings within the City to help shed light on this part of the story. There are, however, a number of monuments in the environs, both secular and ecclesiastical, that date to the Early Christian period.[5]

View of the Grianán of Aileach from exterior

The Grianán of Aileach

The Grianán of Aileach, some 11km (7 miles) to the north-west of the city centre, is one of the most impressive Early Christian forts in the whole of Ireland.[6] It is a circular, stone-built fort or cashel, dramatically positioned on top of Greenan Mountain. It has been identified as Aileach, one of chief forts, indeed 'capital', of the Northern Uí Néill who ruled most of what is now modern Counties Donegal, Londonderry and Tyrone. It may have originally been built and controlled by the Cenél Conaill and was deliberately erected on a very prominent location to be seen from a long distance. In turn, it commands a marvellous panorama along Loughs Swilly and Foyle, and across parts of Counties Donegal, Londonderry and Tyrone. It is also intervisible with the later Elagh Castle discussed in the next chapter.

The Grianán, which was much 'restored' by Dr Walter Bernard of Londonderry between 1874 and 1878, is roughly 23m in diameter, and has terraced walls that are some 4m thick and 5m high. As a result of the work by Bernard, it is now uncertain how much of the modern fort is the product of his endeavours. The walls contain chambers for storage, and stone steps on the interior accessed the ramparts on top. The wide entrance has a long lintel above it, and would originally have had stout wooden gates to protect it. At the centre of the fort, the remains of a rectangular structure were recorded in the 19th-century. There are three low, concentric earthen banks surrounding the fort, which may have had palisades on them and could have controlled access to the main fort and central area around it. However, the site wasn't too secure because in AD 900 Aileach was raided by the Vikings and again in AD 939 when they took prisoner the Cenél nEógain king Muircheartach, son of Niall 'and carried him off to their ships'. Aileach suffered once again in AD 1101, when it was taken by the army of Murtough O'Brien, King of

Interior terraces of the Grianán of Aileach

Munster. O'Brien is said to have carried out the attack in revenge for the destruction, in AD 1088, of his own royal fort at Kincora, Co. Clare by Donal Mac Lochlainn, King of Aileach. It is said that he made each of his soldiers take way a stone from the central cashel so that it could not be rebuilt. After this time the Grianán of Aileach seems to have gone into decline and Derry may have become the political centre for the Mac Lochlainn lords of Cenél nEógain.

Although this section has identified the site on Greenan Mountain as the Northern Uí Néill capital Aileach, it has been suggested that there was an earlier Aileach located elsewhere. Lacey[7] has proposed that the nearby townland of Elagh More (5km east of the Grianán) derives its name from the Irish *Aileach Mór* and that an original Cenél nEógain royal site called Aileach was located there. His theory runs that when the Cenél nEógain effectively took control of the Northern Uí Néill kingship in the late AD 700s – early AD 800s they needed a new regional royal site to reflect this. Accordingly, they built one (the Grianán) in a commanding position on top of Greenan Mountain and named it Aileach after their nearby existing royal site. The remains of an important Later-Medieval O'Doherty castle exist at Elagh More today but there are no visible remains of any Early Christian site. Lacey suggests that this evidence could have been destroyed when the original Aileach site had its materials recycled to build the later O'Doherty castle.

View over Lough Swilly from the Grianán of Aileach

The 'White Fort' cashel near Dungiven with Tamniarin rath in the field behind (and to the left)

Raths, Cashels and Crannogs

Although The Grianán of Aileach was a stone built cashel, the most numerous kind of monument in Ireland and the predominant domestic settlement type of the Early Christian period is the 'rath' or 'ringfort'.[8] These were enclosures, typically surrounded by between one-three ditches and earthen banks. The earthen banks were formed from the soil dug out of the ditch and may have had a wooden palisade on top for added defence. A stout wooden gate would have guarded the causeway over the ditch and through the banks. The simpler forms of rath enclosed the farmsteads of prosperous farmers but the more elaborate examples would have housed someone of high status. Three-ringed forts (known as trivallate raths) are commonly taken to denote a royal site, which can be seen as a central or capital-like place in a territory. There were also unenclosed farmsteads, but these are more difficult to identify, as they do not leave any aboveground remains. The different types of settlement, enclosed or unenclosed, may have reflected differences in status within Gaelic society with only certain people being allowed to build raths or cashels. It has also been argued that because cattle and dairy products were so central to the Irish life in this period that the need to protect cattle may have led to the construction of the defensive features of banks and ditches that we see around many Irish raths in the 6th-8th centuries.[9] It has been also been suggested, based on evidence recovered from archaeological excavations, that from the end of the 8th-century that there was a change in the building styles of raths with the development of 'raised raths', such as the one excavated at Deer Park Farms in Co. Antrim.[10] These raths used the material dug out of the protective ditch, if one had been created, or else soil brought in from elsewhere to raise the inside of the enclosure and create a flat circular platform. The resulting structure placed more emphasis on the protection of the people living there than on their livestock. It may be that the development of raised raths coincided with the increasing use

Tamniarin Rath near Dungiven

Excavation of the ditch of a rath at Longfield Beg in 2006. Note the discarded quernstone in the ditch fill

Complete quernstone and fragments of two others recovered from the fill of the ditch of the Early Christian period rath at Longfield Beg in 2006

of land for growing and processing cereals leading to an increase in the use of slave labour for this agricultural work.[11] Certainly one of the reasons for Viking raids in Ireland was to seize slaves and the port of Viking Dublin was a major centre of the international trade in slaves in the 9th and 10th centuries.

Recorded raths in the Derry area include the scheduled example at Gortinure[12], at Coshquin[13] where there is also a souterrain (see below), and at Kittybane, where the rath also has an accompanying souterrain[14]. There are also a number of enclosures or mounds that may be raths, which include the monuments at Ballougry[15], Culmore[16], Termonbacca[17] and Managh Beg.[18] At Ballynagalliagh[19] there is the recorded site where a rath once stood, but which has since been destroyed or left no visible remains above ground.

A feature commonly associated with settlements throughout Ireland during this period, including raths and cashels, are souterrains – artificial underground chambers and connecting passages. Normally they were constructed with stone walls and roofs, though earthen examples were also built.[20] These subterranean structures, many of which have defensive features, were used as refuges during enemy raids, a feature of this era, while they also appear to have been used to store food, for generally they had a cold, even temperature. A more recent interpretation is that they may also have been used to hide slaves, an increasingly important commodity in Irish society after the 9th-century, during times when a settlement was under attack.[21] Many souterrains have been recorded within a twenty mile radius of the city, while surviving examples within close proximity of the city include those at Enagh[22], Ballynagalliagh[23], two from Coshquin[24], and Shantallow[25]. Other examples, now unlocated or destroyed, have been recorded from Fincairn[26], Glenderowen[27] and New Buildings.[28]

Given the preponderance of lakes and rivers around Lough Foyle, it is unsurprising that crannogs (Irish for 'little tree') were used in this part of Ulster. This was an alternative to the rath, only it was built in a lake.[29]. An artificial platform was created by driving stakes into a lakebed, and infilling the area enclosed with stones to create a level platform above the waterline. After this, houses and defensive palisades were erected on layers laid down over the basal platform. This technique of building was used in Ireland from at least the Bronze Age. Several examples of crannog settlements are known from around the City, including at Campsey Lower[30] and Green Island and Rough Island in Lough Enagh East.[31] Green Island, now connected to the shore by a narrow modern promontory, is composed of a natural core with stone piled around the edge. An unlocated crannog is also recorded from Carrakeel.[32]

Aerial view of the Grianán of Aileach

Island City. The Archaeology of Derry~Londonderry

Early church lintel in the churchyard of Carndonagh Church, Co Donegal. In the centre of the lintel's face is a wheeled cross. To the left is a group of figures, while to the right is interlaced decoration.

Ecclesiastical Monuments

In the early days of Christianity in Ireland the churches were small, rectangular buildings constructed of timber, which have left few aboveground traces.[33] Many later stone churches were also built on the same sites as the original buildings, so that archaeological evidence for early churches is sparse. Unfortunately, no remains of any of the Early Christian churches or other ecclesiastical foundations have yet been discovered on the 'Island' at Derry. The church and graveyard of Killea may have their origins in the Early Christian period[34]. The boundary wall of the ruined Killea church, itself possibly of medieval date, encloses an octagonal area, almost certainly respecting an older circular/sub-circular enclosure. To the west of the site it actually encloses an arc of a much earlier bank that is roughly 7m wide and 0.7m high. This bank has been altered by graves, but it is still possible to follow its line.

A church thought until recently to have early origins, known variously as St Columb's or St Brecan's, is located in modern St Columb's Park in the townland of Clooney, several hundred metres to the north-east of the modern Ebrington Barracks.[35] The only substantial remains of a church are its east and west gables that probably date to the 1590s. Although tradition suggests that it may have been built on the site of an earlier foundation, excavations in the church interior in 1939 found no trace of any earlier building. Another small investigation of the site was carried out in 2012 by archaeologists from the Centre for Archaeological Fieldwork, QUB.[36] The evaluation work followed a programme of geophysical survey, which identified a number of targets for further investigation. Four trenches were located over these anomalies, but no archaeological remains associated with St Brecan's Church were uncovered, and any remains exposed relate to more recent landscaping and cultivation of the area.

A well located downslope from the Grianán of Aileach.

Late Victorian cast iron pump on the site of earlier holy wells known as 'St Columb's Wells', located at St. Columb's Terrace between Lecky Road and the City Walls.

Other recorded churches that have not survived include St Comgal's church, convent and graveyard at Rossnagalliagh[37], and one supposedly founded by St Colum Cille at Ballymagrorty.[38] Two other indicators of the presence of early church sites are bullaun stones, holy wells and pillar stones. Local tradition says that Enagh Church[39], also known as Domnach Dola, was founded by St Cannice. A simple stone cross 18m to the east of the main gate may also suggest an Early Christian origin for the site.

A feature frequently associated with Early Christian churches, many of which may have served as baptismal fonts, are ballaun stones. built into the Calvary at the modern Long Tower Church and St Columb's Well, near where the stone originally stood, may suggest the presence of an early church there. Two bullaun stones are recorded in Altnagelvin townland.[40] Unfortunately, they have been moved from their original setting(s), and it is not known from which church or churches they came originally. Another stone, now lost, was recorded in the 19th-century on the 1st edition OS 6-inch map at the site known as St Columb's Wells (see below). Thomas Colby recorded that it was known as 'St Columb's Stone', and popularly believed to bear the imprints of the Saint's knees.[41]

A possibly early survival from the first foundation on the 'Island' is the group of three holy wells, known collectively as 'St Columb's Wells', located close to a terrace of the same name between Lecky Road and the City walls.[42] They are now represented by a late-19th-century ornamental cast-iron water pump and manhole set in a concrete slab. There are also two holy wells recorded at New Buildings,[43] but they have now disappeared, and another at Rossnagalliagh, known as St Comgall's Well.[44] This was recorded along with the church and convent and still survives as an

Island City. The Archaeology of Derry~Londonderry

The High Cross and Church at Clonca, Co Donegal. The cross head (partially restored) has interlace and geometric designs, while the top and bottom panels of the shaft are also decorated with interlace design. The central panel is divided; the upper section has two lions, while the bottom has two-seated figures, probably saints, with their hands folded.

The Cross of St. Mura at Fahan showing the east face with a Greek cross mounted on a stem in a broad double-edged interlaced ribbon. There is a boss in the cross centre and two concentric circles around bosses in each of the hollowed cross angles. The cross may be of 7th or 8th-century date.

Detail of the Clonca High Cross showing carved decoration on the centre panel of the west face

oval, water-filled hollow (2.0m by 2.4m diameter) with a rough overflow outlet to south-west.[45] In 1905, this well was still venerated locally, and as recently as 1978 was still being looked after, with evidence of a concrete surround and access via steps from the road on the north-west. In recent times the site has been more neglected. In the townland of Clooney a holy well was known to have been located near the ruins of St Columb's Church, but the area has now been re-developed and the site is no longer visible.[46] Another holy well was located in Gobnascale, close to where the Craigavon Bridge meets the eastern bank of the River Foyle, on land once owned by Colonel John Mitchelburne, famed for his actions in the 1689 siege of the city.[47] The site of this holy well is now lost.

A feature frequently found during the Early Christian period in Ireland are the upright pillar stones, which were often decorated. The best known example in Ulster, and most heavily ornamented with Christian symbols, is at Kilnasaggart in Edenappa townland in County Armagh.[48] In the environs of Derry, at Lisglass, there is a pillar stone with a small cross-inscribed on the middle of its east face. Whether this was original or simply the later Christianising of a 'pagan' religious monument is uncertain. Many decorated carved stone crosses, stone slabs and pillar stones can be seen at or close to ecclesiastical sites in Donegal.[49] Some of these decorated stones and crosses are burial markers, some served as foci for prayers and other religious activities and some stood or indicated boundaries, land grants or important routes.

Particularly fine and important decorated crosses and cross-slabs are found at Carndonagh and Fahan, to the north of Derry in the Inishowen. At Carndonagh, which was one of the main early ecclesiastical sites in Donegal, stands the well known Donagh Cross (aka St. Patrick's Cross), a simple high cross with short arms, flanked each side by stele. This red sandstone cross,

Stele at Carndonagh. From left to right these are David the Warrior; animal-headed figure, possibly with two discs and a hammer; David the Psalmist; a bishop carrying a crozier, book and hand bell.

which is 2.5m high, has a depiction of Christ with outstretched arms on its east face below broad ribbon interlace, symbolic of the tree of life. The braid patterns on this cross were compared by the late Françoise Henry to the 7th-century Book of Durrow, and this has led some to believe that this cross may be among the earliest of its kind in Ireland. It's flanking pillar stones have carving depicting David the Warrior and David the Harpist on one stone and on the other a bishop carrying a crozier, book and hand bell. A short distant away, with the churchyard is a 12th-century decorated church lintel and a cross-slab known as 'The Marigold Stone', whose west face is decorated with a *flabellum*, whose head bears a large circle within which is a seven-petalled marigold (Mary's Gold), the 'herb of the sun'. A *flabellum* was a liturgical fan used in early churches to keep flies off the chalice on the altar; one of St Columba's relics was a flabellum, and some believe that this depiction on the cross-slab may be a copy of this very relic, flanked each side by two pilgrims.

In the 10th and 11th centuries in Europe the Christian Church underwent a period of reform that established a clear hierarchical system of rule from the Pope, as the head of the Church, down through clearly defined bishoprics to the priests, all of whom were now located in a new institution, a clearly defined parcel of land called the parish. This new system was introduced into all the Christian countries of Europe. Older monastic orders such as the Benedictines were also reformed, putting them under the clear control of a nominated bishop, and new orders such as the Cistercians and Augustinians were founded. The Church in Ireland, located on the fringe of Europe, was one of the last to introduce the reforms but through the 12th-century the Irish church was brought into line with the rest of Christian Western Europe. In the medieval period, discussed in the next chapter, we see the coming of some of the new monastic orders to Derry.

The Marigold Stone

Conjectural reconstruction of the Early Christian monastery at Derry as it might have appeared in 700 AD. The monastery was founded by St. Colum Cille (Columba or 'dove of the church') around 546 AD after he had completed his education at Clonard, Co. Meath. Prior to this, St. Colum Cille, who was apparently born at Gartan in Co. Donegal, had been taught by St. Finnian at Movilla in Co. Down. According to an often repeated tale, the saint became involved in a dispute with his former teacher, St. Finnian, after he had copied a manuscript without permission; this dispute led to a pitched battle (at Cúl Dreimhne) in 561 AD resulting in many deaths. This and other grievances resulted in the exile of St. Colum Cille from Ireland and he left his community Derry in 563 AD with twelve companions to found the great monastery of Iona (also known as 'Hy'), on an island off the west coast of Scotland. He only subsequently returned to Ireland once and died in AD 593.

Although St. Colum Cille founded a number of Irish monasteries, it would appear that Derry was his principal residence until he left Ireland. The name itself, Doire (sometimes Doire Colum Cille), means 'the oakgrove of Colum Cille', a sacred grove of trees, which may have pre-dated the monastery.

St. Colum Cille's association with Derry helped the prestige of the monastery to develop in later centuries. The Rathbreasail Assembly of 1111 AD considered it as a possible location for the seat of the bishopric of Tír Conaill, but Raphoe was finally chosen and Derry was left as a great monastic centre, which a few decades later experienced a monastic revival under Flaithbertach O Brolcháin.

Lack of on-site archaeological evidence means that we can only surmise the former appearance of the Derry monastery, but other known examples provide material for a tentative reconstruction. Life in these early religious communities was undoubtably extremely harsh and ascetic and all the buildings, including the church, would have been of wood, wattle or mud. Irish monks did not build in stone until the 9th-century and in most cases not until the 12th-century.

Island City. The Archaeology of Derry~Londonderry

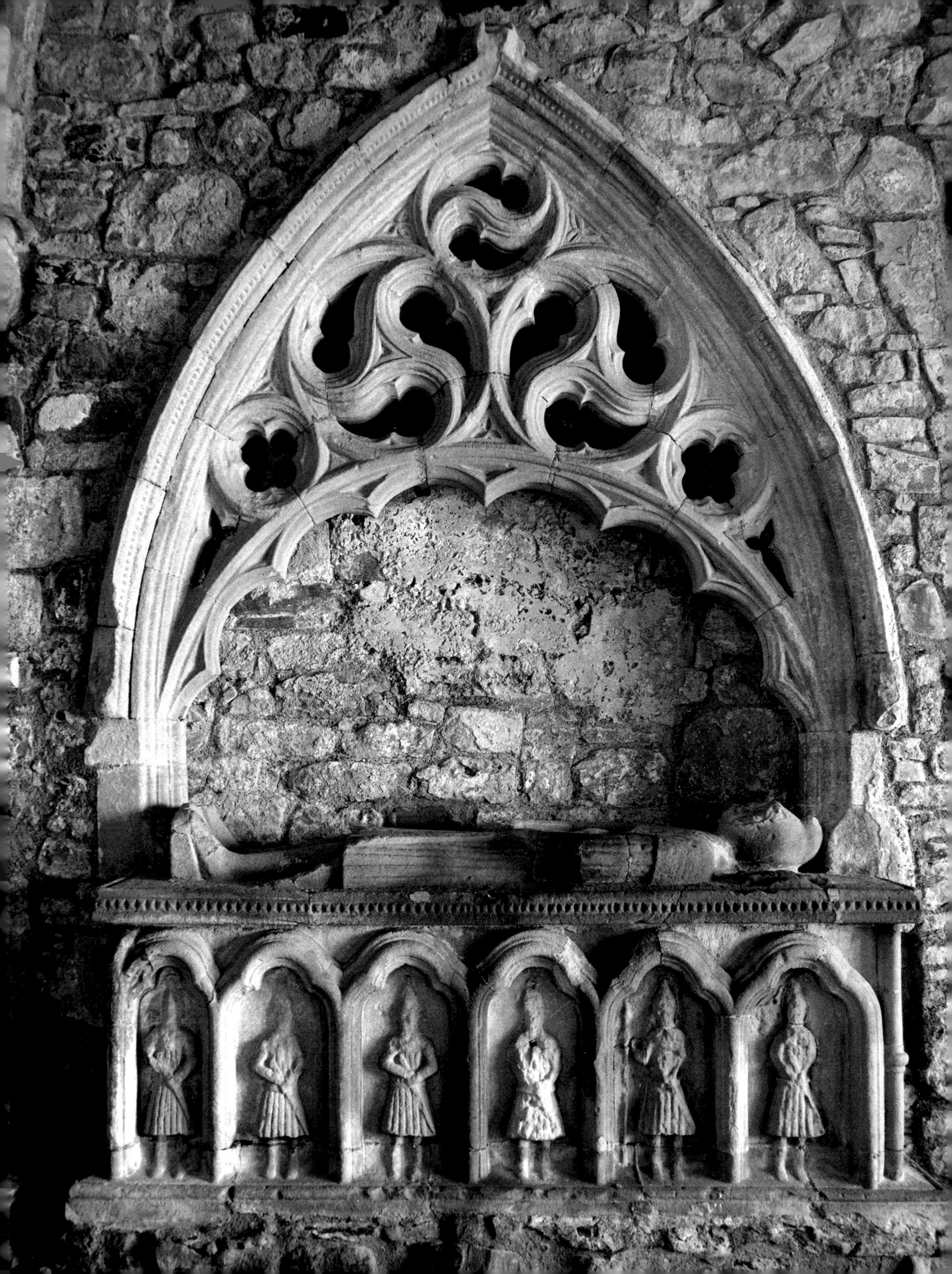

The Medieval Period

During the Medieval period (*c.* 1200 – *c.* 1600) the ecclesiastical settlement at Derry greatly expanded from the monastic foundation created by St Colum Cille. The church reforms of the 12th-century and the arrival of the Normans in Ireland at the end of the same century all affected how this ecclesiastical settlement developed. Although the Norman Earl of Ulster Richard de Burgo built an impressive castle at nearby Greencastle (originally called Northburgh) in the 14th-century the Normans did not construct a new town at Derry and throughout the medieval period the settlement remained under the control of the O'Donnell lords of Donegal. By the end of the medieval period, just prior to the English conquest of Ireland, we know that a number of religious houses and a tower house castle had been constructed on or close to the Island of Derry. We also know that Derry had become an important place of pilgrimage connected with St Colum Cille and we have some details of the route of this pilgrimage. Sir Henry Docwra's map of the Island, which dates to 1600 and is the first map of Derry, illustrates how the medieval buildings at Derry might have looked.

We get much information about how Derry developed in the medieval period, and events related to it, from the various Irish annalistic histories. Later, as Elizabethan interest in Ireland increased, there is additional information from English documents and maps. At the start of the 17th-century the armies of Queen Elizabeth 1 defeated the Gaelic lords of Ireland, including those who had patronized the religious houses at Derry, in the Nine Years' War (1594-1603). Sir Henry Docwra, one of Elizabeth's generals in Ireland, founded a new English settlement at Derry. The medieval buildings were all taken down or adapted for secular use and none survive today. Docwra's new settlement at Derry was later destroyed in the revolt of Sir Cahir O'Doherty in 1608, leading to the construction of the more substantial walled city a decade later and which is described in a later chapter.

Previous: The 'O'Cahan' tomb in Dungiven Priory. Magnificent canopied niche tomb in the south wall of the nave of Dungiven Priory (Canons Regular). Below the recumbent effigy are six weepers, while the arch above is filled with flamboyant tracery. The weepers are gallowglasses (Scottish mercenaries) and like the effigy are armed with swords with pommels of 'acorn' type; one has a spear. It is traditionally dated to the 14th-century and said to be the tomb of Cooey na nGall O'Cahan. However, the late John Hunt observed that they are dressed in a similar fashion to one of the Irish soldiers drawn by Dürer in 1521, noting 'the aketons are alike in the general arrangement of the quilted folds, type of sleeve and length of garment'. Hunt also noted similarities with an effigy at Glinsk, Co Galway and suggested the tomb was made in the late 15th-century, probably for a member of the O'Cahan family.

The Development of Medieval Derry

The association with St Colum Cille was vitally important to the success of the religious foundation in Derry, which remained an important religious centre throughout the medieval period. It may have also developed as a place of pilgrimage related to the saint. In 1122 the *Annals of Ulster* tell how 'Mael Coluim Ua Brolcháin, bishop of Ard Macha, died on pilgrimage in the hermitage of Daire, with victory of Martyrdom and repentance'.[1] According to *Annals of the Four Masters*, from the 1150s the renowned abbot of Derry, Flaithbertach Ua Brolcháin († 1175), started calling himself *coarb* (successor) to Colum Cille. Following a rivalry that had been pursued over a decade, in 1162 the great Columban church at Kells, in modern Co. Meath, acknowledged the dominant position of Derry as the principal church in the *familia* of Colum Cille. This may have spurred the building of new churches in Derry and we know, from descriptions in the Annals, that Derry had three more churches and a round tower by the late-12th-century.

It was Flaithbertach Ua Brolcháin who oversaw the new phase of building at Derry. The *Annals of the Four Masters* for the year 1162 describe that a *'separation of the houses from the church of Doire was caused by the successor of Colum-Cille, Flaithbertach Ua Brolcháin, and by Muirceartach Ua Lochlainn, King of Ireland; and they removed eighty houses, or more, from the place where they were. And the Caiseal-an-urlair was erected by the successor of Colum-Cille, who pronounced a curse against anyone who should come over it'.*

The *Caiseal an Urlair* was a boundary wall built to separate the secular and religious parts of the settlement at Derry. The reference to eighty domestic houses in the annalistic references shows that an extensive settlement had grown up around the ecclesiastical foundations.

We get an idea of the scale of the new building works in 1163 when the *Annals of the Four Masters* record that a 'lime-kiln, measuring seventy feet every way' was made 'by the successor of Colum-Cille Flaithbertach Ua Brolcháin, and the clergy of Colum-Cille, in the space of twenty days'. The wall and lime kiln of 1162 and 1163 where presumably constructed as part of an overall building project which was to culminate in the erection of the *Tempull Mór*, or new cathedral.

In 1164, we are told that the 'great church (*Tempull Mór*) of Doire, which is eighty feet long, was erected by the successor of Colum-Cille, Flaithbertach Ua Brolcháin, by the clergy of Colum-Cille, and by Muircertach Ua Lochlainn, King of Ireland; and they completed its erection in the space of forty days'. In time, this important church gave the parish of Templemore its name.[2] The 'Long Tower' – a high, circular stone tower or round tower – was subsequently constructed as part of the *Tempull Mór* religious complex, which is presumed to have been located in the area of modern Long Tower Street. Some of the new buildings may also have been constructed to house relics that emphasised its important position, including possibly the Soiscela Martain, an important holy book.[3]

The first references to the other important church dedicated to Colum Cille come soon afterwards in the *Annals of the Four Masters* and the *Annals of Ulster* for the year 1166, where it is referred to as the *Duibreiclés Coluim Cille* – 'the black seminary of Colum Cille'. This Augustinian church – normally referred to as the *Dubh Regles* – was built on the site probably now occupied by St Augustine's Church on Society Street. Subsequent references in the annals to the *Dubh*

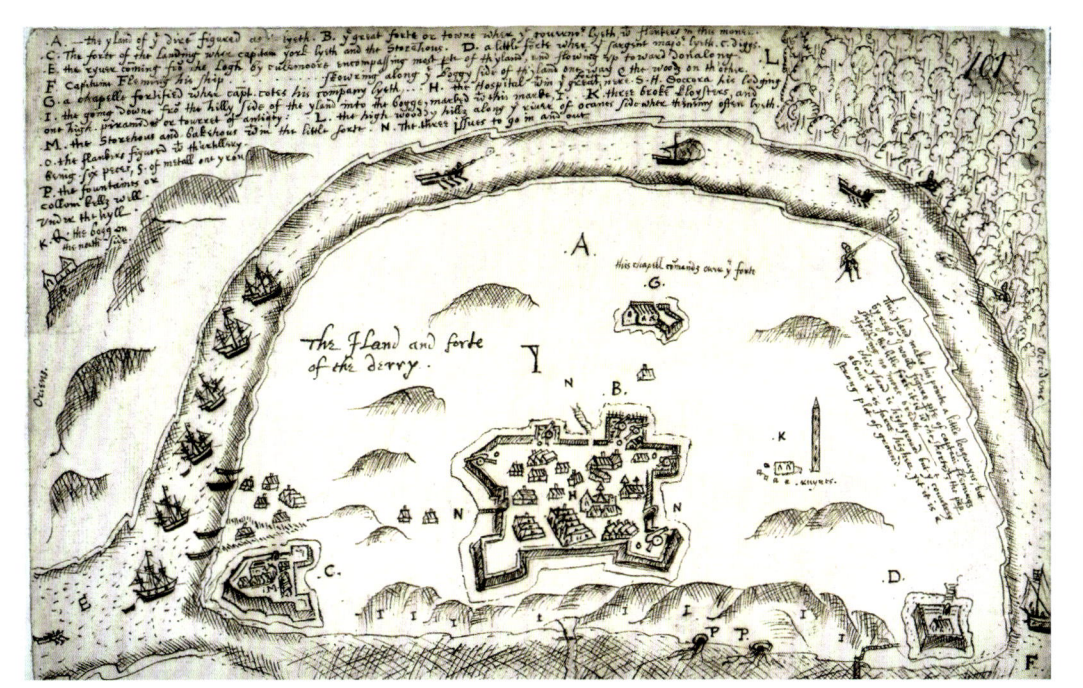

The map known as 'The Iland and forte of the derry' drawn for Sir Henry Docwra around 1600 to illustrate the new fortified English settlement erected on the Island during the Nine Years' War. It shows many of the medieval ecclesiastical buildings that were mostly demolished during or shortly after the creation of the walled city in the early 17th century. The medieval sites and buildings depicted include the holy wells known as St. Columb's Wells; the Dubh Regles church; the *Tempull Mór*, the Round Tower; the Dominican Friary, possibly the Cistercian Nunnery; the O'Doherty towerhouse and St Brecan's Church on the Waterside.

Regles church in the later-12th-century (e.g. 1173, 1175 and 1195) note the deaths of important clerics, while one for 1192 mentions a new doorway being made for its refectory, which was paid for by an O'Cahan lord.[4]

Because of its important churches, the ecclesiastical settlement was raided for plunder on a number of occasions and in the descriptions of these raids in the Irish Annals we get snippets of information about the settlement in the medieval period. The Anglo-Normans invaded Ireland in 1169 and the Somerset Knight John de Courcy subsequently conquered parts of eastern Ulster after basing himself at Carrickfergus in 1177. In the succeeding decades The *Annals of Ulster* describe raids by the Anglo-Normans into Irish territory west of the Bann. In such a raid in 1197, troops based at the motte at Mount Sandel outside Coleraine, under the command of a knight called Rotsel Fitton 'came on a foray to the Port of Doire, so that he pillaged [the churches of] Cluain-I (Clooney), Enach (Enagh) and Derc-bruach (Gransha)'. These three churches were located on the eastern side of the Foyle, downstream from Derry. Unfortunately for the Normans, 'Flaithbertach Ua Maeldoraidh (namely, king of Cenel Conaill and the Cenel nEogain), overtook them with a small force of the Cenel Conaill and the Cenel nEogain, so that he inflicted defeat upon them on the strand of the Nuathcongbhail [probably at Faughanvale, near modern day Eglinton] [and] they were slaughtered to a large number (namely, around the son of Ardgal Ua Lochlainn), through miracle of Colum-cille and Cainnech [Cannice] and Brecan [whose churches] they pillaged there'.

That same year Flaithbertach Ua Maeldoraidh died. He was succeeded by Echmarcach Ua Dochartaich, who took 'the kingship of Cenel-Conaill immediately. And he was but a fortnight in the kingship, when John De-Courcy came with a large force under him past Tuaim [present day Toome where the road still crosses the Bann] into Tir-Eogain. From here to Ard-sratha [Ardstraw, Co Tyrone]; after that, around to Doire of Colum-cille, so that they were five nights

Island City. The Archaeology of Derry~Londonderry

Detail from Griffin Cocket's Map of Derry, 1602

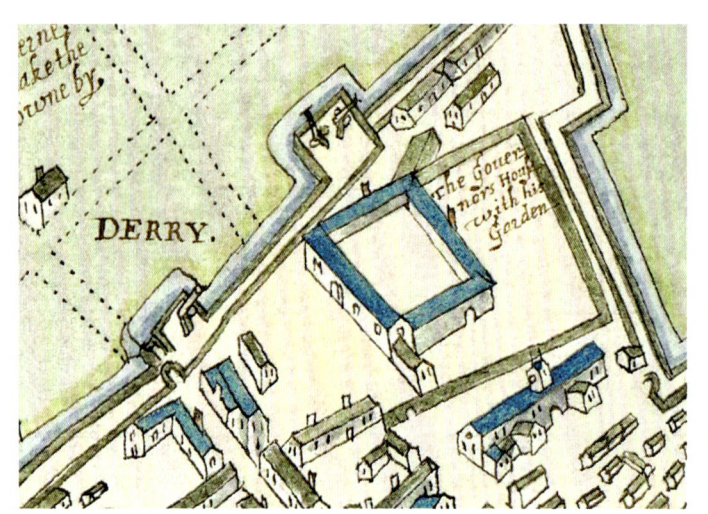

The Augustinian Monastery

The monastery of Arrouaise Augustinian regular canons was founded in Derry probably in the 1230s, and may have either incorporated or been located close to the old monastery of Doire-Colum-Cille (Doire-Calgach). It was sometimes known as the 'Black Abbey', most likely a reference to the long black cassocks and hoods worn by the 'Black Cannons'. According to the Register of John Bole, Archbishop of Armagh (1457-71) the monastery was filial to the abbey of St Peter and St Paul in Armagh. In the later Middle Ages it evidently suffered from the unstable

Detail from Nicholas Pynnar's Survey of 1618-19

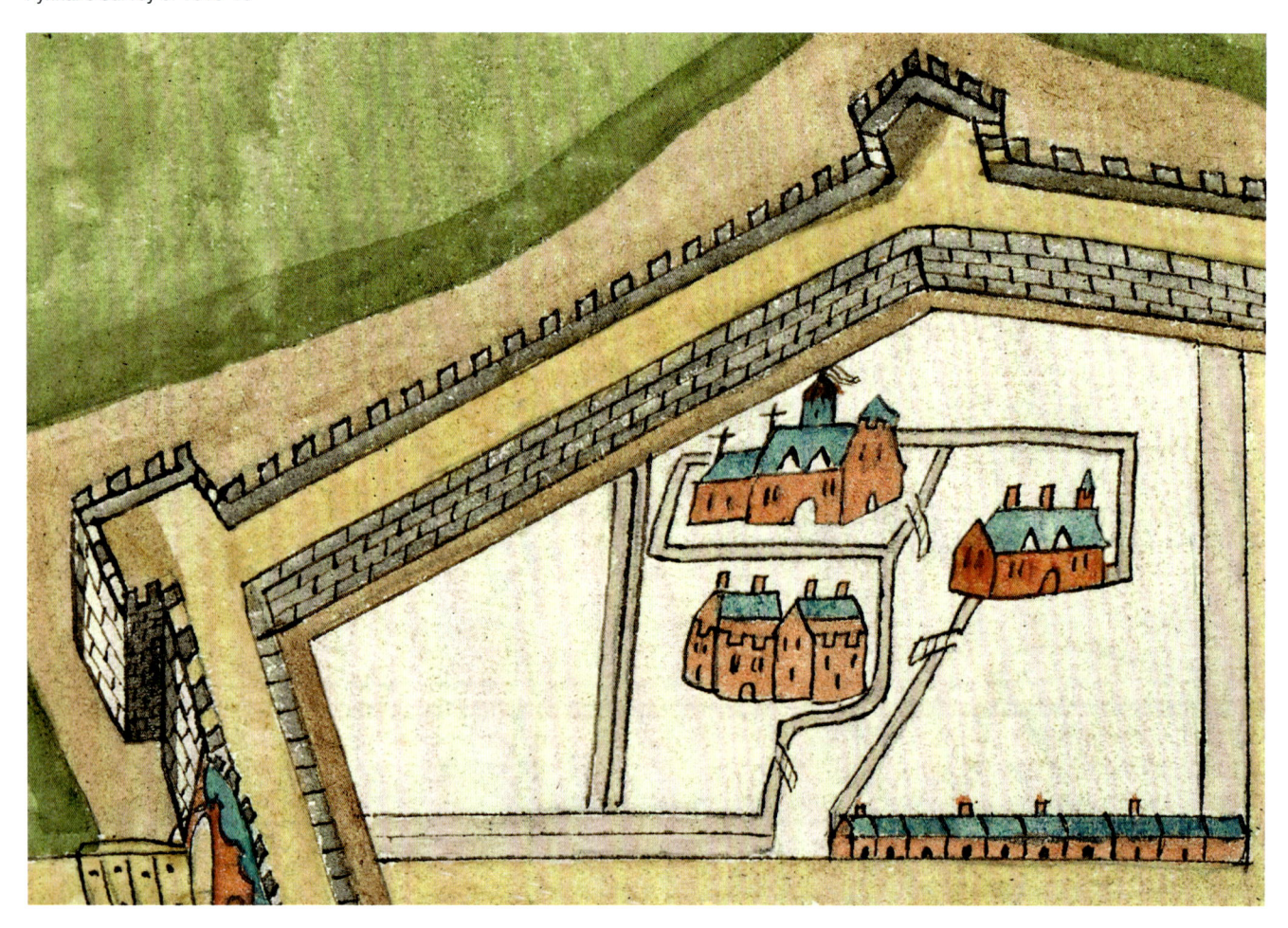

Island City. The Archaeology of Derry~Londonderry

political climate within the area for in 1411 it was so poor that many canons could not be properly maintained and one of them asked to be transferred to the Arrouaisian priory of Cloontuskert, Co Roscommon. An indulgence was granted in 1423 because the buildings were in a ruined state and needed repair. The canons apparently remained into the mid-16th century, but were presumably evicted when the abbey was occupied by Colonel Randolph and his English troops in 1566. The buildings are clearly depicted on Cocket's c.1602 Map of Derry, as well as on Pynnar's survey of 1618-19 and Raven's 1622 and 1625 surveys.

Detail from Thomas Raven's Plan of the City of Londonderry, 1622

Aerial photograph of the area formerly occupied by the Augustinian monastery in the city (left centre ground)

Island City. The Archaeology of Derry~Londonderry

therein… [before raiding into Donegal].' Coleraine was the base from which the Anglo-Normans advanced in the late-12th and early 13th centuries, and their control even extended briefly into Inishowen. But the settlement at Derry continued to be occupied as an Irish ecclesiastical centre. In 1204, the *Annals of Ulster* describe how 'Doire was burned from the Cemetery of St Martin to the Well of St. Adomnán (named after St Colum Cille's famous biographer)'. The Well of St Adomnán may have been one of the wells that became collectively known as 'St Colm's Wells'. The Cemetery of St Martin may have been in the modern area from Fox's Corner to Rossville Street, or else perhaps on the opposite side of Fahan Street down to the Lecky Road.[5]

In the same year a second incident at Derry is recorded where 'Diarmait, son of Muircertach Ua [Mac] Lochlainn, with a force of Foreigners [Normans] came on a foray into Tir-Eogain, so that they plundered the Shrine of St Colum-cille, until a party of the Cenel-Eogain overtook them and defeat was inflicted upon the Foreigners and Diarmait was killed through miracles of the Shrine'.

Another reference in the *Annals of the Four Masters*, this time for 1213, states that Thomas MacUchtry and Rory Mac Randal, Scots from the lordship of Galloway, are said to have, 'plundered Doire completely and took the [religious] treasures of the Community of Daire and the North of Ireland besides from out of the midst of the church of the Monastery'. The plunder was taken back to the Anglo-Norman outpost at Coleraine, which had been granted to them by King John. In the entry for 1215, there is yet another account of a raid when the *Annals of Ulster* record that, 'a foray was made by Aedh, son of Mael-Sechlainn Mac Lochlainn upon the successor [coarb] of St Colum-cille and a herd of cattle was carried off by him'. These presumably belonged to the church and would have been a heavy loss, as cattle counted as wealth in Gaelic society. In more practical terms, they were a source of food and milk for the religious community, and their hides were also used as a source of the vellum on which illuminated manuscripts were created. But the same entry recounts that Aedh's actions did not go unpunished as he 'was killed by the Foreigners [the Normans] in the same year through miracle of Colum-cille'. In 1223 Niall O' Neill plundered Derry, the *Annals of Ulster* recording that he 'profaned Daire, respecting the daughter of Ua Cathain. And God and Colum-cille wrought a miracle, so that his thread of life was shortened'. Such were the experiences of many ecclesiastical centres in Ireland throughout the medieval period.

A medieval convent or nunnery was founded at Derry in 1218 by the branch of the O' Neills based in Strabane in modern Co. Tyrone, and there may have been an earlier foundation at the start of the 12th-century. A reference in 1512 describes the house of St Mary, Derry, of Cistercian nuns being without either an Abbess or nuns.[6] There are no visible remains of the Convent and the site is not securely located. However, it may have been close to the present location of St Columb's Cathedral, which is built on the highest point of the Island. The maps drawn up 1600 and 1601, when the English captured Derry, both appear to show the ruins of the nunnery.

As a result of church reforms in the 12th-century, the monastery at Derry had adopted the rule of Canons Regular of St Augustine by about 1207.[7] For political reasons the seat of the Cenél nEógain diocese was at Maghera, Co. Londonderry, although some bishops may have lived in Derry itself.

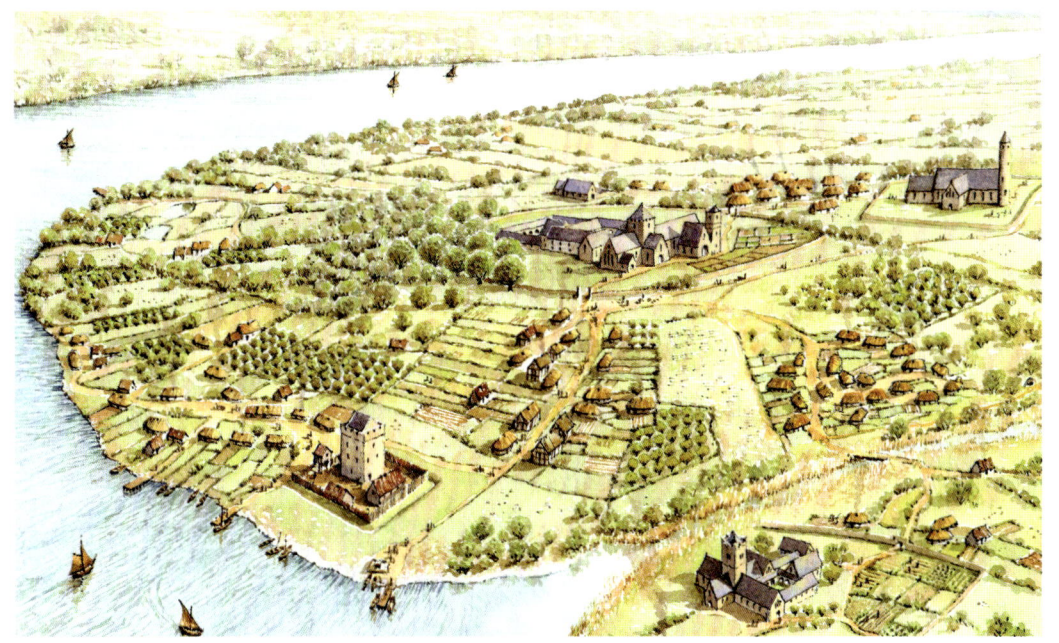

Reconstruction painting showing how the ecclesiastical settlement at Derry might have looked c. 1500. In the foreground, bottom right, is the Dominican Abbey and on left is the O' Doherty towerhouse, roughly where the Tower Museum now stands. Between the Dominican Abbey and the prominent Dubh Regles Augustinian church is the Graveyard of St Martin. Beyond the Dubh Regles church, on the left, is the Cistercian nunnery in the area now occupied by St. Columb's Cathedral. To the right is the *Tempull Mór* and the Long Tower.

Although the Dominicans had come to Ireland in 1224, it was not until 1274 that a Dominican Priory was founded in Derry by one of the O'Donnell chiefs of Co. Donegal.[8] Its exact location is unknown, but tradition suggests that it was not founded on the 'Island', but to the north-west of it, possibly in the region of modern Abbey Street, close to St Columb's Wells. The 'foundations of a church' discovered in the Abbey Street/William Street/Rossville Street area in the early 19th-century may have been part of the Priory.[9] On the map portraying the fortifications erected by Docwra at 'the Derrie' following his arrival in AD 1600, the ruins of the Priory appear to be depicted. The Dominicans themselves were only expelled from what became the City in 1689, just before the famous siege of that year commenced.

It has been suggested that a Franciscan Friary was also founded at Derry in the medieval period.[10] Very little is known about it, and there may be some confusion with the Dominican Priory in the sources. It would seem that there is no hard evidence to prove that the Franciscans were established in Derry before the second half of the 17th-century, and there are no visible remains of such a Friary, the site of which is unlocated.

In AD 1305 Richard de Burgh, known as the Red Earl of Ulster, built a castle at Greencastle (originally called Northburgh) in modern Co. Donegal to control the entrance to Lough Foyle. In AD 1311 King Edward II granted the settlement at Derry to the Earl and his heirs, but de Burgh handed over half of the 'Island' to the Bishop of Raphoe in 1322.[11] This division of the 'Island' meant that it was now split between the Cenél Conaill diocese of Raphoe and the Cenél nEógain diocese of Derry, although this accommodation may possibly have had its roots in an earlier agreement between those competing dynasties. In any case the 1322 division remained in place until the army of Elizabeth I took Derry at the end of the 16th-century. If de Burgh had intended to develop a town at Derry this never materialised and because of its distant location in north-west Ulster, it was only ever on the periphery of the area of Ireland controlled by the Normans.

In the 15th-century there was a resurgence of Gaelic power. During the late Medieval period

Island City. The Archaeology of Derry~Londonderry

Belmont-Shantallow Knight's effigy

Effigy of a Unknown Knight

This badly mutilated effigy of a knight, now on display in the Tower Museum, is said to have been found in Derry city during the 19th century and subsequently relocated to the garden of Belmont House, Shantallow. The figure, which is missing its head and lower legs, is dressed in white or *alwyte* plate armour, characteristic of the later middle ages. The late John Hunt suggested a date of 1560-70 on the basis of its form of trunk-hose (breeches) and similarities with English provincial armour of this date. The cuirass, which covers the breast, is of one plate, below which is a skirt of four over-lapping thin steel plates (lames) with hanging gothic tasses. The shoulders are defended by overlapping dome shaped metal pieces (pauldrons) of moderate size, while the elbows are protected by articulated plate guards (cowters). The sword, which has a straight cross and a pronounced iron strap down the wooden shaft (langet), is suspended diagonally across the abdomen from a loosely buckled belt.

Belmont-Shantallow Knight's effigy-detail of shoulder armour

Belmont-Shantallow Knight's effigy-detail of swords and hip-belt.

Belmont-Shantallow Knight's effigy-side view of trunk-hose and plates

Island City. The Archaeology of Derry~Londonderry

Bishop Street Excavation of 2013 – the Medieval Deposits

The site of the current car park off Bishop Street, within the walls, has been identified as the location of the Augustinian monastery through cartographic and documentary evidence. The research excavation undertaken in September 2013, at the north-western corner of the car park adjacent to St Augustine's Church, was conducted to determine whether medieval archaeology survived here and, if it did, the nature of that archaeology.

Below modern car park deposits, extensive layers of garden soils and part of a graveyard of seventeenth-century date were uncovered. These post-medieval horizons sealed up to two metres of medieval deposits which comprised multiple layers along with a couple of small pits and postholes and the inside edge of a ditch. The ditch was the earliest feature uncovered by the dig and extended for approximately a metre and a half in depth with silt, boulders and slump material, all sterile, making up the basal fills. The principal finds from the medieval features were disarticulated animal bone (representing food and butchery waste), and pottery which included both local and imported glazed tablewares and local coarse cooking wares. Preliminary examination of the pottery indicates the presence of imported medieval jugs from the Saintonge area in southern France, now modern Charente-Maritime. The Saintonge pottery probably made its way to Derry as a part of the wine trade and is typically found on high status sites. This area of southern Atlantic coast France later became a centre for Huguenots and Saintonge pottery of a different later type was also imported into the plantation city. The dig also uncovered sherds of Redcliffe pottery jugs from Bristol, England. Both the Saintonge and Redcliffe jugs can be dated to the late-thirteenth to early-fourteenth centuries. Two contemporary silver coins were also recovered, although both were poorly preserved and heavily corroded. Preliminary identification of these indicates that they are a medieval penny dating to between 1279 and the 1360s and an early thirteenth-century (1247-1253) Henry III longcross halfpenny which had been cut in half. The presence of the latter indicates monetisation in the town at this time. Other finds included a corroded iron key and a barbed fish hook. A cut and dressed stone was also recovered from a later, probable late-sixteenth or early-seventeenth century, informal hearth. Clearly this was in secondary use and must derive from a medieval stone building that would once have stood close-by.

The range and wealth of ceramic types discovered, coupled with the coins, suggests that there was a thriving medieval settlement on the island of Derry in the thirteenth and fourteenth centuries. The imported and high-status table wares that were found would not be out of place on the high table in an Augustinian monastery. It is not certain, however, whether the medieval features uncovered are located within the confines of the medieval monastery or not, and indeed whether there are earlier horizons still waiting to be discovered. These and other questions will require further investigation.

Two sherds of brown-coloured medieval unglazed Derry pottery. The fabric of these pots is very coarse and utilitarian containing many small pieces of quartz and stone. It represents the unglamorous everyday cooking ware made in Derry and used to prepare meals in kitchens throughout the ecclesiastical town. It is variously known as Everted Rim Ware or, more commonly now, Medieval Ulster Coarse Ware.

Images of the internal and external faces of sherds from a broken green glazed jug dating to the later 1200s or early 1300s. The jug was manufactured in the Redcliffe area of Bristol and came to Derry as a trade item. Bristol traded extensively with Ireland during the medieval period and from the 1170s onwards Dublin and Bristol were very closely linked.

One of the more unusual finds from the Bishop's Street excavation this sherd comes from the top of a handle on a glazed medieval pouring jug. The decoration is of a human face and the vessel may have been made in Bristol, like the Redcliffe examples. It was something that would have been used at dinner in finer surroundings, not an everyday item.

This image shows the handle of another pouring jug but is particularly important as sherds of this fabric and glaze type are usually taken to represent locally produced products, not imported items. Thus, with the finding of this handle and a few other similar fragments we may be seeing the first evidence for a medieval glazed pottery industry in Derry.

Island City. The Archaeology of Derry~Londonderry

Above: The furthest travelled of the medieval pottery found on the excavation these sherds come from vessels made around Saintonge in south-western France. Like the Bristol wares they represent parts of pouring jugs and would have been traded to Derry as a by-product of the wine trade. These finely made jugs would have been more widely used in pouring wine for consumption at table rather than as part of a liturgy.

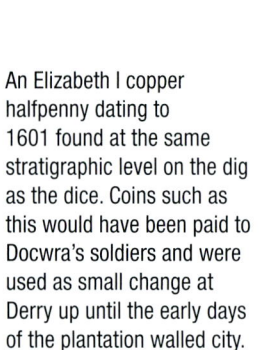

Four dice made from animal bone recovered during the excavation by sieving. They came from pre-plantation city levels that date to Sir Henry Docwra's town (1600-1608). Soldiers have gambled away their wages for time immemorial and playing at dice was a favourite sport of the Elizabethans.

An Elizabeth I copper halfpenny dating to 1601 found at the same stratigraphic level on the dig as the dice. Coins such as this would have been paid to Docwra's soldiers and were used as small change at Derry up until the early days of the plantation walled city.

68   Island City. The Archaeology of Derry~Londonderry

The Dominican Chalice. This richly decorated mid-17th century silver chalice, with a gilt interior, is clear evidence for the continued survival of a community of Dominicans (the Order of Preachers) in Derry following the plantation. At its base it has the inscription in Latin *Frater Dominicus Connor prior Conventus Derenis ordinis predicatorium me fiere fecit anon 1640,* which means 'Brother Dominic Connor, Prior of the Convent of the Order of Preachers in Derry had me made [in the] year 1640'. The Dominican Friary, established in Derry during the 13th century, escaped the suppression in the time of Henry VIII. The friars were apparently expelled by English troops in 1566, but were back again a few years later and were certainly present in 1600 when Docwra provided the then prior, Father O'Luinin, with a piece of land to live in peace for the rest of his days. However, a community of friars continued to operate in the city and in 1683 there is a record of fifteen friars attached to the community. Their numbers were drastically reduced in the 18th century, and the last of the Dominicans of Derry, Father Valentine O'Donnell, died between 1789 and 1793.

Large sandstone slab, known as 'St Columb's Stone,' sits in the grounds of Belmont School, Shantallow. It has the impression of two shod feet in it. Tradition says that the stone was brought to Derry from the Grianán of Aileach, but this seems unlikely given its size. The stone has been interpreted as an inauguration stone, where the ceremony to declare a new Irish lord was carried out.

Derry sat at the intersection of four powerful Gaelic lordships – the O'Donnells and O'Dohertys of Tír Conaill to the west of the River Foyle, and the O' Neills and O'Cahans of Tír Eoghain, to the east of the Foyle. A fine depiction of an armoured figure popularly identified as Cooey na nGall O'Cahan and dating to the period c. AD 1475–1500 is preserved on the 'O'Cahan' tomb in St Mary's Abbey in Dungiven, Co. Londonderry.[12]

Another stone effigy of a knight in armour, lacking head and feet, but with hands joined in prayer was found in Derry City during the nineteenth-century and relocated to Belmont House, now Belmont School, Shantallow. This superb sculpture is now on display in the Tower Museum. The renowned Irish medievalist John Hunt believed that it probably dated to around 1560–1570.[13] We do not know which chieftain the sculpture is meant to commemorate, but in 1566 the death is recorded of an important chief, Calvagh O' Donnell, son of Manus O' Donnell. This is within the date range that has been allocated to the carving of the effigy by John Hunt and it is tempting to think that the sculpture might be a representation of one of the last O'Donnell lords that would have known Derry well in the late medieval period.

A large sandstone slab, known as 'St Columb's Stone,' that sits in the grounds of Belmont School, Shantallow, has the impression of two shod feet in it.[14] The stone is roughly 2m long x 1.65m wide and is 0.4m thick and is marked in about the same location on the 1689 Neville map of the siege of Londonderry. Tradition says that St. Patrick brought the stone to Derry from the Grianán of Aileach.[15] Colby also states that there was an artificial mound, 7.5m square by 1.2m high, close to the stone, of which nothing now remains. The stone has been interpreted as an inauguration stone, where the ceremony to declare a new Irish lord was carried out.[16] We cannot be sure as to which dynastic family used the inauguration stone.

In the late 1400s or early 1500s the O'Dohertys, under the overlordship of the O'Donnells,

Medieval Ulster Coarse Ware pottery dating to *c.*1500, found on Bishop Street Carpark excavation in 2013. This is an example of the type of unglazed and locally-made pottery using for cooking and storing liquids that would have been used in Medieval Derry, along with glazed pottery vessels imported from Britain and elsewhere in Europe.

built a towerhouse on the Island of Derry.[17] It was sited close to the present Magazine Gate, in the area of the modern Tower Museum, and was built in lieu of certain taxes, on land purchased from the Mac Lochlainns for 20 cows.[18] The castle was converted into a magazine and store after the English capture of Derry in 1600, and is illustrated on several early 17th-century maps.

At the present time the excavation at Bishop's Street Without is one of only two excavations on the Island where artefacts of pre-plantation date have been uncovered.[19] These included two groups of broken pottery vessels. The first group was made up of locally made pottery dating to the 1400s and 1500s. It contained sherds of Medieval Ulster Coarse Ware pottery, which would have been used in cooking and everyday purposes, and also higher quality tableware jugs, termed transitional ware. The second group of pottery sherds was of higher quality again and represented imports from France during the 1500s. The first type of imported pottery identified was from Saintonge in southern France and represented chafing dishes for keeping food warm at table. The other imported sherds were from ceramic flasks made in the area of Martin-camp in northern France. Unfortunately, most of these artefacts were found in 17th-century deposits along with artefacts of that date so they have clearly been removed from their original location close by. However, the fact that earlier material survives on the Island gives hope that in future excavations more and more evidence for this important period in the city's history will come to light.

St. Colum Cille and his Churches at Derry

St. Colum Cille is probably the most famous individual connected with the history of Derry and much has been written about his life and works.[20] According to tradition, Colum Cille was born at Gartan, outside Letterkenny in Co. Donegal on 7 December, AD 520 or 521.[21] He was born into one of the most powerful families in Ireland that also had connections with Irish migrant kingdoms in Scotland. On entering the priesthood, Colum Cille was taught by St Finnian at

Detail from Griffin Cocket's map of 'Derry', inset to 'A true description of the north part of Ireland…by Mr Griffin Cocket…' c.1602 showing the O'Doherty towerhouse, built in the late 1400s or 1500s by the O'Dohertys, under the overlordship of the O'Donnells, to guard the harbour at Derry. The castle was later utilised by Sir Henry Docwra in the early years of the 17th century, both as a defensive outpost and as a warehouse. It survived the building of the city walls, being shown on Raven's map of 1625, but was subsequently demolished.

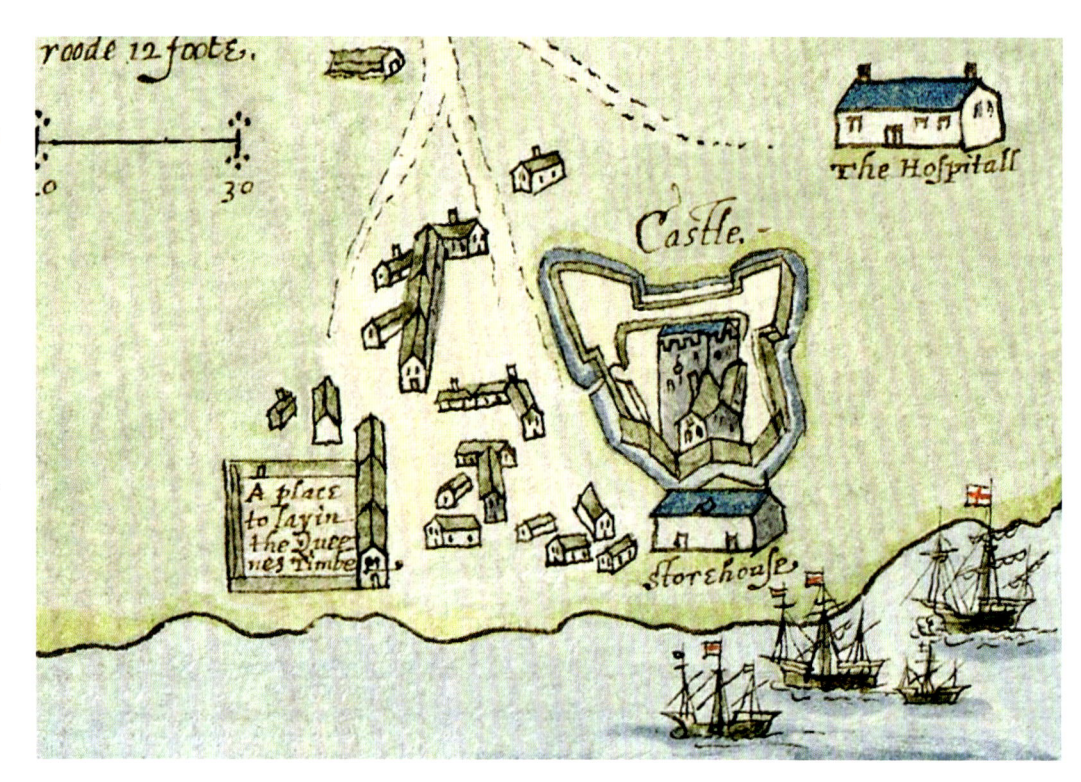

Aerial photograph showing the site of O'Doherty's towerhouse, now partially built over by an imaginative reconstruction occupied by the Tower Museum.

72   Island City. The Archaeology of Derry~Londonderry

Movilla in Co. Down and, later, at Clonard in Co. Meath. After completing his education, he began to found a number of churches (collectively known as the Columban Familia), including Durrow and Derry. Colum Cille was censured by Díarmait mac Cerbaill, king of Tara, for copying a Latin Psalter (prayer book) brought back from Rome by Saint Finnian of Moville, where the well-known judgement "To every cow her calf and to every book its copy" was pronounced. This prayer book was later enclosed in a metal shrine known as the Cathach or 'Battle Book' and carried in battle by the O' Donnell's as a sacred relic to help them overcome their enemies. Colum Cille was again slighted when the son of the King of Connaught was seized from his protective company and killed by Díarmait's soldiers because the young man had killed someone man during a game of hurley. Because of these incidents, Colum Cille went back north, rallied the men of Ulster and Connaught and defeated, with great slaughter, the army of king Díarmait at the battle of Cúl Dreimmne, near Sligo, in AD 560. A synod of Bishops held at Tailtiu (Teltown) in Co. Meath censured Colum Cille again, at the behest of Díarmait mac Cerbaill. As a result Colum Cille sailed from Derry in AD 562 or 563 with 12 companions and founded the great monastery of Iona (also known as 'Hy'), on an island off the west coast of Scotland.[22] It is for this that he is principally famous, as Iona became a great centre for missionaries who travelled throughout Scotland and northern Britain, bringing Christianity to the peoples there. One of the best-known episodes in the life of Colum Cille took place in around AD 578 or 579 when, on a rare trip back to Ireland, he was heavily involved in the great Synod of Druim Cett (now identified as having taken place at a mound in the Roe Park at Limavady). There the churchmen and secular lords discussed the independence of monastic foundations as well as toleration for bards who were in danger of being banished for satirising Áed mac Ainmire, king of the Cenél Conaill.

Colum Cille died in AD 593, and in the centuries following, his legacy was jealously argued over by the various ecclesiastical foundations with which he had been associated. We know much about the saint because of a manuscript called the 'Life of St Columba', composed around AD 700, more than a century after his death, by Adomnán, an Abbot of Iona and a relation of his.[23]

It would appear that Derry was Colum Cille's principal residence until he left Ireland to found the monastery in Iona in AD 563. The name itself, Doire (sometimes Doire Colum Cille), means 'the oakgrove of Colum Cille'. That the oak trees on the island were in now regarded as a Christian sacred place seems to bear out the suggestion that they had also been a sacred place in prehistoric times but were adopted or 'Christianised' by the monks. Lacey notes another tradition relating to pre-Christian Derry tells us that it was the dun or fort of Áed Mac Ainmire, who is said to have given the site to Colum Cille.[24] In this account it is said that Colum Cille burned down the fort when he took possession of the site, the story possibly preserving some memory of a rite of exorcism or consecration.

In 1532, Manus O'Donnell, who later became chief of the O'Donnells, completed his 'Life of Colum Cille', a compilation of sources about the saint. O'Donnell describes the early life and mission of Colum Cille at Derry:

'Having received, moreover, the very noble and very honourable order of the priesthood, and having been chosen against his will as the abbot of the black monks in that settlement of Derry, and having blessed it and made his dwelling there, he took it in hand to feed a hundred poor people every day for the sake of God. And he had a particular person to give that food to the poor. One day, after the poor had been fed, another poor man came begging. But Colum Cille's servant said that he had already fed the customary number, so he told the poor man to return on the following day when he would get alms like the rest of the poor. But he did not come on the following day until after all the poor had been fed, and again he begged alms. He got nothing from the servant but the same answer. And he came begging a third day after the poor had been fed but only got the same answer from Colum Cille's servant'.

At that point the poor man said: 'Go to Colum Cille and tell him that unless it be from himself that he gets what he gives to the poor he should not decide just to provide only for a hundred each day.'

'The servant went to Colum Cille and told him what the poor man had said to him. When Colum Cille heard this, he rose suddenly, not staying for his cloak or shoes, but pursed the poor man and overtook him eventually at a place that is called An t-Iomodh Deisiul ['The Righthand-wise Turn'] on the southwest side of the Tempoll Mór ['The Great Church'] of Derry. He recognised that it was the Lord that was there and he fell to his knees before Him and spoke with Him and he spoke to Him face to face, and was filled with the grace of the Holy Spirit. Among all the gifts that he got from God that time, he receive knowledge of all the mysteries in the scriptures…And from then on he provided not only for a hundred, but the great gifts that he got without measure from God, he gave them out without stint for the sake of God'.[25]

This story about Colum Cille's seems to have in later times inspired an Irish tradition of a pilgrimage, or turas, in honour of the saint in Derry, where the pilgrims would walk around various 'stations', in a sunwise (deiseal) direction.[26] The starting point and end point of the pilgrimage are given as:

'…the place …that the pilgrimage should be made was from the penitential station [altar] at the ship quay (*port na long* meaning 'landing place') at the east end of the settlement to 'the Righthand-wise Turn' at the west end'

Later in O'Donnell's text the end-point of the pilgrimage is further described as 'the place that is called the Righthand-wise Turn' to the south-west of the Great Church (thempoll mór) of Derry', the place where Our Lord appeared to Saint Colum Cille. The pilgrimage appears to have started from the bottom of modern Magazine Street (which itself may be a fossilised remnant of the turas), where the waters of the River Foyle lapped against the Island of Derry, and ended in the area around where the modern Long Tower Church is located. Lacey suggests that the original Columban Church, and the medieval monastery that succeeded it, are roughly halfway between the start and end of the turas.[27] The route probably ran uphill close to or along the line which Magazine Street runs today, skirted around the outside of the *Dubh Regles* church in the vicinity of present day St Augustine's and finally descended to the Righthand-wise Turn' beside modern day Long Tower (beside the *Tempull Mór*). Lacey further observes that:

'…the unusual curve of the former Long Tower Street outside the [17th-century city] walls might be an indication of an original route which has survived from medieval times, perhaps the last section of the tura' [28]

The tradition of the turas was lost with the change in settlement at Derry to a walled, Protestant

Carved wooden figure, probably representing the Virgin Mary, found at Lettershendony in 1978, now on display in the Tower Museum. This rare survival of a wooden religious statue was carved from a single piece of elm and was probably carried in processions. Although radiocarbon-dated to the 18th century, the statue is carved in a late medieval style and represents a native Irish tradition of religious sculpture.

Plantation city in the 17th-century. However, Colum Cille remains one of the most popular of Irish saints and folklorists were still collecting stories about him from people in Irish-speaking areas of Co. Donegal in the 1970s.[29]

When Derry was a prominent ecclesiastical centre in the Early Christian and Medieval periods, the two most important churches were the *Dubh Regles* and *Tempull Mór*. The *Dubh Regles* probably stood in the area occupied by the modern St Augustine's Church of Ireland 'chapel of ease' (whose origins were in the 17th-century) which may be the site of the original Columban monastery. Although local tradition holds that St Colum Cille established the monastery, the earliest written evidence for this claim only dates to about 500 years later. The original church was probably re-built as an Augustinian Priory in the medieval period, and Magazine Street may have developed as the route of an ancient pilgrimage or turas leading up to it.[30]

The Archbishop of Armagh, John Colton, made a famous visitation in 1397, and the description of this visit confirms the *Dubh Regles* as the site of the abbey of the Canons Regular or Augustinians

'The Venerable father [Archbishop Colton]…proceeded towards Derry, and having crossed the river [Foyle] by means of boats, advanced towards the city, Dr William McCamayll [Mac Cathmhaoil], Dean of the Cathedral church of Derry, with many others, clerks, friars and laymen, reverently came forth to meet the said Father, and conducted the said Father to the monastery of the Canons Regular [Augustinians], called the Black Abbey of Derry, and reverently lodged him and his attendants, and placed them in suitable chambers…'[31]

Both the Cenél nEógain and Cenél Conaill had an erenagh family – Mac Lochlainn (of the Cenél nEógain) and O'Deery (of the Cenél Conaill) – living in Derry until 1609, although the church had fallen into ruins by the later part of the 15th-century.

The *Tempull Mór*, which gives its name to the present city parish of Templemore, was built in 1164, close to the site of the current Long Tower Church. Later, the Long Tower, a high, circular stone tower or round tower, was also constructed in the area of modern Long Tower Street. It is portrayed on the early 17th-century English maps of Derry.

By the middle of the 13th-century the *Tempull Mór* had been elevated to the status of a cathedral. There is a documentary reference in 1250 in the *Annals of Ulster* to the collapse of a spire, which may have been associated with *Tempull Mór* ("The pinnacle of the great church of Daire of St Colum-cille fell…"). In 1254, the *Tempull Mór* became the cathedral of the diocese of Derry, despite opposition from the Cenél Conaill. In 1566 Derry was garrisoned by English forces, and at that time the *Tempull Mór* was in a ruinous condition. The gunpowder explosion in 1567 that led to the withdrawal of the troops may have destroyed much of what was left. It is shown on several 17th-century maps as being located in the area of Charlotte Street/Long Tower Street/Long Tower Primary School/St Columba's Church. Evidently there were still traces of the *Tempull Mór* in 1689 when Neville drew his map of the City, depicting the 'Great Siege', as it is marked on this. However the round tower beside the church is conspicuously absent from this illustration of the city. Although the church is shown on the plan of the city printed in 1751 in Tindal's Continuation this may have been copied from earlier maps, and we cannot be certain when the *Tempull Mór* was finally demolished. In the 1970s, excavations uncovered evidence of an earthwork of unknown date on Long Tower Street.[32] While it is tempting to think that this may have been part of the medieval church enclosure, this cannot be proved.

Medieval Sites in the Vicinity of Derry

Despite the paucity of discovered medieval archaeological finds on the Island of Derry, medieval buildings and finds have been recorded close by. A notable example is the ruin of an important O'Doherty castle, known as Elagh (Aileach) Castle, located at Elagh More.[33] It comprise the remains of a later Medieval stone castle and earthwork enclosure, though it may have earlier origins (see section on the Grianán of Aileach in the previous chapter). McNeill suggested that Elagh castle may date to the middle 14th-century, but added that although the physical remains hint at that date 'the only reference to a castle at Elagh comes from long after 1350'.[34] There is a local tradition that the castle was built by Nechtan O'Donnell for his father-in-law, an O' Doherty.[35] As Nechtan died in 1452, this would date the castle to the first half of the 15th-century. It remained the chief O' Doherty stronghold until 16 May 1600, when it was abandoned by Sir John O' Doherty in the face of Sir Henry Docwra and his English troops. Subsequently, Captain Ellis Floudd was put in charge of the castle with a garrison of 150 men. The O'Dohertys reclaimed it during the local rebellion of 1608, but lost it to Sir Arthur Chichester, who then used it once more for a garrison. By 1621 it had been leased out to Peter Benson, the builder of the City walls, but by 1665 had fallen into disrepair. The existing tower, which retains traces of a portcullis slot, is probably the surviving portion of a double-towered gateway. In March 2013 a small evaluation was carried out at the site and later, in August 2013, a larger excavation took place.[36] During the excavations of August 2013 three trenches were opened up. One (Trench 1) was in the flat area to the north of the rock outcrop and the footings of a large masonry structure were revealed in it. This was interpreted as being an outer perimeter wall of the castle. A post-built wooden structure was detected beyond it farther to the north. In another trench located in the terraced field to the south of the rock outcrop, a deep ditch with an internal earthen, stone faced, bank

Detail of a map known as 'The Derry' from c.1600 which is a general map of the River Foyle area and the country between the Foyle and Lough Swilly. Shown on the map are Docwra's settlement at Derry (D), the forts at Culmore (B) and Dunnalong (E), Elagh Castle (C) and at the bottom of the map, unlettered, the castle at Inch Island

Elagh (Aileach) Castle, once the site of a major O'Doherty castle. As it survives, it comprises the remains of a later medieval stone castle and earthwork enclosure, though it may have earlier origins. It remained the chief O'Doherty stronghold until May 1600 when it was captured by Sir Henry Docwra.

Aerial view of Elagh (Aileach) Castle in 2013 shortly before excavations took place. Some believe this important O'Doherty castle occupied the site of the ancient capital of the northern Uí Néill, rather than the Grianán of Aileach.

were uncovered. On the interior of this bank there was a paved area. The features identified in these two trenches were interpreted as being from two different periods of occupation at the site. The earthen bank and ditch may date to the Early Christian period, perhaps strengthening Elagh Castle's claim to be the real Aileach. The stone foundations in the area to the north of the rock outcrop may date to the later medieval period and are probably associated with the masonry castle.

A third trench, located on the top of the rock outcrop towards its southwest "corner" uncovered the remains of a rock-cut gulley that was ancient, but of uncertain date. This appears to have been the target of treasure hunters, possibly in the early 20th-century, and the soil that they had removed was found piled up beside the feature. The rock-cut gully was cut through an earlier occupation layer in which burnt bone, charcoal and a Bronze Age flint "thumb nail" scraper were found. A second gully dug into the clay on top of the rock was also found. It ran at roughly at right angles to the rock-cut one and was flanked on one side with larger stones. The small-scale of the excavation on the rock outcrop made interpretation of these features difficult although it is possible that the gullies and stones flanking them might represent the fragmentary remains of robbed-out wall footings.

Although there were significant structural remains uncovered in all three trenches excavated in August 2013 very few artefacts were found. However, in the smaller evaluation of March 2013 pottery sherds were uncovered dating from both the period of the O' Doherty occupation and also from the 17th-century English occupation of the castle. Taken together, the 2013 excavations

The southern trench of the 2013 excavation at Elagh Castle showing the deep ditch with an internal earthen stone-faced bank and exterior paved area. The features in this trench have been interpreted by the excavation director as possibly dating to the Early Medieval period, perhaps strengthening the claim of Elagh Castle to be the real Aileach!

Above right: Trench showing ditch south of castle

show the great potential for further archaeological work at Elagh, both on the rock outcrop but especially in the area immediately around the site where archaeological features and strata have been left relatively undisturbed and well preserved.

Another significant former castle was built on a crannog known as Green Island in the south-east corner of Lough Enagh, close to the eastern bank of the Foyle.[37] A smaller crannog known as Rough Island lies north-west of Green Island in the same lough.[38] It is not clear when it was built, but during the 16th-century Enagh Castle was an O'Cahan stronghold. Its remains were demolished during the 19th-century after a causeway was built out to the island, and the remaining foundations of the castle, which stood on a slight mound, were removed and the island levelled. During this work a dugout canoe was discovered along with a quern and other artefacts. The 4th edition OS 6"map marks it as 'Castle (in ruins)', showing a promontory extending out to the island. The island is now connected to the mainland by a causeway 11m wide, and while there are no visible traces on the island of the castle other than a slightly higher central area that may be the mound, a geophysical survey carried out in 2008 revealed the possible outline of the foundations.[39] In the 1980s a cast-iron cannon ball came to light, that would appear to relate to the brief siege in June 1601 when the English troops of Sir Henry Docwra put the Irish garrison of the castle to flight after bringing a cannon to bear on the castle.[40]

The view of the Grianán of Aileach from Elagh Castle. The fact that both sites are intervisible may be deliberate and strengthen the associations between them.

Set on top of a drumlin ridge between Enagh Lough East and West, Enagh Church (also known as Domnach Dola) overlooks the crannog and the site of O'Cahan's castle in the Eastern lough.[41] The church is almost totally ruinous, with only the eastern end standing to gable height and a portion of the south-east corner of the south transept or side-chapel. It measures approximately 28m by 7m internally and is built of local schist, dressed on the outside face, with a tall and narrow lancet window in the east gable. The masonry of its south transept is of a superior quality than the rest of the surviving building and is possibly of a different date. The interior of the church is very uneven, largely due to the number of burials within it. Enagh Church may be the site of the church recorded in the *Annals of Ulster* as having been pillaged by the Norman knight Rotsel Fitton in 1197.

In 1948, a carved stone head dating to the medieval period was recorded by Oliver Davies in the garden of Ashbrook House, Currynierin.[42] He speculated that the carving, possibly of a woman, might have come from one of the churches in the area, probably from Clondermot. The head may originally have been depicted as wearing a close-fitting cap or diadem, and would have been part of a life-sized sculpture that may have stood inside a church.

Derry from the Sixteenth to early Seventeenth Centuries

During the 16th-century, particularly after the accession of Elizabeth I in 1558, Gaelic Ulster came into increasing conflict with the post-Reformation English government as the part of Ireland that had most vigorously resisted the attempted imposition of Crown authority. There was increasing Elizabethan interest in the reconquest of Ireland, partly to ensure that the Catholic island did not become a springboard for the invasion of England by her European Catholic enemies such

Aerial view of Enagh Lough East, looking east. The crannog on Rough Island, excavated in 1941, is in the middle of the picture along with the modern causeway that now links the crannog to the shoreline. The site of the O'Cahan castle, on Green Island, is on the right of the picture. The ruins of the church are in the trees to the left of Enagh House.

as Spain. England was also aware of the plentiful resources (especially timber) to be exploited in Ireland.

The coastal location became strategically important as a gateway for getting troops into the heartland of north-western Ulster, controlled by the powerful lordships, the O'Donnells and O'Neills, in Counties Donegal and Tyrone. In September 1566, during the revolt of Shane O'Neill, Derry was garrisoned by English forces under Colonel Edward Randolph. Although Randolph was killed in fighting in November 1566, the garrison of some 700 troops inflicted serious losses on the forces of O'Neill. But in April 1567, the powder magazine, which some accounts say was housed in the *Tempull Mór*, was destroyed by an accidental gunpowder explosion. The church, however, survived in ruins into at least until the end of the 17th-century. Short of supplies and marooned in a place that was completely surrounded by hostile forces, the garrison was evacuated, and the settlement reverted to Gaelic control. The English were not to return until late in the Nine Years' War (1594–1603), a deployment that led to the ultimate defeat of the Gaelic lords of Ulster.[43]

From 1594-1603 a conflict was fought in Ireland known as the Nine Years' War. Much of the war took place in Ulster where the English Crown sought to defeat an alliance of Gaelic lords under Hugh O'Neill and Hugh O'Donnell. In AD 1600, late in the war the Crown landed an

Carved stone grave slab at Clonca Old Church, Co Donegal inscribed with the words (translated) as 'Fergus Mac Allan made this stone, Magnus Mac Orristin [buried] under this'. The grave slab is also decorated with a cross, foliage, a sword, a hurley stick or a shinty stick and ball. Mac Orristin may have been a Scot, probably a gallowglass.

Inscribed stone set into the outside wall of Clonca Church, reading (translated) 'O'Dubdagan who made… this stone for Domnall O R.' Above the inscription are a mallet and chisel device, a mason's mark. Probably late 15th century.

Island City. The Archaeology of Derry~Londonderry

A restored Bellarmine jug found in Londonderry

The Many Faces of a Cardinal

Most archaeologists will be familiar with the distinctive Cologne-Frechen produced German stoneware 'Bartmann' (German for 'Bearded man') jugs and bottles exported across Europe for over two centuries from the mid 1500s. They are easily recognised by their iron-rich brown surface and mottled 'tiger' or speckled salt glaze, but it's the stamp of a bearded man that is their most striking characteristic. While originally these facemasks appear to have represented the 'Wild Man' of European myths, they became associated with Cardinal Roberto Bellarmino (1542-1631), a theologian and opponent of Protestantism. Consequently, these vessels, whose importation often ran parallel to the wine trade, are commonly known as 'Bellarmine' jugs and jars. Their relief decoration, which often also included a medallion or heraldic devise on the belly of the vessel, was made from separate moulds. As these moulds were shortlived there are many different variations of applied decoration on Bellarmine vessels.

Six Sherds of Bellarmine jugs showing the bearded face of the Cardinal

Island City. The Archaeology of Derry~Londonderry

army at Derry as part of a plan to drive a wedge between O'Donnell's and O' Neill's forces. The Derry army was to drive into the area that is now Counties Londonderry, Donegal and Tyrone cutting Gaelic supply lines and engaging O'Donnell's and O' Neill's men while other English forces advanced into Tyrone from the south and east.

In May 1600, an English force of 4,000 men and 200 cavalry under the command of Sir Henry Docwra sailed up Lough Foyle and landed close to Culmore Point.[44] Having seized Culmore and Elagh Castle, and with his route back to the sea secure, Docwra then occupied Derry, which appears to have been undefended and probably unoccupied. He fortified a position on the Island by building earthwork defences around some of the Medieval buildings and repairing and refortifying the O' Doherty towerhouse. It is said that he used masonry from the medieval buildings in these new fortifications, none of which have been archaeologically identified. In his Narrative written in 1614, Docwra described what he found on the Island when his force arrived:

'…wee went to the Derry [from their fortification at Culmore] 4 myles of upon the River side a place in manner of an Iland Comprehending within it 40 acres [16.1ha] Ground, wherein were the Ruins of an old Abbay, of a Bishopp's house, of two churches. & at one ends of it an Old Castle, the River called loughfoyle encompassing it all on one side, & a bogg most commonlie wett & not easily passable except in two or three places dividing it from the main land. This peece of Ground we possest our selves of without Resistaunce, & judging it a fit place to make our maine plantation in, being somewhat hie [high], & therefore dry, and healthie to dwell upon, att that end where the old Castle stood, being close to the water side, I pressentlie resolved to raise a fforte to keep our store of Munition & vivtuells in, & in the other a little above, where the walls of an old Cathedral church were yet standing, to evert [convert] annother for our future safetie & retreate unto upon all occasions'[45]

In his account, Docwra thus described the size and topography of the 'Island', the adjacent marshes, and the ruins of the various ecclesiastical buildings there. This passage also records his intention to re-use the O'Doherty castle at the eastern side of the Island as his magazine and storehouse, and to refortify the '*Dubh Regles*' Cathedral as the new citadel of his fortification.

As with all contested history there are two sides to the story. The Irish account of Docwra's arrival is given in the entry for AD 1600 in *Annals of the Four Masters*.[46] It is broadly similar but has different emphasis, especially in relation to the re-use of the existing medieval buildings on the Island:

'The English fleet…arrived in the harbour of Dublin in the month of April of this year. From thence they set out in the very beginning of summer…and they were ordered to put into the harbour of the Lake of Feabhal [Lough Foyle], son of Lodan. They then sailed, keeping their left to Ireland, until they put into the harbour of that place, as they had been directed. After landing, they erected on both sides of the harbour three forts, with trenches sunk in the earth, as they had been ordered in England. One of these forts, i.e. Dun-na-long, was erected on O'Neill's part of the country, in the neighbourhood of Oireacht-Ui-Chathain; and two in O'Donnell's country, one at Cuil-mor [Culmore], in O'Doherty's country, in the cantred of Inishowen, and the other to the south-west of that, at Derry-Columbkille. The English immediately commenced sinking ditches around themselves, and raising a strong mound of earth and a large rampart, so that they were in a state to hold out against enemies. These were stronger and more secure than courts of lime and stone, or stone forts, in the erection of which much time and *great labour might be spent. After this they tore down the monastery and cathedral, and destroyed all the ecclesiastical edifices in the town, and erected houses and apartments of them. Henry Docwra was the name of the general who was over them. He was an illustrious Knight, of wisdom and prudence, a pillar of battle and conflict.'*

In a letter dated 19 December 1600 from Docwra to Sir Robert Cecil, contained in the Calendar of State Papers for Ireland, Docwra gives another 'Description of Lough Foyle and the country next adjoining':

'Derry…is an island made with the river on one side and a bog on the other. It lies in form of a bow bent, whereof the bog is the string, and the river the bow. The bog is passable in all places in the summer, but in winter hardly, but in one or two, especially now the little fort is made at the upper end, where the ground was. only hard and passable, both for foot and horse. "This island is a high uneven ground, and so is the country over against it on both sides. It is in length about a small mile, and in breadth a quarter, and I think it containeth about 1,000 acres of ground, most part sown with corn, when we came to it. It hath under the foot of 'the high ground next the bog, about the middle thereof, two very good springs of fresh water hard together, and lies so as a chapel, standing upon the height of it, commands in a manner all the rest. This place is distant from Lough Swilly, where it makes a neck of a land, about six miles, and stands fitly to keep O'Dogherty's country in awe, and to make incursions into Tyrconnell. Both the island and main almost to Birt [Burt] is all Church land belonging to the Bishop. There is in this island plenty of stone from the ruins of old buildings, and besides good quarries within the island, as also a vein of good slate, if it were dressed and wrought for the purpose…' [47]

Such is the layout of the new settlement is portrayed on the map 'The Island and Forte of the Derry', drawn up in 1600, more than one thousand years after the first annalistic references to the settlement there.[48] The 1600 map is the first-ever detailed illustration of buildings on the Island. It shows on high ground a large earthen fortification, whose defences rely on are punctuated by at least six bastions of different sizes, and five of which contain cannon, while inside the fort are a number of buildings including a hospital for the soldiers and Docwra's lodgings. To the right of the map, the *Tempull Mór* and round tower are shown in the area of modern day Long Tower. To the left of the map the fortified storehouse and magazine (encompassing the O' Doherty tower house) is depicted on low ground near the river. On higher ground above the main fort the map depicts a 'chapell' which 'commands over ye forte'. This 'chapell' would appear to be the remains of the medieval nunnery and as it overlooked the main fort Docwra put some soldiers into it. The map shows a defensive earthen bank thrown up around the nunnery ruins. Whether Docwra had this defence built or whether it was the repair of an earlier English fortification dating to their occupation of Derry for several years in the 1560s is uncertain.

At the bottom right hand corner of the map a 'little forte', surrounded by a ditch is illustrated, while just to the left of that' two wells (now known as St Columb's Wells) are shown and two causeways across the bog. Bottom left of the map on the opposite side of the bog from the refortified tower house two ruinous buildings are shown, probably representing the ruins of the Medieval Dominican Priory. Finally, almost in the very centre of the map, a gallows is located prominently outside the fort.

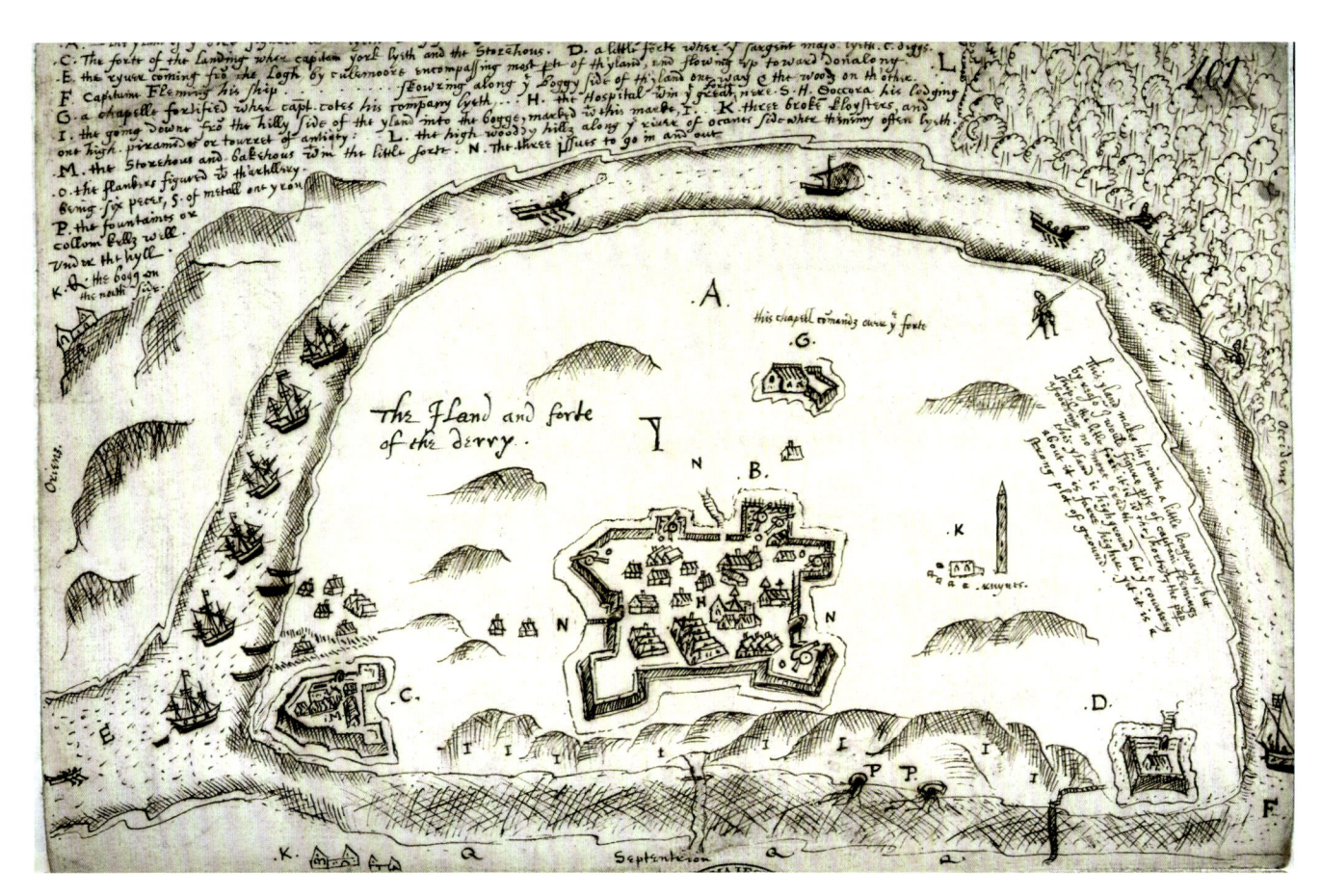

'The Island and Forte of the Derry' dating to 1600 and the first-ever detailed illustration of buildings on the Island.

Soon after, another map of Derry was drawn up by one Griffin Cocket in c.1601.[49] This shows in detail the main fort illustrated in the 1600 map, though here the perspective is looking up from the small fort around the tower house (marked 'Castle') at the riverside. More buildings, including 'the Governor's House with his Garden' are shown within the great fort, and a large defended house and bawn, 'Babington's House', and the 'Hospitall' are shown between it and the 'Castle'. For the first time streets within the new settlement are marked, as is the outline of potential extension to the settlement ('A Paterne to make the Towne by') on to the high ground outside the great fort. At the top of the map a building, 'The Governor's Horstalls' may have occupied the site of the 'chapell commanding ye fort' shown on the 1600 map.

Despite the potential for expanding the settlement, it seems as if this did not happen, as Docwra became disillusioned and in 1606 sold his interest in the fledgling town to Sir George Paulett, who took over as Vice-Provost and Commander of the Garrison. Docwra left Derry and returned to England, although by 1616 he was back in Ireland as Treasurer of War. Docwra then stayed in Ireland and when he died in 1631 was buried in Christ Church Cathedral, Dublin.

In 1608 Sir George Paulett, the governor of Derry, fell out badly with the local Gaelic nobles led by Sir Cahir O'Doherty. Sir Cahir rose up in a revolt that was quickly crushed, though not before Paulett had been killed and the settlement at Derry burnt to the ground. This event, along with the flight of the Ulster Gaelic lords to Europe in September 1607 – The Flight of the Earls – led to Gaelic Ulster being opened up for British colonisation. The Plantation of Ulster commenced a few years later.

Island City. The Archaeology of Derry~Londonderry

Detail of the general map of the Foyle/Swilly area drawn up by Robert Ashby in 1601. Shown on the map are Docwra's settlement at Derry, the forts at Culmore and Dunnalong, Elagh Castle, the Grianán of Aileach, and the abbey and castle at Rathmullan.

Late 16th and early 17th-Century Sites in the Vicinity of Derry

Prominently located on a hilltop some 11km (7 miles) west of the city lies Burt Castle, which was first mentioned in a land grant to Sir John O'Doherty in 1587, probably a few years after it had been completed.[50] The castle is of the Scottish Z-plan with two round turrets at diagonally opposite corners of a roughly square tower with three stories and an attic. The north turret contains the staircase and lies adjacent to a tier of small rectangular mural chambers over the entrance. In 1601 the castle was captured by Sir Henry Docwra and around this time it was illustrated on a map depicting it with a strong bawn made up of an earthen rampart, an extra-mural ditch and defensive blockhouses at two corners, all now vanished; the drawing also shows over half a dozen beehive hunts within the bawn. Burt was then garrisoned by the English, but was returned to Sir Cahir O'Doherty in 1603, only to be besieged by the English and captured again in the rebellion of 1608. It was later granted to Thomas Chichester, who repaired it and added further buildings both inside and outside the bawn. The site seems to have been occupied until the end of the 17th-century.

Much closer to the city is Culmore fort, which was an integral part of the city's defences in earlier times, guarding the access to and from Lough Foyle. It seems originally to have been a late-medieval O'Doherty fortification that was captured by Sir Henry Docwra in 1600 and re-fortified by him immediately before his occupation of the Island of Derry. In this regard it

Burt Castle, eleven kilometres (seven miles) north-west of Derry~Londonderry was another O'Doherty castle. It dates to the late 16th century and was one of their main fortresses.

is illustrated on a map of 1600 as a triangular earthwork and ditch with cannon, enclosing the earlier towerhouse.[51] Between 1609 and 1629, the London Companies spent £1,100 in building and garrisoning a fort here. It was later fortified by the Jacobites during the siege of Londonderry in 1689. The current fort here is a stone blockhouse dating to the 19th-century.[52]

To the south of the city on the border between Counties Tyrone and Londonderry lay Dunnalong Fort, the largest of Henry Docwra's key strongholds in his early 17th-century campaign in the Foyle region.[53] The fort was already the location of an O'Neill castle, but records indicate that Docwra bolstered its strength by the creation of bastioned earthworks enclosing the old castle, as well as his garrison's quarters and a brewery on the banks of the Foyle. Contemporary maps show that his fort was of considerable size and strength, but for all this, its use as a military camp was short lived. Its strategic importance declined after the surrender of the Gaelic lords and the Treaty of Mellifont in 1603, and it was completely abandoned by c.1608.

In summer 2012 geophysical survey and an evaluative excavation took place at the fort, which is documented in contemporary maps and accounts, while cartographic sources and aerial photography provide an indication of its location.[54] The 2012 work consolidated existing information; the geophysical survey enabled the precise identification of its location and defined its perimeter, as well as informing the excavation strategy, which focused on the western bastion. The excavation targeted the perimeter defences, as well as the site of a building identified by

Burt Castle, Co Donegal, is a prominently sited Z-plan house (a Scottish form with towers at opposing corners). It was probably quite new when first mentioned in a land grant to Sir John O'Doherty 1587. Captured by Docwra in 1601, it was depicted on a map that year with a squarish bawn, now gone. The building has pistol loops and no vaults. It passed to Sir Cahir O'Doherty but was taken again by the Crown following his rebellion in 1608.

Island City. The Archaeology of Derry~Londonderry

Culmore Fort. Detail from the general map of the Foyle/Swilly area drawn up by Robert Ashby in 1601. Originally a late-medieval O'Doherty fortification, Culmore Fort was captured by Sir Henry Docwra in 1600 and re-fortified before his occupation of the Island of Derry.

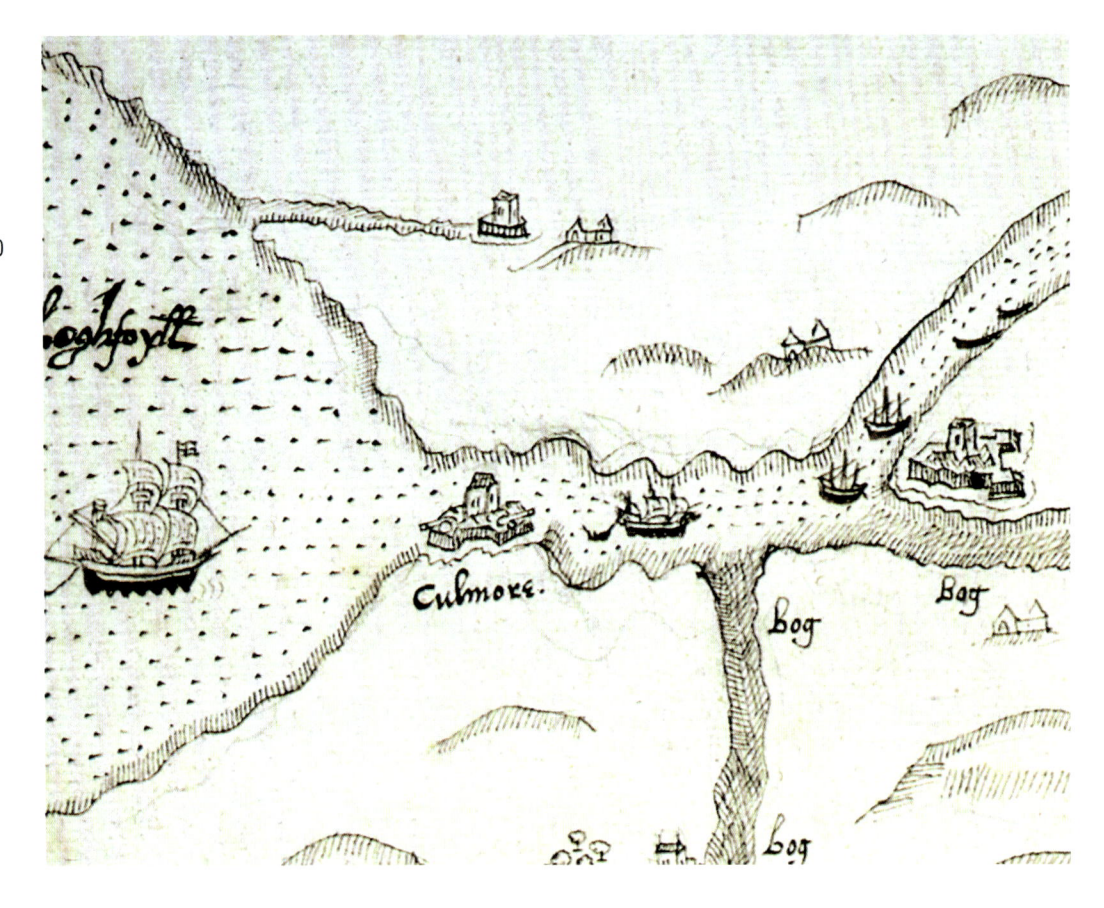

The 19th century Culmore Fort at Culmore Point, a stone blockhouse which replaced the earlier fortifications.

Island City. The Archaeology of Derry~Londonderry

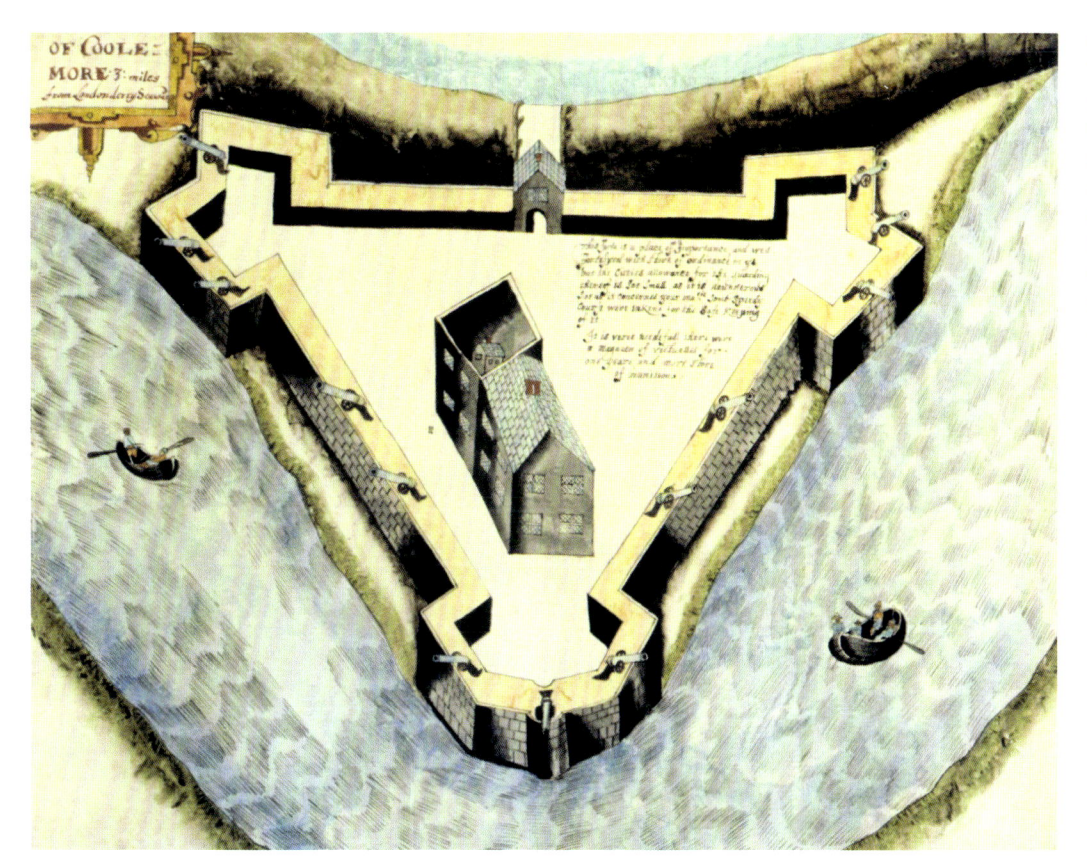

Culmore Fort illustrated by Thomas Raven in 1622. Between 1609 and 1629, the London Companies spent £1,100 in building and garrisoning a fort here because of it's important location protecting access to both Lough Foyle and also access from there downstream.

Aerial view from Culmore Point along the River Foyle to the walled city and beyond, showing the importance of Culmore's location.

Island City. The Archaeology of Derry~Londonderry

Map of 'Dounalong' c.1600, possibly drawn up by military engineer and mapmaker Robert Ashby. Originally an O'Neill castle built in the 16th century, Dunnalong was occupied by the English troops of Sir Henry Docwra in July 1600. They refortified the site with a view to it later becoming a mercantile settlement like Derry. This did not happen and within a decade the fort and settlement were vacated and abandoned. The map marks the ditch surrounding 'the ruins of the walls' of Sir Art O'Neill's Irish castle as well as newly built structures within the English fortification such as 'the great brewhous', for making beer for the garrison.

the survey. Archaeologists from the Northern Ireland Environment Agency and the Centre for Archaeological Fieldwork (CAF), Queens University Belfast oversaw the survey and excavations. They were assisted by staff from Derry City Council Heritage and Museum Service, Foyle Civic Trust, The Centre for Maritime Archaeology at the University of Ulster. Most of the excavation crew was made up of local volunteers, participants on the 'Plantation to Partition' programme funded by the 'Peace III Initiative', as well as other members of the public. The exploration took the form of a 'keyhole' evaluation of targeted areas rather than a full, open-plan excavation of the site. Small, narrow, trenches were positioned over locations highlighted by the geophysics, so that the nature of the remains could be investigated with minimum disturbance.

The work confirmed 17th-century reports that in the area of the western bastion at least, the curtain consisted of a significant ditch enclosing an internal earthen rampart. The ditch was up to 6.5m wide and was cut to a depth of almost 2m below the modern ground surface. Its outer slope was notably the more gradual, sloping down to a rounded, U-shaped base, before rising more sharply to the interior of the fort in a gradient punctuated by a pronounced step. The remains of the base of the rampart, also 6.5m wide, survived immediately inside the ditch and confirmed the formidable nature of the defences. The largest deposit within the ditch occurred approximately 60cm below the ground surface and consisted of a layer of yellow clay which contained 17th-century artefacts, including red brick fragments, a clay pipe stem, lead shot and sherds of 17th-century pottery. This deposit was interpreted as an early, deliberate, attempt to fill in the ditch sometime in the 17th-century probably soon after the fort had gone out of military use. Few artefacts were found in the earlier ditch fills. The relative sterility of these lower layers may indicate that these deposits had accumulated during the three years of Docwra's campaign while the ditch was still open and maintained as a defensive feature.

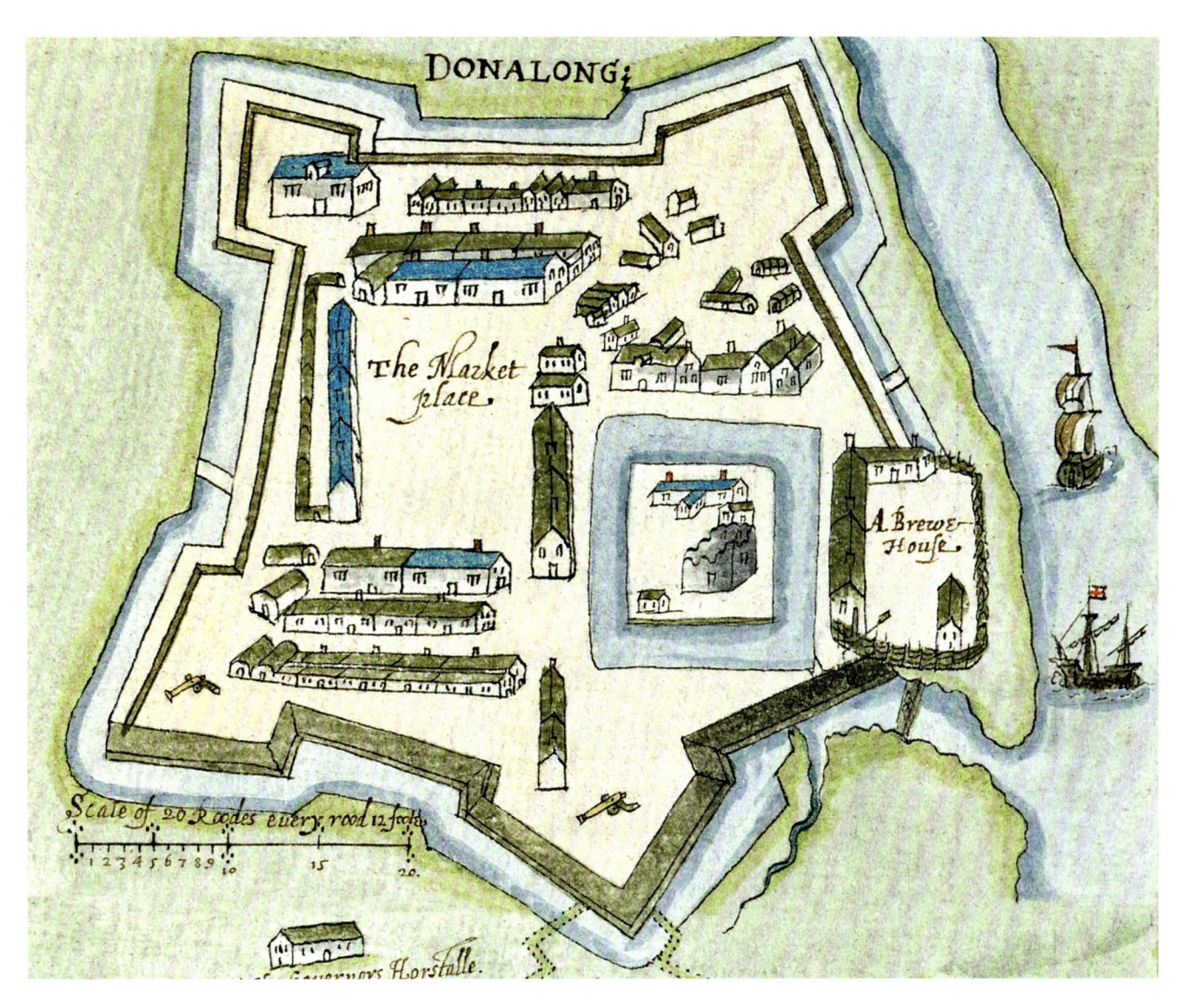

In the area immediately inside the western bastion, the excavation unearthed a cluster of post-holes, coinciding with a zone of intensive burning, indicated by the geophysics results. The use of fir posts in the construction of buildings at Dunnalong was recorded in contemporary records, and the position of the post-holes in the site stratigraphy suggests that they were probably contemporary with the earthen rampart. It is probable that, although only a small corner was unearthed, the post-holes represented the remains of a wooden building dating to the period of the occupation of the fort. The 17th-century maps of Dunnalong depict rows of wooden buildings within the fort and it may be that these post-holes formed part of such a structure,

Map of 'Donalong' fort, inset to 'A true description of the north part of Ireland', by Griffin Cocket, 1602. In 2012 an archaeological excavation investigated a section of the substantial defensive ditch and rampart that surrounded the fort as well as uncovering evidence of a wooden building within.

Island City. The Archaeology of Derry~Londonderry

Detail of Dunnalong fort from the general map of the Foyle/Swilly area drawn up by Robert Ashby in 1601.

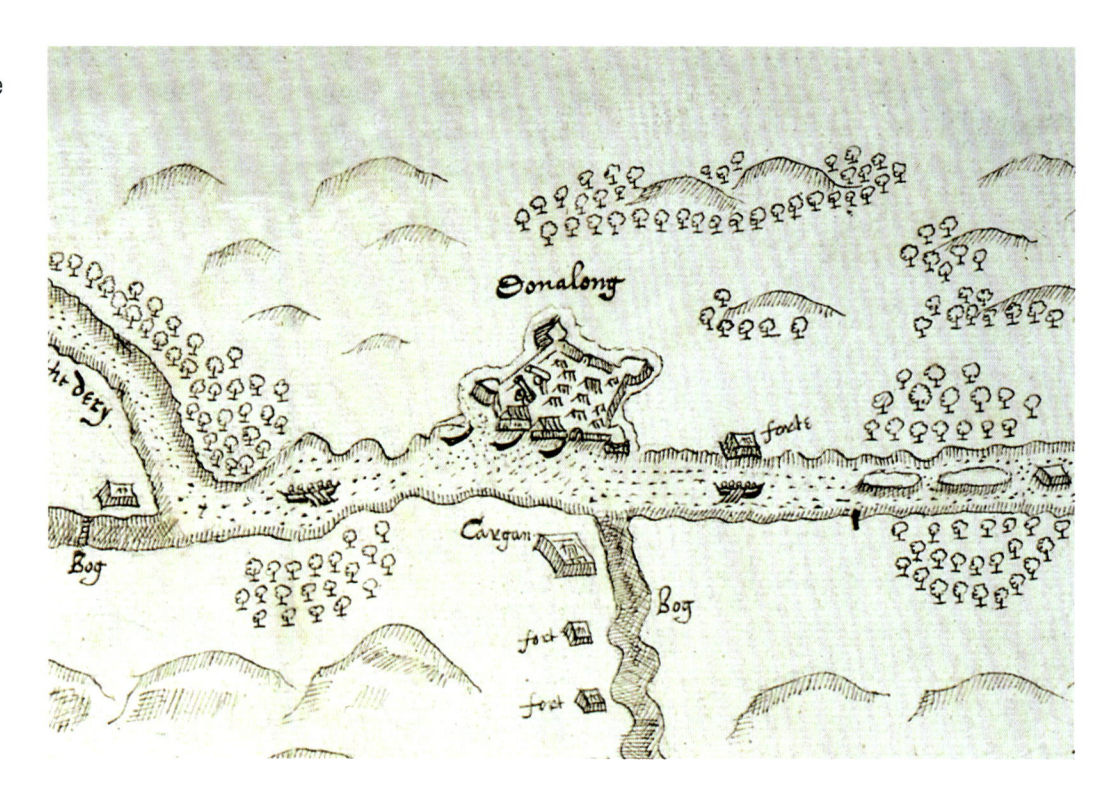

Aerial photograph of the site of Dunnalong fort. The fort surrounded the area of the later farmyard in the foreground but only the faint outline of the ditches remains visible above ground today.

96   Island City. The Archaeology of Derry~Londonderry

perhaps housing soldiers of Docwra's garrison during his campaign. A later wooden structure was partially superimposed on the plan of this earlier building and a large pit containing iron slag was dug into the remains of the fort. However, neither of these features has yet been definitively dated so cannot, at this stage, be tied into the period of use of the fort.

The Glengalliagh Bell – An Armada Legacy?

One of the many interesting artefacts held in St. Columb's Cathedral is a bronze bell on permanent loan from the Hamilton family of Glengalliagh Hall. The bell is roughly 30 cm high and has four panels of decoration in relief. These appear to represent the 'Madonna and Child', 'Christ on the Cross', a bishop and 'Christ in Majesty'. The Glengalliagh Bell has previously been incorrectly dated to 1411 due to the misreading of casting flaws and later damage as numerals. It is now thought to date to the later 1500s and be overtly Catholic in symbolism. As the bell at Carndonagh Church of Ireland parish church is said to have come from the Spanish armada ship *La Trinidad Valencera,* it may be asked could the Glengalliagh Bell also be an Armada bell? One possible Armada link is shown by casting marks on cannons found from the Armada ship *La Juliana,* which foundered in 1588 at Streedagh Strand, Co Sligo. Some of the cannons recovered from the wreck bear the image of Saint Severo, bishop of Barcelona in AD 290. That image is very similar to the image of the bishop on the Glengalliagh Bell. A second possible Armada link comes with the location of the Glengalliagh Bell find. The Hamilton family believe that it was found in the 1930s during the building of workers cottages close to the site of Elagh Castle. In 1588, *La Trinidad Valencera* went down in Kinnegoe Bay, Inishowen. Fortunately for those onboard it sank slowly enough that the vast majority of them were first rowed to shore. The survivors moved south towards Elagh Castle where they expected to receive help. While some made it to the castle, many were killed and captured in the nearby fields by the Earl of Tyrone's troops. Presumably the Armada survivors gave the Carndonagh bell as a gift or payment when they first landed in Inishowen. Was the Glengalliagh Bell similarly gifted, or buried, to be found hundreds of years later? Further research will hopefully answer that question.

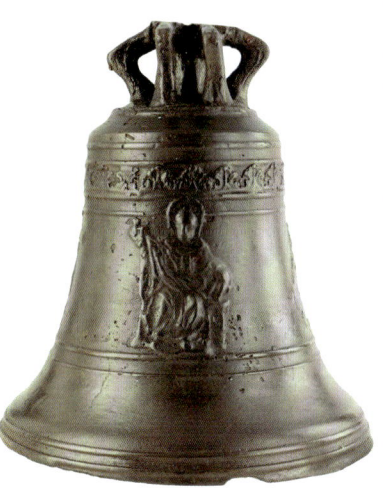

Griffin Cocket's map known as 'Derry' c.1602 shows the great fort illustrated in the 1600 map, though here the perspective is looking up from the small fort, now described as a 'Castle', defending the river crossing and the 'Storehouse' between it and the edge of the river. More buildings, including 'the Governor's House with his Garden' are shown within the great fort, and a large defended house and bawn, 'Babington's House', and the 'Hospitall' are shown between it and the 'Castle'. For the first time streets within the new settlement are marked, as is the outline of potential extension to the settlement ('A Paterne to make the Towne by') to the south-east of the great fort. At the top of the map a building, 'The Governor's Horstalls' may have occupied the site of the 'chapell commanding ye fort' shown on the 1600 map.

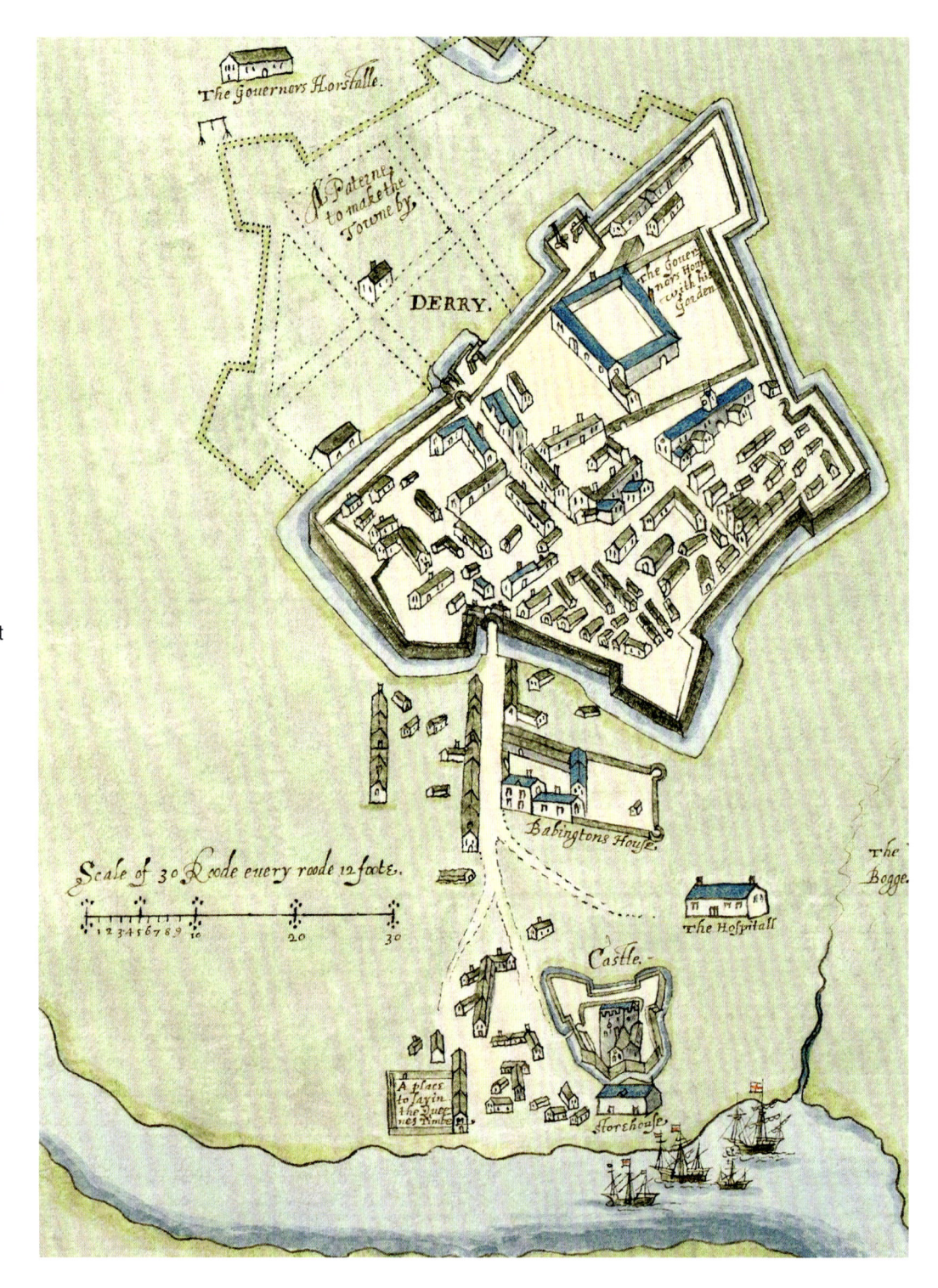

98   Island City. The Archaeology of Derry~Londonderry

Sir Henry Docwra's Town of Merchandise and War

Derry as it might have looked at the end of the Nine Years' War in 1603. The immediately noticeable fact is the ruination or abandonment of the ecclesiastical buildings apart from those reused by Docwra's men. On the high ground of the Island is the large earthen fort constructed by Docwra's troops, whose ramparts and bastions were only finally swept away during the building of the plantation city. Inside the fort are new military buildings but also the Dubh Regles which was initially taken over as a storehouse and hospital. Beside this the cloister has been adapted into a courtyard home for Sir Henry and beyond the defences are the ruins of the nunnery temporarily occupied by the soldiers as a strong point. To the right the round tower now stands more prominently as a testament to the once ecclesiastical city. At the bottom of the hill the O'Doherty tower house has been lowered in height, re-roofed and surrounded by new earthwork ramparts like those on the hill above. To the left of it are storehouses and quays for landing goods. Uphill to the right of the landing place a civilian settlement has begun to grow outside the defences. Within this new town stands Mr Babington's house and bawn from where many of the survivors of the O'Doherty 1608 attack on Derry held out till given terms.

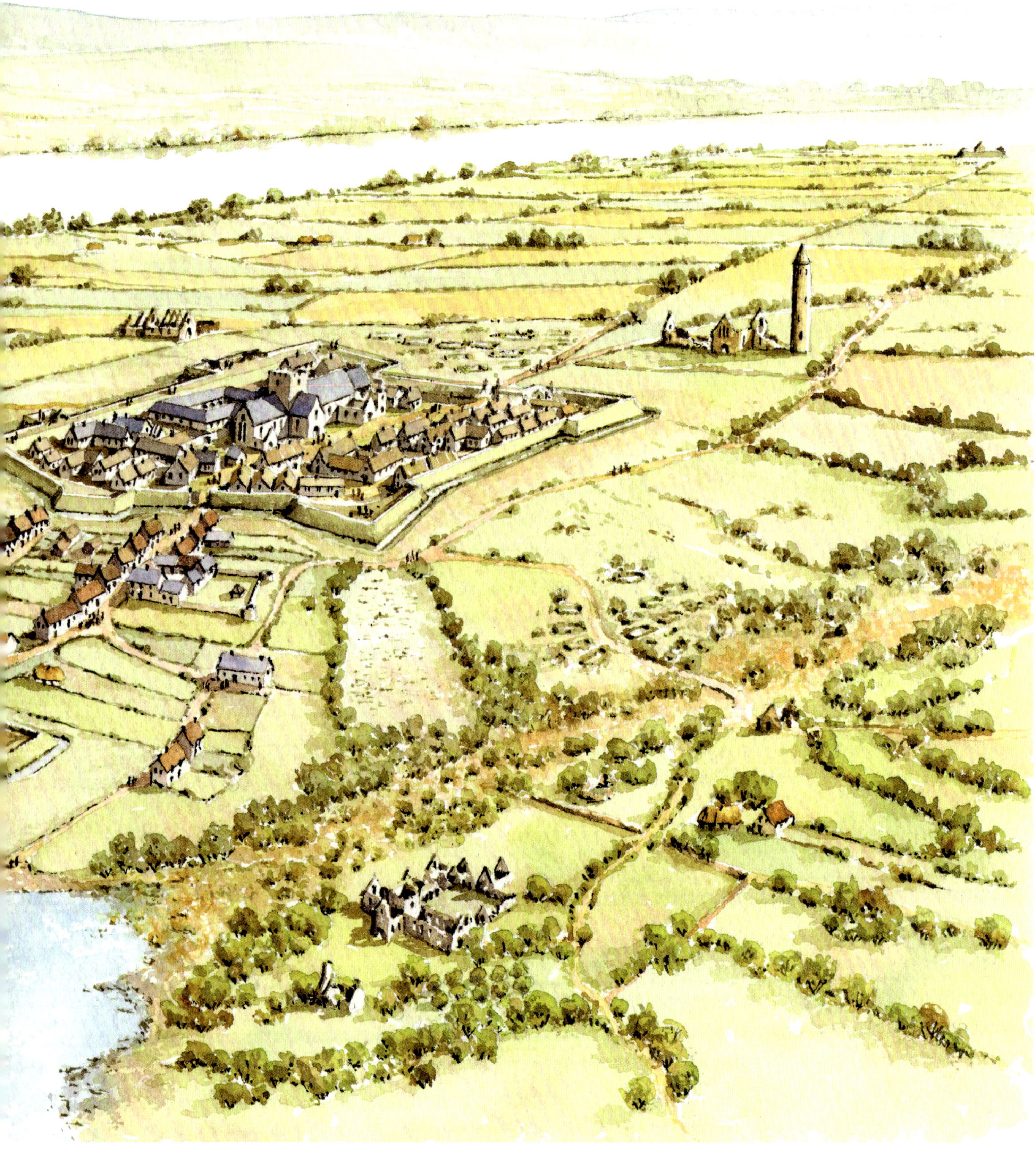

The 1611 map known as 'The Platt of the Derrie' drawn up by Thomas Raven shows a design for a new town at Derry. There is a perimeter wall with bastions, gates, drawbridges and an external ditch shown around the town except along the shoreline of the River Foyle, though a pier is shown extending into the river here. Sir Henry Docwra's earthworks are marked enclosing a church and bishop's house, up near where the modern St. Augustine's Church stands. The O'Doherty towerhouse is also depicted. The street layout is gridded, but although the spaces between the streets are marked out as being for gardens and back properties no new buildings are shown.

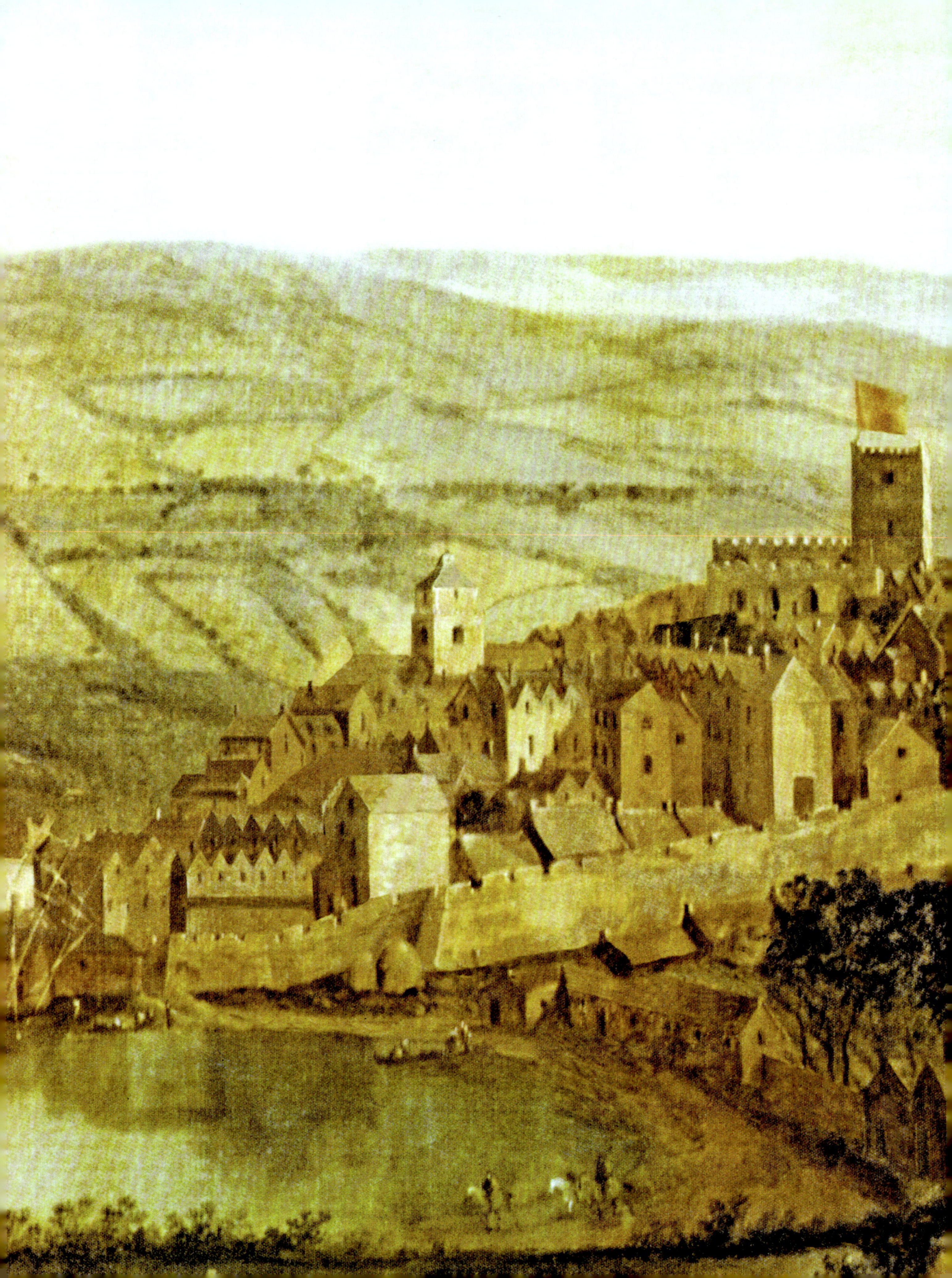

Detail from 'Londonderry' (oil on canvas, now lost), attributed to Willem Van Der Hagen, *c.* 1718-21. Colonel Michelburn's crimson flag (signifying 'No Surrender') can be seen on the cathedral.

The Plantation City of Londonderry

From the beginning of the 17th-century onwards, Derry underwent perhaps the most dramatic change in its long history of settlement. This came about due to what is called the Plantation of Ulster, which was ushered in from 1609 under the instruction of King James I.[1] The O'Doherty uprising of 1608, following so close on the heels of the 1607 Flight of the Earls, reinforced in the English Crown mind the need for stability. The convenient answer was to plant the land with 'reliable' subjects, such as Protestant settlers. As a consequence of this thinking, James induced the London trade guilds to take land in the north-west of Ulster in a newly created 'County of Londonderry', which was an amalgam of the old County of Coleraine along with parts of Counties Tyrone and Donegal. Twelve 'Great' companies, trade guilds of the City of London, were given land grants and told to create viable settlements, including two walled towns at Derry and Coleraine. These companies were the Mercers, Drapers, Salters, Vintners, Grocers, Haberdashers, Ironmongers, Merchant Taylors, Goldsmiths, Skinners, Fishmongers and Clothworkers. The Londonderry plantation was a substantial enterprise and initial details on how to proceed were not agreed between the companies and the crown until January 1610. A body representing all these companies and their affiliates, and whose purpose was to oversee the plantation scheme agreed with the crown, was established in 1611. It was known as *The Honourable The Irish Society* and still exists today. On 29 March 1613, the Society was given a new Patent or Charter to complete the building of the new settlement at Derry. This royal document, called the 'Charter of Londonderry', took the name of the previous settlement and combined it with the name of the home of the guilds to mark the creation of a new city. It replaced the charter awarded to Docwra in 1604 and so Derry became Londonderry.[2]

The individual guilds involved in the plantation were allocated estates by lottery within the newly established county of Londonderrry and the area granted to the companies amounted to 15,595ha (38,520 acres) of land. This included the proposed settlements at Derry and Coleraine located close to the coast to make trading and commercial ventures easier. As part of the agreement *The Honourable The Irish Society* was to construct walled defences around the new settlement at Derry. The fortifications meant the town could attract settlers, mostly merchants, craftsmen and their families, and act as both a market and port so that goods and commodities could be traded through it. The building of the new City walls saw the sweeping away of the remains of Docwra's town and fort on top of the hill. Part of the new city's land grant of *c.* 1620ha (4000 acres) allowed for each house within the walls to have a garden outside the walls on the island and a larger plot beyond to grow food for the new settlement.

The Walls of Derry~Londonderry

In August 1613 two officials of *The Honourable The Irish Society*, Alderman George Smithes and Mathias Springham, merchant-taylor, were sent to Londonderry to manage and direct the plantation.[3] In their report of 15th October 1613 they described the actual mechanics of marking out the new walled city:

> Touching the fortification of Derry, wee, with the assistance of Captain Panton and of other captines, of spiall noate [special note] and good experience being ten in number, have viewed and trode out the ground at Derry for the fortification there, and have conferred and advised with them concerning the same…their advise is, that materials should be first laid in place afore the wall be gone in hande; and we think it fit that the same fortificacon and worke for the same, be begunne and sett forward with all convenient speed.

The walls of Londonderry are still the most visible aspect of this new phase of settlement on the Island and they were constructed between late 1613 and March 1619.[4] The city has the most complete circuit of historic walls of any in Ireland and is a striking example of 17th-century urban fortification. The walls stand up to 8m (26ft) high, measure almost 1.3km (1 mile) around, and enclose an area of roughly 13ha (32 acres). Along with Carrickfergus[5] in Co. Antrim, Derry~Londonderry is one of only two settlements in Ulster to have been entirely walled in stone. The walls are now 400 years old, and have withstood both sieges and the urban expansion of the city far beyond the historic core. They are both a legacy of the history of the City, and very much part of its thriving life today.[6] Across Europe, from the end of the 15th-century, urban defences changed to meet the threat of attack involving the use of artillery. Walls were reduced in height to present less of a target to the enemy than their medieval predecessors, they were often sloped

Aerial photograph of the walled city taken in 2013, looking north-east.

outwards ('battered'), and large banks of earth were placed behind them to provide support and to absorb the impact of cannon balls. Bastions, angular projections on which artillery could be mounted, were shaped so that in addition to facing directly outwards, artillery and small-arms fire could be directed parallel to the walls to protect against enemy attempts to storm the defences.

The walls were initially designed and built under the general supervision of Capt. Sir Edward Doddington but due to his long absence Captain John Baker, commander of Culmore Fort, oversaw most of the works.[7] Captain Thomas Raven carried out the surveying and measuring of the walls and they were built by Peter Benson of London (a specialist tile and brick layer). Benson had also been granted lands in Donegal and stayed on at Londonderry to later become Mayor.[8] He built the City wall from blocks of local schist that splits easily into layers, with an earthen bank behind. The structure varies in height from roughly 6–8m (20–26ft) and in width from 4.5–9m (15–30ft). Some parts of the walls have a steep batter at the base, whilst other sections rise almost vertically. Along the wall top are embrasures (openings) for artillery and, in places, smaller openings for the use of muskets (musket loops) can also still be seen. The wall head is finished with dressed sandstone, and this was also used to dress the exterior corners of the bastions. Outside, from near Water Bastion round clockwise to just beyond Double Bastion, the walls were enclosed by a ditch which is now filled in but which has been shown by excavation to have been some 10m (33ft) wide and 2m (7ft) deep. Originally eight bastions were built around the circuit of the walls, and today five of these survive intact. Two circular sentry boxes are still preserved on the walls near St Columb's Cathedral, although there would have been many more in the past. In comparison with contemporary fortifications in Britain or Europe, the defences

Island City. The Archaeology of Derry~Londonderry

Map of the walled city showing the principal buildings and features of the 17th century fortifications

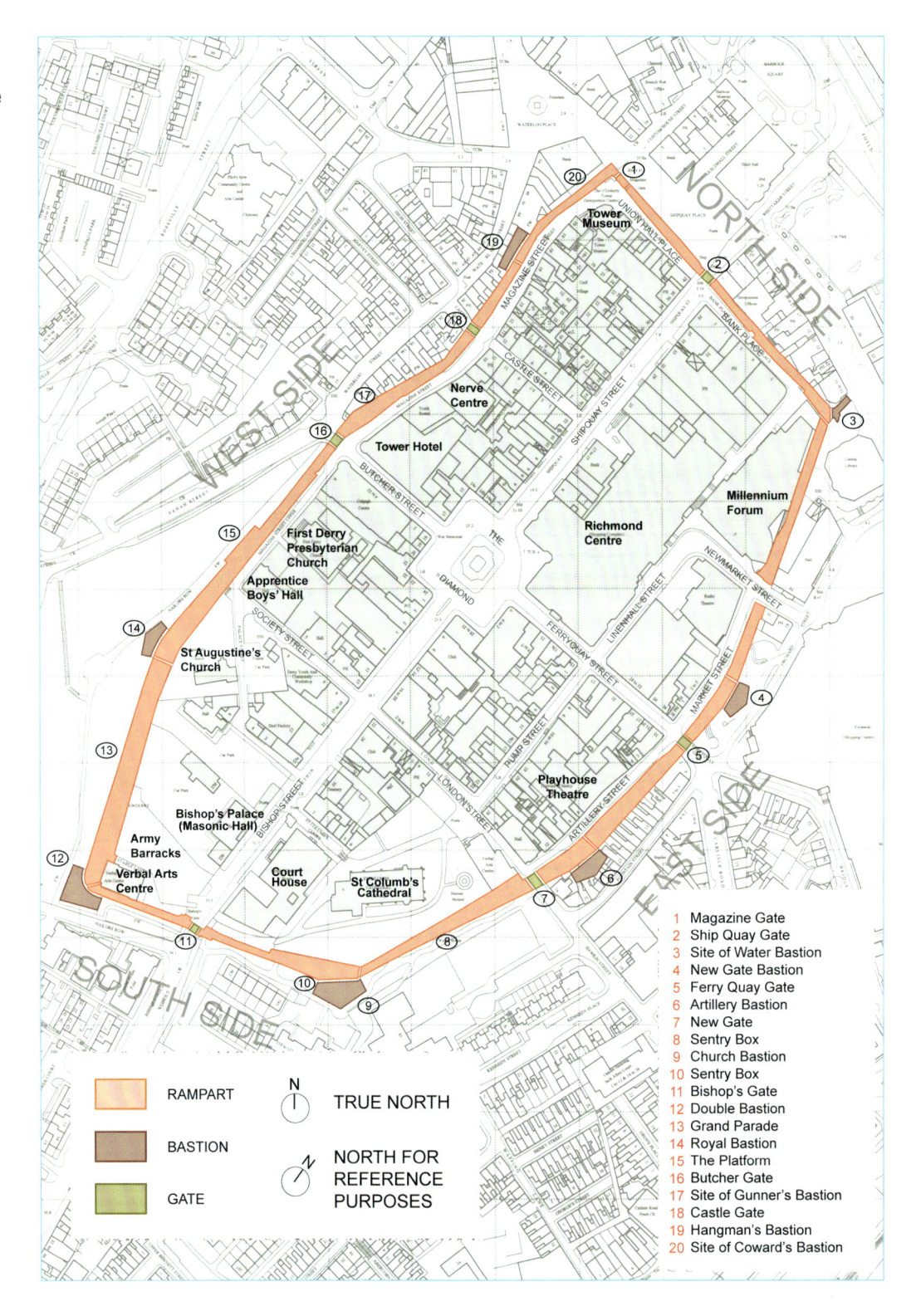

1. Magazine Gate
2. Ship Quay Gate
3. Site of Water Bastion
4. New Gate Bastion
5. Ferry Quay Gate
6. Artillery Bastion
7. New Gate
8. Sentry Box
9. Church Bastion
10. Sentry Box
11. Bishop's Gate
12. Double Bastion
13. Grand Parade
14. Royal Bastion
15. The Platform
16. Butcher Gate
17. Site of Gunner's Bastion
18. Castle Gate
19. Hangman's Bastion
20. Site of Coward's Bastion

RAMPART
BASTION
GATE

N — TRUE NORTH
NORTH FOR REFERENCE PURPOSES

Island City. The Archaeology of Derry~Londonderry

are quite plain, with none of the complex outworks to be found elsewhere. The reason is simple. At the time when the walls were built, there was no threat of artillery attack by the native Irish, and it was not envisaged that an invading foreign army would land here with heavy cannon.[9] The wide flat walkway on top of the rampart is known as the *terreplein*, and was used originally by the garrison to transport cannon speedily to the place of danger using a gun carriage. This greatly added to the defensive capabilities, because during a siege ordnance and men could be moved quickly to any section under immediate threat. Although many more defended the city at various times, there are twenty cannon ranging in date from 1590 to *c*. 1642 currently displayed at various points along the walls.[10]

Gates and Bastions

Originally there were only four gates into the city positioned at the four cardinal points. These entrances to the Walled City still exist today, but they were much altered in the late-18th and 19th centuries, and none of their original features now remain. The other three gates (Magazine Gate, New Gate and Castle Gate) were also added at this time. There are fine views of the modern city from many points around the walls, which emphasises their original important strategic function. The layout of the walls can be appreciated best by following the circuit anti-clockwise from Magazine Gate and Shipquay Gate at Guildhall Square. We have used the current names of gates and bastions around the walls, but the earlier names are also shown for information. The 1622 names are taken from the map commissioned by Sir Thomas Phillips and probably prepared by Thomas Raven. The 1689 details are from Captain Thomas Neville's map and *Description of the Towne and Workes about it*.

We begin with the last of the gates to be cut through the city walls, the Magazine Gate, located on the north side of the old city, close to the Tower Museum. It was built in 1865 though plans had been prepared over thirty years previously. It's keystones have carved heads representing Adam Murray and David Cairnes, both of whom played an important role in the 1688-89 siege. Looking out from the walls you can see the Guildhall and Shipquay Square (popularly known as Guildhall Square), built on land reclaimed from the river, and behind them the River Foyle and the Peace Bridge. Looking back from the walls into the city, up to the War Memorial in The Diamond, it is clear how the land rises steeply from the river and bog. It was on this high point of the original island that the medieval *Dubh Regles* church and Docwra's early 17th-century fortifications were located. On the rampart walkway is a row of recently restored cannon, mounted on replicas of mid-17th-century block carriages, with their barrels protruding through the embrasures (openings) in the outer wall. The two cannon closest to Shipquay Gate are of particular interest as they date to the time of Sir Henry Docwra and bear the Tudor rose-and-crown emblem, one having a date stamp of 1590, and the initials of the gun founder, Thomas Johnson.

To the south-east, roughly in the centre of the north wall of the city is Shipquay Gate (*Water Gate,* 1622), one of the four original gates into the 17th-century city, although the present opening was built in 1805. It is interesting to note that *Port na Long* or 'ship quay' is a placename of ancient origin that dates from the time of the Gaelic settlement. The gate gets

Looking through Shipquay Gate up to the War Memorial in The Diamond. This gate was rebuilt in 1805-06 at a cost of around £400

Historic cannon on the town walls overlooking Shipquay Place

Engraving by John Nixon published in the European Magazine, dated February 1800. Visible in this picture is the late 17th century Market and Assembly House in the centre of The Diamond, later to be replaced by the Corporation Hall in 1823. This building, badly damaged by fire in 1903, was demolished in 1910 and replaced in 1927 by the War Memorial

its name from the fact that, in the 17th-century, the River Foyle came right up to the foot of the city walls here and ships that entered Lough Foyle moored close by for people and goods to be unloaded. From Shipquay Gate, the rampart descends gently towards the site of the former Water Bastion, and a number of blocked up gun loops can be seen along this section. The red sandstone blocks built into the wall may be indicative of high-status buildings, and there is a local tradition that they were removed from the Medieval churches for re-use in the construction of the walls.

South-east of Shipquay Gate, at the east corner of the north wall of the city, lies the Water Bastion (*Governor of the Plantation's Bulwark, 1622; Water Bastion, 1689*), which got its present name from the fact that the River Foyle originally came right up to the walls at this point. Sadly, most of the bastion was demolished around 1850 to improve access to and from Foyle Street, and all that now remains is a small platform. However, the foundations were uncovered during the excavation in 1983, which showed that the original walls had an external batter, were nearly 7ft (2m) thick, and were decorated with sandstone quoins.

From the Water Bastion, the rampart rises steeply, and this stretch terminates at a broad flight of steps giving access to Newmarket Street. It is the only place where the circuit of the walls is broken, and the opening was created in the 1860s to allow carts access to a new covered market. There is an excellent view of the impressive outer face of the walls here from Orchard Street, just around the corner. This street takes its name from an orchard that was located here at the time of the 1689 siege, and it is traditionally believed that it was by using a tree in this orchard that Robert Lundy, the deposed Governor, escaped over the walls on December 18th 1688. This area is close to the edge of the 17th-century ditch that once also added to the strength of these defences.

A view along the top of the city wall, with the Millennium Forum on the right, looking south towards New Gate Bastion

Island City. The Archaeology of Derry~Londonderry

The city wall alongside Market Street in the 1920s looking north to Newmarket Street. The street gets its name from the vegetable and fish markets that used to be here. The stuccoed Palazzo-style building on the left is still present

Across Newmarket Street and further up the rampart walkway is New Gate Bastion *(London Bulwark, 1622; New Gate Bastion, 1689)*, where there are two demi-culverin cannon mounted on authentic replicas of 17th-century field carriages. Two gun loops, can be seen, and four embrasures, which would have allowed artillery to provide covering fire along the adjacent wall face. authentic replicas of 17th-century field carriages. Two gun loops, can be seen, and four embrasures, which would have allowed artillery to provide covering fire along the adjacent wall face.

The next short section of rampart rises steeply towards Ferryquay Gate defences *(Ferry Gate, 1622)*, which is located on the site of one of the four original gates in the centre of the east wall of the city. The gate may originally have led down via Bridge Street to the ferry and, later, to the first city bridge which was built in 1791. It was the original Ferryquay Gate that was closed on December 7th 1688 by 13 apprentices to prevent the Earl of Antrim and his troops from entering the city, leading directly led to the siege of 1689. The present gate was built in 1866 and the heads carved on the keystones represent the Revs George Walker and James Gordon.

Looking from Ferryquay Gate, past the War Memorial in The Diamond, Butcher's Gate, on the western side of the walls can be seen, giving a good feel for how narrow the 17th-century city actually was. A little further on, the sandstone surround of the gun loops has a number of very clear indented lines. Similar markings on stones in Carrickfergus town and Castle have been interpreted as the result of soldiers using the stone to sharpen the blades of their weapons.

The outer face of the wall often overlooks the rear yards of residential properties, and this is particularly obvious at the Artillery Bastion *(Lord Deputy's Bulwark, 1622; Ferry Bastion 1689)*,

Island City. The Archaeology of Derry~Londonderry

The original gateway here, which was famously closed by thirteen apprentices on 7th December 1688, included a drawbridge over a large fosse. The gate was widened in the 1790s, while the present entrance of Scottish Giffnock sandstone dates to 1866

New Gate Bastion with the Ferryquay gate on the left. This salient bastion, also called 'The London Bulwark', has four sides with single gun loops and four cannon embrasures

110   Island City. The Archaeology of Derry~Londonderry

The Church Wall with sentinel turret looking north east towards New Gate. On the left is the sallyport entrance leading into the churchyard of St. Columb's Cathedral

which lies close to New Gate, roughly midway between the Ferryquay Gate and the Church Bastion. Its situation would have been very similar in the 17th-century, as suburbs grew up in the shadow of the walls. In times of war or siege however, such as in 1649 and again in 1689, such buildings were levelled to provide clear fields of fire for the defenders. Within the Artillery Bastion are two cannon. The first is an English saker with a City of London shield on it, one of a batch sent by the City of London in 1620. The second is a demi-culverin sent to the city in 1642 by the London Salters Company, one of a group of fifteen gifted by the London Companies to strengthen the defences. A number of gun loops and embrasures can still be seen in the outer wall face, although they have mostly been blocked up in modern times.

Close to the Artillery Bastion lies New Gate, which was first opened in 1787 and probably represented the first significant breach of the original walls. It was replaced by the present gate in 1866. Continuing past St Columb's Cathedral, there are a large number of gun loops and embrasures along this section of the walls. The outer wall increases in height and one of the last two surviving circular sentry boxes is located here. Originally there were others but they were shot off by Jacobite cannon during the siege in 1689. The fact that the sentry box survives here probably reflects the lesser amount of cannon fire aimed at this part of the wall during that siege. Just beyond the sentry box the extra height probably reflects the one time presence of a 'banquette' or firing platform for musketeers, something suggested also by the square holes that would have held supporting timbers.

The Church Bastion (*King James' Bulwark, 1622; Church Bastion, 1689*) lies at thje southmost point of the city walls. It was from here that King James II was fired upon as he approached the City on 18 April 1689, an occasion when the defenders were traditionally supposed to have cried 'No Surrender' and when the siege began in earnest. Another sandstone block with scratch marks that come from being used to sharpen weapons can be seen. There are two demi-culverin cannon

View along the Church Walk with a sentinel tower looking south west towards the Church Bastion. Only two of these towers now survive on the walls but originally there were many more. Most were destroyed during the 1689 siege.

A sketch of the same sentinel tower in the 1830s, then roofless, from the Ordnance Survey Memoirs

Island City. The Archaeology of Derry~Londonderry

View of the city walls outside the Church Walk looking towards Church Bastion, with sentinel turret above. This four sided salient bastion was originally known as King James Bulwark

A 'defenders view' through one of the gun loops on the Church Bastion looking north east along the wall below the Church Walk

Island City. The Archaeology of Derry~Londonderry

Pen and ink drawing dated 1892 showing the Church Bastion and adjacent sentinel turret. At that time the bastion was separated from the walk by a low fence

here, and looking out of the embrasures, back north-east towards New Gate, gives a superb view of the outside face of the wall. Along the bottom of the wall face is a small gateway, known as a 'sally port'; tradition has it that it was used during the siege, and leads into St Columb's Cathedral. After Church Bastion, past the second surviving sentry box, is Bishop's Gate. Here the walkway splits with one flight of steps descending to Bishop's Street Within and another rising steeply over the top of Bishop's Gate.

The Bishop's Gate and the southern stretch of the wall were weak points during the Jacobite siege of 1689. They provided the easiest approach to the City, which was overlooked by Windmill Hill and was the scene of some of the fiercest fighting. It was here, during excavations in 1999 at Bishop's Street Without, that traces of a defensive earthwork and ditch known as a 'ravelin' were uncovered just outside the walls. This was one of the four original entrances, but the current gate here was erected in 1789 as part of a centenary commemoration of the 1689 siege. The keystones have carved warrior heads that represent the Rivers Boyne and Foyle, and were executed by the renowned sculptor Edward Smyth.

114 Island City. The Archaeology of Derry~Londonderry

The Church Bastion and the wall walk around 1930 showing the railing which then fenced off the bastion

The open access to Church Bastion and wall walk today with the adjacent sentinel turret

Island City. The Archaeology of Derry~Londonderry

The Double Bastion (*Prince Charles' Bulwark, 1622; Double Bastion, 1689*) at the south-west corner of the city walls, is the site of two demi-culverins, one of which is the famous 'Roaring Meg', the best known of the cannons deployed by the defenders in the siege of 1689. 'Roaring Meg', sent to the City in 1642 by the Worshipful Company of Fishmongers, got its name from the deep sound that it made when it was fired. The bastion is separated from the rampart walkway by a low stone wall and, during the nineteenth-century, was planted as a private garden. From Double Bastion there is a fine panoramic view over the Bogside and up to Creggan Heights. During the 1689 siege there were Jacobite guns positioned on the slopes above the Bogside. Double Bastion got its new name from the fact that the well-sited Jacobite artillery blew off the defensive parapets and could skip cannon balls right across the bastion causing mayhem. To counter this, the defenders constructed a line of gabions (large wicker baskets filled with earth) down the middle, behind which they could take cover. This divided the bastion in two and thus gave rise to a new name. In July 1689 Marshal Conrad de Rosen, the Jacobite commander, rounded up at least 200 of the local Protestants living outside the walls and forced them towards Butcher's Gate. His intention was for them to be admitted to the city and so speed up depletion of resources and starve the garrison and townspeople into surrender. In retaliation, the defenders erected a large wooden gallows on Double Bastion and threatened to hang all of their Jacobite prisoners. Because of this threat, de Rosen backed down and the civilian hostages outside the

The Church Bastion on the south-east corner of the walls with a pair of cannon. The one remaining tower from the old Londonderry gaol can be seen in the background left of centre

The view looking into the city and Bishop's Street Within through Bishop's Gate, c.1960

View of the city walls from Creggan with the Double Bastion, Grand Parade, Bishop's Gate, the Verbal Arts Centre (First Derry Primary School), the Bishop's Palace and St. Columb's Cathedral all prominently visible

The Double Bastion and cannon behind railings looking along the Grand Parade towards the Walker Testimonial *c.* 1900

The Double Bastion and its cannon today with the Grand Parade on the right

118   Island City. The Archaeology of Derry~Londonderry

Grand Parade, Royal Bastion and the Walker memorial pillar from a photograph taken c.1915. The testimonial was erected in 1822-6 to designs of John Henry for £4,200 including £100 for the statue by John Smyth of Dublin. The monument was blown up in 1973, but the base remains; a few (only) of the young trees in the picture have now survived to become mature specimens

The base of the Walker memorial pillar as it exists in 2013. The memorial plinth was restored for the three hundredth anniversary of the siege

Island City. The Archaeology of Derry~Londonderry

Aerial picture showing the section of the city walls between the Royal Bastion and the Double Bastion, with Grand Parade, St. Augustine' Church, Bishop's Street car park and the Verbal Arts Centre. In the bottom left of Bishop's Street car park can be seen the archaeological excavation that took place there in 2013 which uncovered prehistoric, medieval and 17th century artefacts and features

walls were allowed to return to their homes.

The walls now turn north on to Grand Parade, which is one of the most formal sections of the monument. The wide, straight walkway here is the last surviving trace of a designed, formal landscape and stretches back to its use as a promenade in the nineteenth-century. The sycamore trees here were planted to commemorate the Apprentice Boys who closed the gates on King James' soldiers: the fruit of sycamore trees is said to resemble a bunch of keys, symbolic of the locked gates. A defensive ditch extended from Double Bastion to about half way along the outside of this stretch of wall, but because the ground fell away so steeply, beyond this point there was no need for it to continue. The level grassed area, extending out from the foot of the walls before falling sharply towards the Bogside, was originally much steeper. It had been terraced and flattened out to build houses, which were later levelled in the mid-20th-century. There are three cannon positioned here, the third of which has a very well-preserved shield of the City of London, and is another of the batch of guns sent over in 1620.

Northwards from the Double Bastion is the Royal Bastion (*Lord Docwra's Bulwark, 1622; Royal Bastion, 1689*) on which Governor Walker memorial pillar was erected in 1826-28 to commemorate the shutting of the city gates by the Apprentice Boys of Derry. The pillar, which was 24.7m (81ft) high, was surmounted by a statue of the Rev. George Walker, Governor of the city throughout the siege. It was blown up in 1973, but the stonework at the base was restored in

1993. The statue of Governor Walker survived the blast and after restoration, can now be seen in the Apprentice Boys Memorial Hall. There are also two late-18th-century 6-pounder cannons within the bastion, one on either side of the pillar.

Past the Royal Bastion, a long rectangular gun platform protrudes out from the walls. It does not seem to have ever had a name and was simply described on some maps of the city as the 'Platform'. A broad flight of steps descends to Society Street, which may mark the line of a Medieval street or one laid out as part of Docwra's 1600 settlement.

Roughly in the centre of the west wall of the city, is Butcher's Gate *(no name, 1622; referred to as New Gate elsewhere)* one of the four original city gates, but the structure here today was rebuilt in 1810. The view back through the gate and past the War Memorial in The Diamond, again gives a good idea of how narrow the 17th-century City was. Butcher's Gate saw some of the fiercest fighting of the Jacobite siege, when the Earl of Clancarty and his regiment of Cork Jacobite troops attacked the walls at this point on 28 June 1689 in the most direct assault on the walls during the siege, and were repulsed with heavy casualties.

A short distance north-east of Butcher's Gate was a demi-bastion, known as the Gunner's Bastion (*Mayor of Londonderry's Bulwark, 1622; Gunner's Bastion, 1689*), named because of its location close to the Master Gunner's house (although it is often misidentified on many later maps as 'Hangman's Bastion'). It was removed sometime between 1843 and 1873. Further north-east is the Castle Gate, the smallest and one of the least elaborate of the city's gates. It was opened through the walls in 1802, and had to undergo significant repairs, following damage, in the 1990s.

The north end of the city's west wall originally had two bastions, but only one of these now survives – the Hangman's Bastion, located a short distant north-east of the City Gate. The bastion here is rectangular in shape and now entirely surrounded by buildings. It got its name from an incident from the 1689 siege when a man trying to escape over the walls at this point got caught in the rope he was using and was almost hanged. Along this section of the walkway, the wall kinks outwards, and this may have been to incorporate the late-Medieval O'Doherty tower house that would have stood here. At the corner, just beside where Magazine Gate now stands, was the last of the bastions. It was known as Coward's Bastion *(Lord Chichester's Bulwark, 1622; Coward's Bastion, 1689)* and was removed in the first half of the 19th-century when the Corn and Butter Market was constructed. The bastion got its name from the fact that it was this section of the walls that was attacked least during the 1689 siege, and so was a popular posting for some members of the garrison.

Archaeological Investigations Around the Walls

A number of archaeological investigations have uncovered interesting information about the walls. The foundations of the Water Bastion (known in 1689 as the 'Governor of the Plantation's Bulwark') were uncovered during an archaeological excavation in 1983 (Brannon 1986). The wall at this point, which was nearly 2m wide, was found to have an external batter and to be decorated with sandstone quoins at its corners. The bastion, which got its modern name from the fact that the River Foyle originally came right up to the walls, had been demolished around

1850 to improve access to and from Foyle Street. All that remains now is a railed-off platform overlooking the public library, from which a flight of steps descends into Foyle Street.

In 1998–99 at The Millennium Complex, East Wall, between the city walls and Bank Place/Linenhall Street/Newmarket Street archaeological excavations uncovered a number of 17th-century vaulted cellars and tunnels.[11] Among the artefacts recovered were sherds of Sgraffito ware and brown earthenware pottery, along with hand-made brick, and animal bone. NIEA records state that one 17th-century tunnel, exposed during rebuilding at the YMCA adjacent to Linenhall Street, had been demolished in 1979. It extended from Linenhall Street to the back of the city wall and consisted of twelve brick-vaulted bays. The two bays adjacent to Linenhall Street were reported to be well-preserved and accessible below the now-demolished YMCA gym. The middle five were described as ruinous and the last five bays, next to the city wall, were intact. The network of bays was surveyed but it is reported that they were then withheld on security grounds. The construction technique was described as follows:

> The tunnels show identical building materials and methods of construction. The walls are usually of brick but stone is used in some parts. The roof consists of approx. 7-foot bays of intersecting barrel vaults and the workmanship is of a very high standard. The bricks appear handmade and show indentations made by straw during the hardening process. They measure 7 x 1½ x 2½, inches, a popular size.

The network of tunnels or cellars may have had a defensive function, as the passages formed a continuous network connecting the cellars of houses with important buildings such as the Magazine and barracks. They were necessary as the city is exposed to view from the higher, surrounding hills, and they were probably used to facilitate the unobserved movement of food, ammunition and troops to the bastions and ramparts. They could also have been used to store gunpowder safely in the event of a siege and as a place of refuge for women and children during attack. The tunnels are likely to pre-date the siege of 1689 and may be a part of the original design for the defences built by 1619. As they were mostly used for storage, the tunnels/cellars must originally have had wooden gates or partitions at various points to protect a particular householder or merchant's goods from theft. The excavations in 1998–99 uncovered a further group of interlinked cellars, in a poor state of repair. It appears they were used over a long period of time and, upon their destruction, the remains were deliberately collapsed and infilled with a mass of rubbish. Their remains are now preserved within the foundations of the Millennium Forum theatre.

A third excavation was undertaken at the Millennium Theatre site in 1999.[12] This examined the construction method of the earthen rampart behind the stone facing of the city wall. The dig found that the outer wall was backed by a clay rampart some 7–8m (23–26ft) wide and 2–3m (7–10ft) high. The clay rampart is made up of the material dug out from the city ditch. The wall was then built on and against the front of this rampart. When completed, it was said to have been 3.6m (12ft) thick within the city, with a wall 7.3m (24ft) high and 1.8m (6ft) thick on the outside. Certain encroachments were made on the walls during the 18th-century in the vicinity of what is now the site of the Millennium Theatre in the north-east of the city, and by 1853 most of the Water Bastion, which faced onto Foyle Street, had been removed.

At Fountain Street, a section of the 17th-century extra-mural town ditch was investigated in 1978 and found to be roughly 10m wide and 2m deep.

The Layout of the New City

The newly planned city was laid out as its defensive walls were being constructed. The street pattern was regular with four main streets crossing at a central square, later called 'The Diamond', and leading straight to the four gates in the city walls. These main streets and gates were:

   a)   Silver Street (now Shipquay Street), leading from The Diamond northwards to Water Gate (now Shipquay Gate).
   b)   Queene's Street (now Bishop's Street Within), from The Diamond southwards to Bishopps Gate (now Bishop's Gate).
   c)   Gracious Street (now Ferryquay Street), from The Diamond eastwards to Ferry Gate (now Ferryquay Gate).
   d)   Shambles Street (now Butcher Street), from The Diamond westwards to New Gate (now Butcher's Gate).

This pattern of the main streets in new settlements emanating from a central 'Diamond' was common in the Ulster Plantation.[13]

A secondary network of streets was also laid out further back from The Diamond. It was agreed initially that 200 houses were to be built within the walls, with room for 300 more. A number of maps of the new settlement survive from the early 1600s and illustrate how it developed.[14] One of the most important is Nicholas Pynnar's 'London-Derry' drawn up in early 1619, which shows the newly built walled city.[15] Within the walls, the four main streets are lined with terraces of houses. What may be the '*Dubh Regles*' Church and tower are shown surrounded by three buildings in the area of modern St Augustine's Church of Ireland church, and on the other side of the town, close to where the modern Tower Museum now stands, the re-edified O'Doherty tower house is depicted, surrounded by four cannon. The streets are laid out in grid pattern with a cannon standing where the modern Diamond is now. Outside the walls is a windmill and roads leading from the three landward town gates, and two parallel piers, forming a small harbour are shown at the bottom of Shipquay Street. In a key attached to the map Pynnar noted that:

The City of London-Derry is now compassed about with a very Strong Wall, excellently made and neatly wrought; being all of good Lime and Stone and in every Place of the Wall it is 24 feet [7.3m] high, and six feet [1.8m] thick. The Rampart within the City is 12 feet [3.7m] thick of Earth… The whole number of Houses within the City is 92 and in them there are 102 Families, which are far too few a number for the Defence of such a Circuit, they being scarce able to man one of the Bullwarks; neither is room enough to set up a 100 Houses more, unless they will make them as little as the first, and name each Room for a House.[16]

Nicholas Pynnar's 'London-Derry' drawn up in 1618–1619, which shows the newly built walled city. Within the walls, the four main streets are lined with terraces of houses. The 'Dubh Regles' Church and tower are shown surrounded by three buildings in the area of modern St Augustine's Church of Ireland church, and on the other side of the town, downslope to where the modern Tower Museum now stands, the re-edified O'Doherty tower house is depicted, surrounded by four cannon. The streets are laid out in grid pattern with a cannon standing where the modern Diamond is now. Outside the walls is a windmill and roads leading from the three landward town gates. Two parallel piers, forming a small harbour are shown at the bottom of Shipquay Street

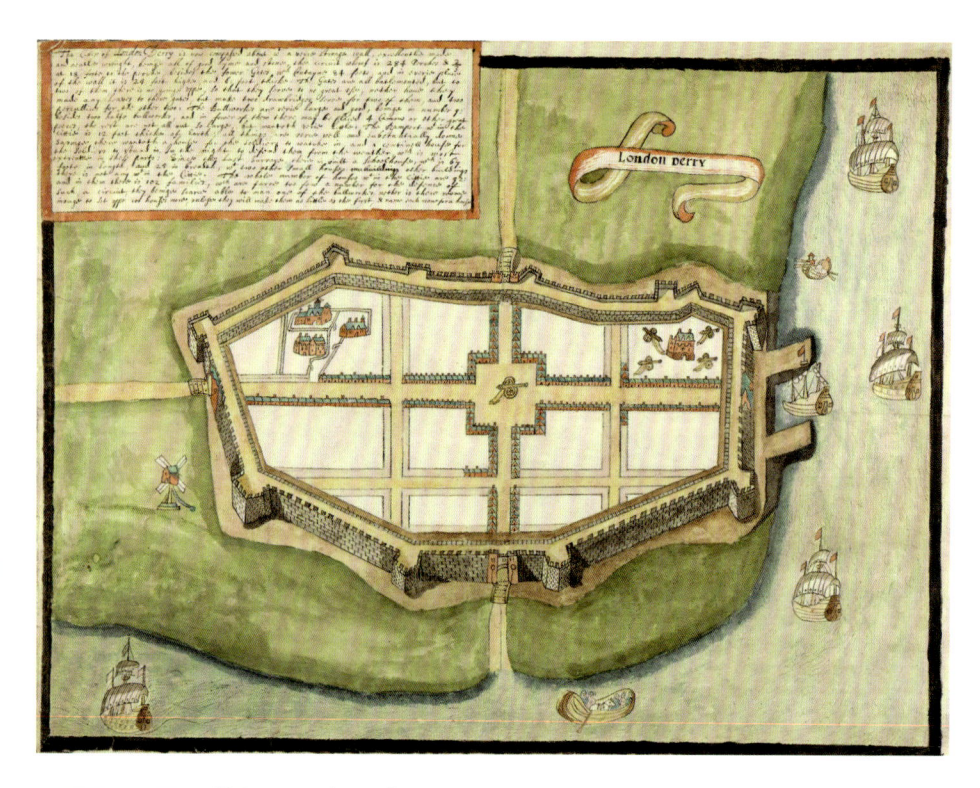

'The Plat of the Citte of Londonderrie as it Stand[s] Built and Fortified', drawn up by Thomas Raven in 1622. It's broadly similar to Pynnar's map as regards the streets, terraced houses (now with back garden plots shown) and town wall, but unbuilt proposed buildings are also illustrated. These include a citadel or fortified market place where The Diamond is now and a large church building in the area of modern Linen Hall Street. Two new, or proposed, quays or landing places are shown at the edge of the river, outside the walls, one at the end of Ferryquay Street, the other outside Shipquay Gate. Finally, garden plots and a few houses are shown outside the town walls, as well as three lime kilns

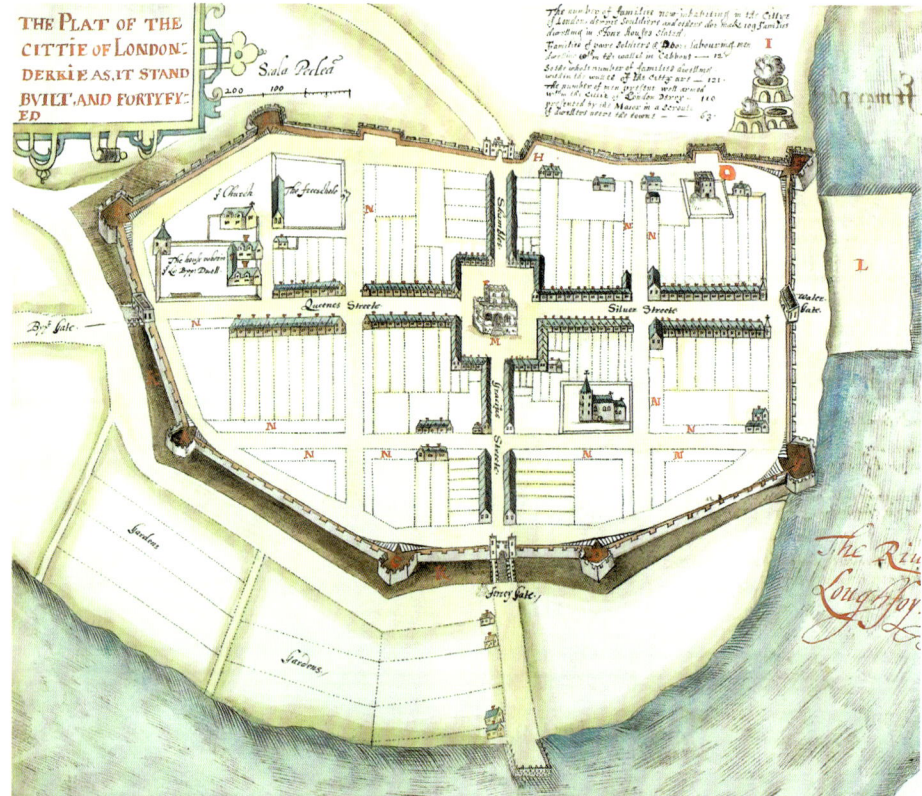

Opposite: Detail of Thomas Raven's 1622 map 'The Plat of the Citte of Londonderrie' showing the area around The Diamond of the new city

124 Island City. The Archaeology of Derry~Londonderry

Pedea

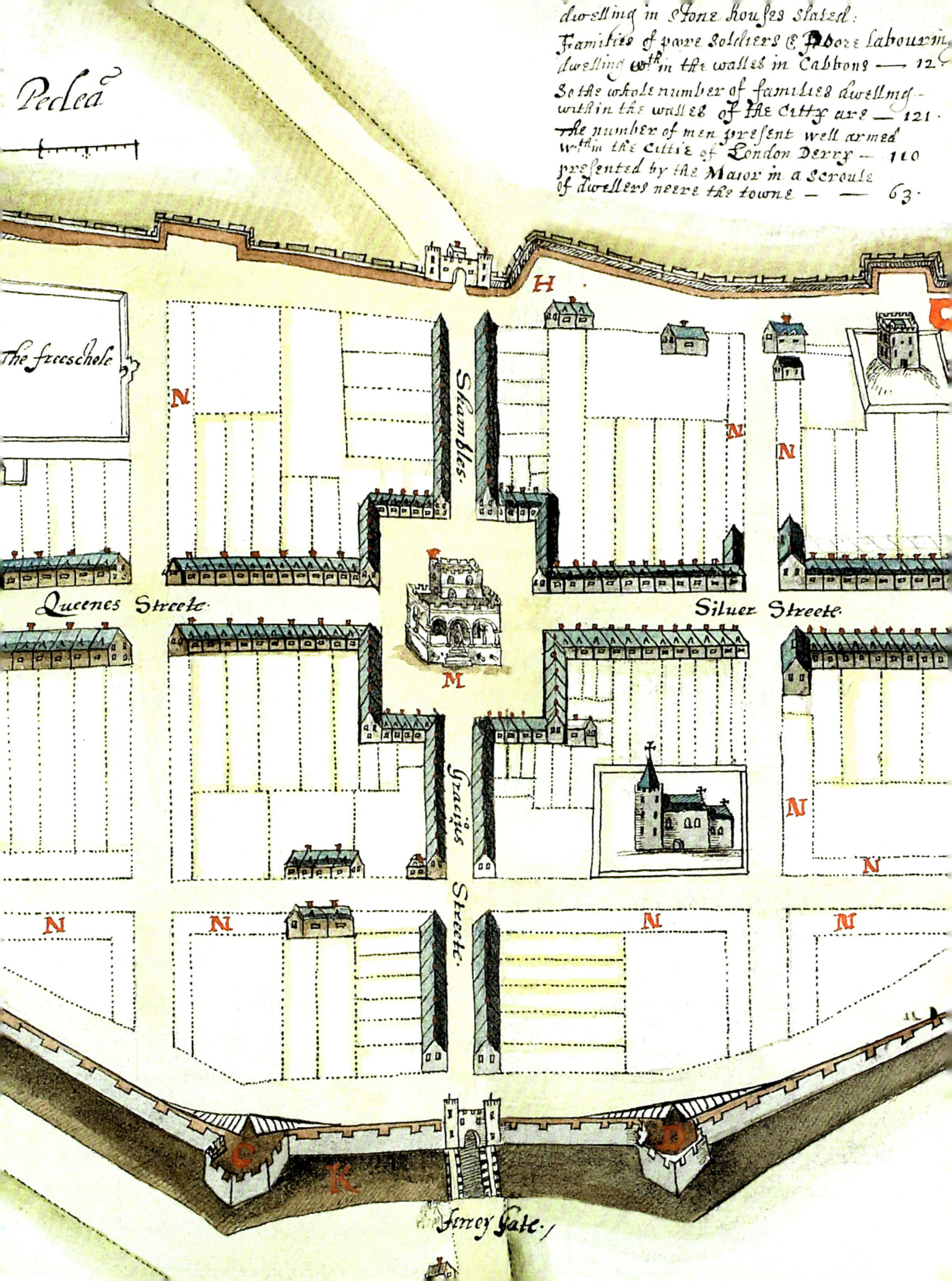

dwelling in Stone houses slated:
Families of poore soldiers & poore labourin
dwelling within the walles in Cabbons — 12
So the whole number of families dwelling
within the walles of the Citty are — 121
The number of men present well armed
within the Cittie of London Derry — 110
presented by the Maior in a scroule
of dwellers neere the towne — 63

The freeschole

Queenes Streete

Shambles

Siluer Streete

Gracius Streete

Ferry Gate

Thomas Raven's 1625 map of 'Londonderry', made in connection with proposals for improving the City's defences. The proposed citadel in The Diamond, shown in the 1622 map, has been replaced by a market house and the late medieval O'Doherty towerhouse is described as a 'store'

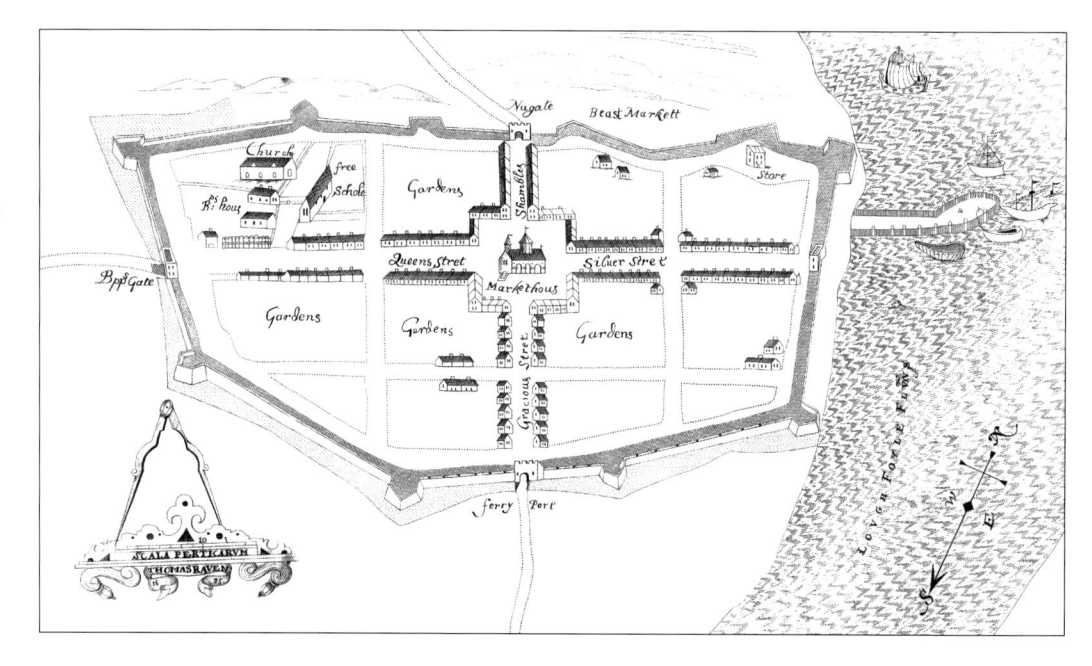

Although Pynnar describes a total of only 92 houses, with 102 families living within the walls more than 92 houses are illustrated on his map, reminding us that maps cannot be regarded as recording settlements with complete accuracy.

Another map of the new city, 'The Plat of the Citte of Londonderrie as it Stand[s] Built and Fortified', was drawn up by Thomas Raven in 1622 and is now held by the Worshipful Company of Drapers and with copies in the Public Record Office Northern Ireland (PRONI). In general terms it is broadly similar to Pynnar's as regards the streets, terraced houses (now with back garden plots shown) and town wall, but new buildings are also illustrated. These include a proposed fortified market place where The Diamond is now, a newly built house and bawn for the Bishop, a church and a school. Two quays or landing places are shown at the edge of the river, outside the walls, one at the end of Ferryquay Street, the other at Shipquay Gate. A large church, possibly the suggested location for a cathedral, is shown in the area of the modern Richmond Centre/Linenhall Street. As the City's cathedral, St Columb's was actually constructed less than a decade later at the other end of the city we should again be cautious about information portrayed on early maps. Finally, Raven's map shows garden plots and a few houses outside the town walls, as well as three limekilns to produce the mortar for all the new buildings. Two ditches, of probable 17th-century date, uncovered during excavations in the 1970s in the Fountain Street area and a series of earthworks at Long Tower Street may all be evidence of the new settlers' property divisions outside the walls. 17th-century extra-mural property boundaries were also uncovered during the 1999 excavations at Bishop's Street Without. When we come to examine the numbers of people in the new city the key to Pynnar's map states that:

> 109 Families dwelling in stone house slated… (i.e. with slate roofs)…the whole number of families dwelling within the walls of the citty are 121… the number of men present well armed within the cittie of London Derry – 110.

As the numbers of families almost correlates to the number of armed men in the city, this might suggest that the majority of the new settlers were young families. Although the numbers fluctuated at various times, the population of the new town rose steadily throughout the 17th-century. In 1622 there were 121 families within the walls and 63 families nearby, and by 1628 there were 155 families increasing to 500 male adults by 1630 (Londonderry Sentinel 1936). This made Londonderry the largest plantation settlement in Ulster at the time. It is uncertain whether the rise in adults recorded meant that the city was attracting new people or simply that original families had stayed on and children not included in the earlier surveys had now grown up to be classed as adults.

Among the important buildings constructed in the new town in the early decades of the 17th-century were a Custom House, the Corporation Hall, St Columb's Cathedral, a school, and a gaol with a gallows. In addition, such diverse buildings as blacksmiths' forges, stores, alehouses and taverns were also erected. Along the riverside, which was also overlooked and protected by the walls, there were shipbuilding facilities and extensive stockpiles of essential goods such as coal and timber. Although much of the original town layout survives, as far as we know, all of the original buildings are gone, with the exception of the 1633 St Columb's Cathedral. Archaeology is, therefore, central to uncovering new information about the development of the city in all periods.

Foundation stone of the St. Columb's Cathedral. The original foundation stone of 1633 used to be in the south porch, but was moved to the main porch in 1825. Below it is placed a modern copy (not in the picture). A smaller stone inserted into the body of the stone was apparently taken from the Columban church of 1164 A.D.

St Columb's Cathedral

St Columb's Cathedral, London Street, was built between 1628 and 1633 and is the oldest known building in the city.[17] One of the most remarkable buildings of the Ulster Plantation, it was the first Protestant cathedral built in either Ireland or Britain after the Reformation. The foundation stone was laid in 1628 and the cathedral was completed in 1633. It was built under the supervision of Sir John Vaughan and constructed of stone from local quarries.[18] An inscription on a stone plaque in the porch reads:

> IF STONES COULD SPEAKE
> THEN LONDON'S PRAYSE
> SHOULD SOUNDE WHO
> BUILT THIS CHURCH AND
> CITTIE FROM THE GROUNDE
> VAUGHAN AED

Like many contemporary London churches, the new cathedral was built in the Gothic style, this being the last large scale example of the use of this style in Ireland until it was revived in the mid to late 18th-century. The building, the first cathedral to be built in the British Isles after

Early photograph shows the east end of the cathedral before the addition of the chancel in 1887

Right: Engraving titled 'South-East prospect of Cathedral Church of London-Derry' by Paul Sandy (1780, The Virtuoisi Museum) shows cathedral just after completion of the new spire.

Below: South Elevation of St. Columb's Cathedral in 1688-9.

The Chancel of St. Columb's Cathedral looking up towards the East Window from the city walls.

the Reformation, comprised a high nave with a six bay clearstory and side aisles with battlements along the exterior aisle and nave walls. The tower at the west end had four stages, the present steeple having been added by the Earl-Bishop of Derry in 1778 and rebuilt in 1802. The tower's base, in the form of an octagon, acts as a porch, while another porch was built off the south aisle by Bishop King in the later 17th-century.

Until the tower was raised in height by 21 feet in 1778 to accommodate a new spire, the cathedral had retained its original form more-or-less unchanged. The south porch was removed in 1825 and in 1827 the eastern turrets, formerly battlemented, were rebuilt and capped with domes. The cathedral interior was remodelled in 1859-62 with the old wooden Georgian galleries in the side aisles were removed and the old box pews replaced. The final significant episode of alterations and additions took place in 1887, when the large chancel was added, though the east window tracery was retained in the enlarged building. Finally, the erection of the Chapter House and choir vestry in 1910 provided accommodation for the clergy and choir.

On 23 October 1641 the descendants of some of the Ulster Gaelic lords who had been dispossessed in the Plantation rose up in a revolt known as the 1641 Rebellion. The conflict became widespread as the English Civil War (1642–1651) effectively spread to Ireland. During more than a decade of fighting in Ireland there were as many as five different armies in the field until the final Parliamentarian victory in 1653. Historians know this conflict as *The Confederate Wars*. From May to August 1649 Derry underwent the first of the two sieges to which it was subjected in the 17th-century.[19] The siege occurred when a Presbyterian army loyal to Charles I sought to capture the city from the Parliamentarian garrison that held it. Before the siege commenced, the

View of interior of the cathedral looking towards the great east window

Parliamentarian garrison under the command of Sir Charles Coote destroyed houses adjacent to the outside of the town walls to deny the Royalists any opportunity to approach the town under cover. After twenty weeks, Eoghan Roe O' Neill and a Catholic Irish army drove off the besiegers and the city was relieved on 8 August 1649.

In around 1653 a Parliamentarian citadel (strong point within the city) was established around the Cathedral, perhaps incorporating its eastern wall.[20] The fortification is mentioned in 1662, two years after the Restoration of King Charles II, when a report on the city states that 'the late Usurpers [the Parliamentarians] made a Kinde of Citadell including the Church [St Columb's Cathedral] and part of the Churchyard, making the Steeple the Magazine'.[21]

The citadel was demolished sometime during the 1670s. During the later siege of 1689 cannon were mounted on the tower and as the Cathedral sits close to the highest point of the city it must have suffered some damage during the Jacobite bombardments.

Amongst the 17th-century artefacts on display in the Cathedral are a silver-gilt chalice (the 'Promise Chalice'), a paten (a small plate to hold the Eucharist) for the Church, still used during special services for celebration of Holy Communion, and a bell with the legend: 'Fear God, Honour the King. Re-cast for Londonderry Steeple in 1614.' Both chalice and bell were sent over by *The*

Honorable The Irish Society in advance of the construction of the Cathedral. The mention of a 'Steeple' in 1614, more than a decade before construction of St Columb's Cathedral commenced, is intriguing and which church it refers to is uncertain.

In the churchyard of St Columb's is a mound of earth known as 'The Siege Heroes' Mound'. The nature of the mound remains uncertain, but it may contain bones of some of those who died in the 1689 siege and whose bodies were uncovered during the remodelling of the interior of the Cathedral in early 1861. St Columb's Cathedral's website (http://www.stcolumbscathedral.org) records that during those works:

The Churchwardens …gave …an assurance that any bones dug up in the future would be buried again…the Apprentice Boys arranged to have the bones collected from the churchyard. They were placed in six coffins, a large deal box and an oaken case and were deposited in a vault in the north aisle of the Cathedral, close under the third window from the East… The Apprentice Boys gathered the soil that had been removed from the Cathedral [during the refurbishment] and formed it into a mound near to the main entrance gates and later placed a monument on

Top left: The Edwards Memorial tablet erected in 1672 in the north aisle wall of the cathedral. Hugh Edwards, Mayor of the City in 1671, died in 1676. Below this memorial can be seen a panel of mortuary symbols of the same period.

Top right: The Tomkins/Elvin memorial tablets erected in 1678 in the North Aisle of Derry Cathedral. John Elvin was Mayor of the City who died in 1672 aged 102. Alexander Tomkins died in 1642

Island City. The Archaeology of Derry~Londonderry

The Promise Chalice. An English silver gilt chalice presented by *The Honourable The Irish Society* in 1613 as a symbol of their promise to build a cathedral (this was the year that the county of Londonderry was established by Royal Charter). The chalice bears the coat of arms of the City of London and is inscribed in Latin, which translated as 'To the Church of God in the City of Derry, the gift of Londoners'. The chalice is still in use in the cathedral during special services for the celebration of Holy Communion

The Wandesford silver Chalice and Paten. They were made in Dublin, 1642, by silversmith William Cooke. The chalice is inscribed 'Michail Wandesford - Decanus obtulit, 1637'. Wandesford was Dean of Derry from 1635 to his death in 1637. The chalice is one of the earliest known examples of Irish hallmarked silver - hallmarking began in Dublin in 1638-39

Pair of silver flagons made in Dublin, 1655. The makers were probably Nicholas Seward and William Lucas. They are the only known pieces of silver to have been hallmarked in Dublin that year. The flagons were presented to the cathedral in 1683 by Bishop Ezekial Hopkins (bishop from 1681-1690). They are inscribed 'The gift of Ezekiel LD Bishop of Derry to the Cath. Church of Derry 1683'

Island City. The Archaeology of Derry~Londonderry

Map showing the location of significant archaeological excavations that have taken place within or close to the walled city between 1976 and 2013

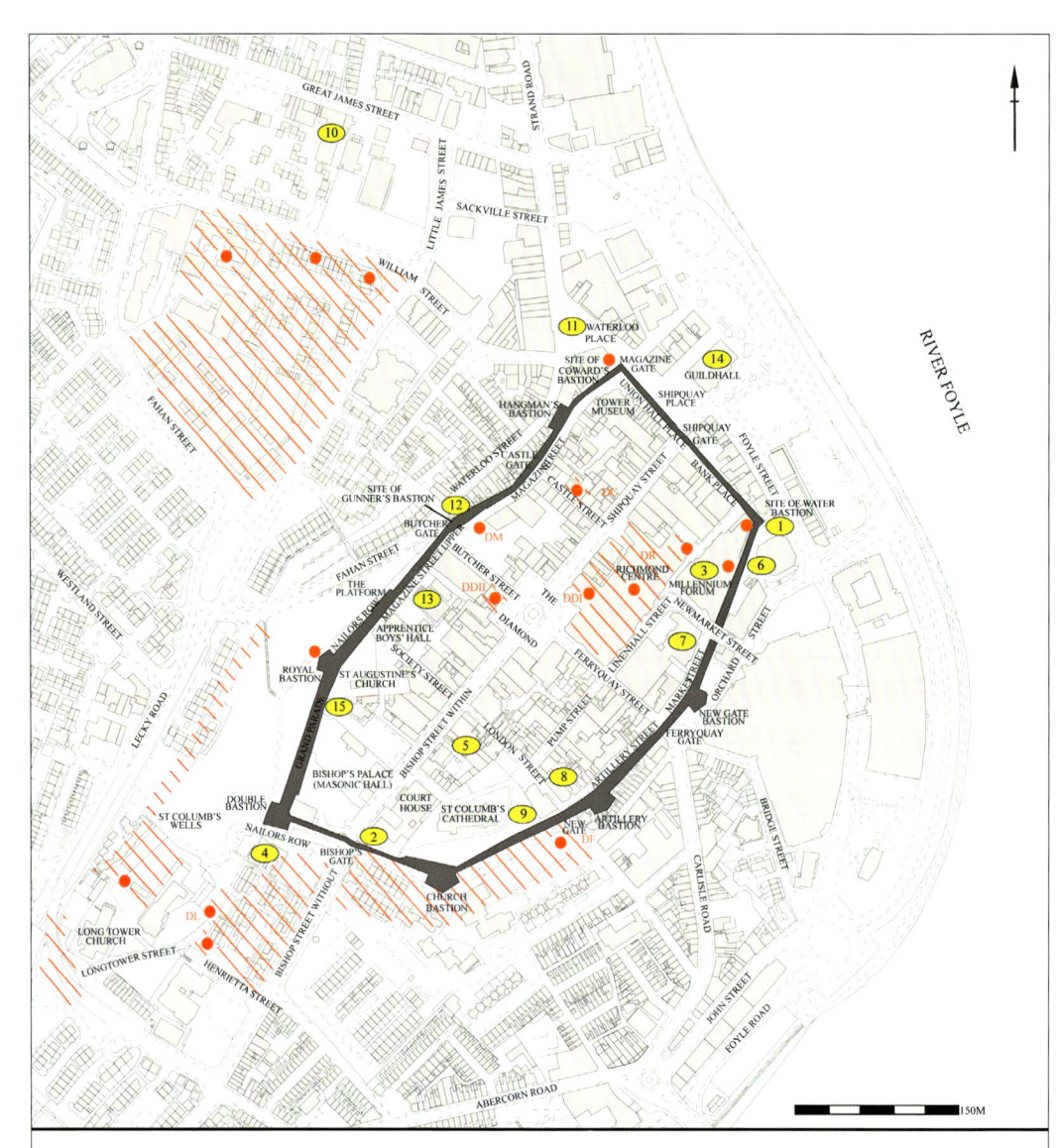

Map of Significant Archaeological Excavations that have take place in the City, 1976-2013

Excavations 1976-1980 (information from Lacey 1980)

DL = Long Tower Street (1976-1979).
DF = Fountain Street/ Nailor's Row (1976-79).
DDI/ DDII = The Diamond (1976-78).
DR = Diamond/ Richmond Street Area (1977-79).
DM = Magazine Street (1977-79).
DC = Castle Street (1978).
Abbey Street (1977-79).
Linenhall Street (1980).

Excavations 1908-2013

1 = Water Bastion (1983).
2 = Bishop's Street Within (1988).
3 = Site of Millennium Theatre (1998-1999).
4 = Bishop's Street Without (1999).
5 = Bishop's Street Within (2000).
6 = St. Columb's Hall, Orchard Street (2002-2003).
7 = Rialto Theatre (2005).
8 = 10-12 Artillery Street (2006).
9 = Siege Heroes Mound, St. Columb's Cathedral (2006)
10 = Great James Street (2008).
11 = Derry City Centre Public Realm (2009-2010).
12 = Waterloo Street (2009).
13 = First Derry Presbyterian Church (2010).
14 = The Guildhall, Shipquay Square (2010).
15 = Bishop's Street Carpark (2013).

top of it with an inscription describing the events outlined above. This mound is now known as "Siege Heroes Mound".

In 2006, archaeological monitoring of work to lower the ground level associated with this monument recovered pieces of disarticulated bone along with sherds of post-medieval pottery.[22]

The Houses within the Walled City

Houses within the city are portrayed on the 17th-century maps as being constructed of brick and stone two or three stories high. Although no complete examples have yet been found, the remains of several 17th-century houses have been uncovered on excavations. The evidence provides information that the maps and documents do not and it gives us a more intimate picture of what life would have been like for the families living in the city. For example, the walls of the houses were built of large mortared stones and appear to have had plastered internal walls, a stone fireplace and a brick oven to cook food in. The floors were composed of flagstones and the roofs of the houses were covered in ceramic tiles or slates. The houses would have had latrines in the back yards as well as cellars for storing food, wells for fresh water and pits where rubbish was deposited. Cobbled surfaces around the houses and in the back yards gave a firm surface for people carrying out tasks around the house and for storing things on.

The best evidence so far of 17th-century houses in the city were the two excavated at Linenhall Street.[23] These houses had brick ovens built-in to the side of stone fireplaces. House 1, in which the oven was almost complete, measured almost 9m long by 5.5m wide internally and had an entrance in one of the long walls. House 2 was very slightly wider than House 1 and although it was not possible to record its full length, it was probably similar to the first. Lacey noted that 'the walls of both houses reflected both current and probably seventeenth-century property lines'.[24] This is exciting evidence that suggests at least some of the house plots marked out when the 17th-century city was being established still survive today, 400 hundred years later.

The walls of both houses were constructed of large mortared stones and were roughly 0.6m thick. The dividing wall between the two houses was only slightly thicker. A section of one of the walls was set into a foundation trench cut into the bedrock. Although neither house survived to full height, the width of the wall foundations means that they could have supported more than one storey. The west wall of House 1 survived to a height of nearly 2.5m above the floor at some points, as did the ovens in both houses. The floor of House 1 was made up of large irregular flagstones with the gaps between the flags filled with small cobbles. The floor of House 2 appears to have been composed of a mix of flagstones along with a greater concentration of cobbled stones. This shows that that no two houses within the city were built identically although there were common features in all. Both houses at Linenhall Street had traces of plaster on their internal walls and there were two square recesses in one of the walls of House 1 that appear to have served as shelves. House 1, at least, seems to have had an internal partition, perhaps of wood, suggesting that the ground floor was divided into two smaller rooms. Given that space would also have been needed for a stairwell to allow access to the upper floors, life within these 17th-century houses was probably quite cramped. The excavation of House 1 also revealed that a

Island City. The Archaeology of Derry~Londonderry

Thomas Philips, 1685. Perspective drawing by Thomas Phillips titled 'Londonderry' one of several ascribed to him in this year. This drawing gives a good impression of how the walled city may have looked in the years just before the Jacobite siege of 1689. The illustration, looking from the west and down river, clearly shows the effect of the topography of the Island on the buildings within it. Apart from the fortifications, which look visually dramatic, St Columb's Cathedral is perhaps portrayed too prominently, with streets within the city sloping down to the Shipquay Gate, beyond which is a small wooden quay projecting out into the river. Garden plots are shown outside the town walls and a causeway across the boggy area (the modern Bogside) beyond. Also prominent in the background is a windmill, the body of which survives today in the grounds of Lumen Christi College

Island City. The Archaeology of Derry~Londonderry

Engraving published in 1793 titled 'Londonderry' by W. & J. Walker is from a drawing by Paul Sanby from an original sketch by the amateur draughtsman John Nixon. This is a view from the Waterside opposite the landing place of the ferry across the River Foyle. The tall spire of St. Columb's Cathedral was erected in 1776-78 by Frederick Augustus Hervey, Bishop of Derry (the Earl Bishop) by his Cork architect, Michael Shanahan

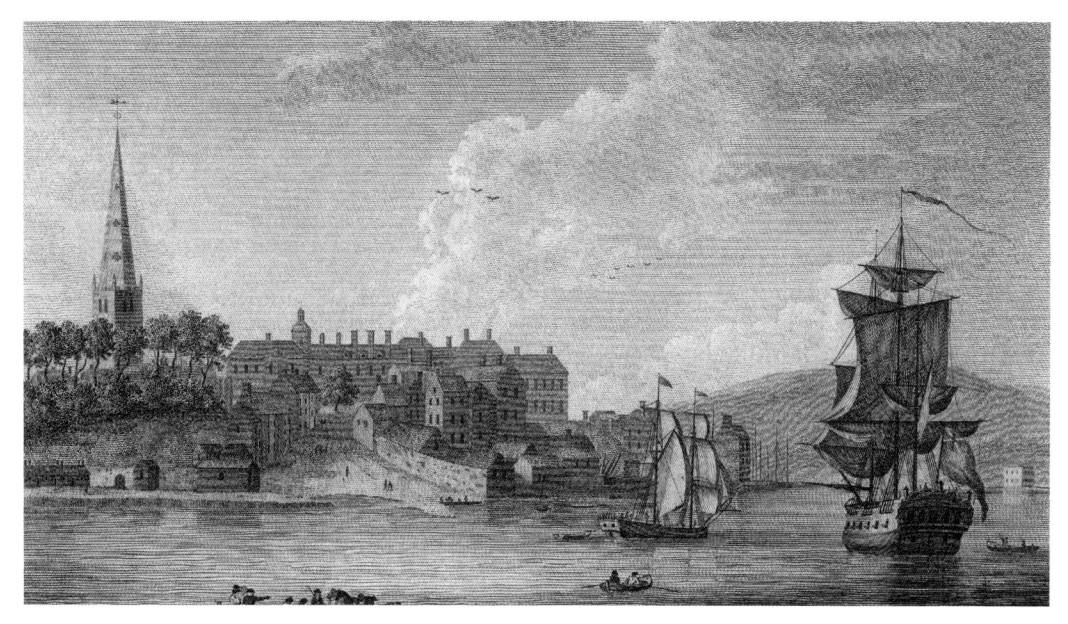

cobbled floor, laid on top of a platform of building rubble, had been inserted at some later stage over the 17th-century floor and showed that there were at least two phases of occupation in this house. Intriguingly a brick-built, bucket-like feature of uncertain function was recorded as sunk below the earlier flagged floor of House 1. In the absence of banks or safes in the 17th-century, perhaps personal possessions or coins were kept hidden in this carefully constructed receptacle below the floor of the house.

Lacey dated the primary settlement of the Linenhall Street houses to *c*. 1630 based on map evidence and also from datable artefacts recovered from the excavation.

In 2005 another excavation uncovered the structural remains of buildings at the site of the Rialto Theatre, not far from Linenhall Street.[25] The earliest building, located at the northern end of the site, comprised the well-preserved remains of a large 17th-century house along with artefacts. The excavated remains of the house were 13m long by 7m wide internally. The walls of the house were constructed of schist, (the same local stone used in the city wall) which had been bonded with lime mortar. They were were 0.5–0.75m thick and built on foundations that varied in depth from 0.1–0.6m deep. Like the 17th-century Linenhall Street houses, the internal faces of the walls of the house uncovered at the Rialto Theatre excavation were coated in a layer of plaster to create a smooth finish. It had a flagstone floor and a brick, rather than stone, fireplace at its southern corner. The excavator dated the construction of the house on artefact and map evidence to between 1625 and 1685 and its demolition to around 1738.

Features within 17th-century houses varied from settlement to settlement in Ulster.[26] Plans for 'howses' were drawn up for some of the new Londonderry plantation settlements, such as those for the Drapers' Company in 1615.[27] However, these house plans normally show fireplaces positioned back to back in a centrally positioned stack, not located in the end walls as found in the Linenhall Street and Rialto Theatre houses. The foundations of a 17th-century stone and red brick terrace that once fronted onto what is now Waring Street in Belfast was also investigated in a number of excavations between 1999 and 2002.[28] As at Linenhall Street, the floors of the houses in the 17th-century Belfast terrace were not identical in each house. Some of the Waring Street houses had beaten clay floors, a basic but functional construction, while another had timber floorboards. The remains of a red brick corner oven, of different construction to those found in the Linenhall Street houses, was also recorded in one of the Waring Street houses.

In 1976 and 1977 excavations took place in the north-east of The Diamond. They uncovered the preserved back yards of 17th-century houses including a cobbled surface, a stone-lined well more than 4.5m deep, several rubbish pits and a large stone-lined pit nearly 3m deep. Lining pits with stone meant they could be periodically emptied and re-used whether for rubbish, storage or as latrines. A series of trial examinations in the Richmond Street area in 1978 and 1979 revealed a number of pits, cobbled areas, 17th-century soil deposits and a stone-built cellar.[29] Roof tiles – both glazed and unglazed- were found during excavations in The Diamond in 1976. At another site excavated in the south-western corner of The Diamond in 1978 a large circular pit, an abandoned well shaft, a 17th-century brick-built kiln and a stone-lined storage pit of late-17th-century date were all recorded.

In 1978 a previously unknown stone-built well was noted in a covered alley between nos 33 and 35 Shipquay Street and a brick-built well was also found at the premises of *Peerless Dry Cleaners* in Magazine Street. In 1979, at Shipquay Street, the probable 17th-century cellar area of a house at the junction of Richmond Street was excavated, and amongst the many finds was a portion of a North Devon sgraffito pottery dish with a date inscription of 1684.

In 1998 the construction of the new Millennium Theatre led to archaeological investigations being carried out. The excavations revealed a series of 17th-century house frontages and associated cellars.[30] In 1999 an excavation undertaken outside the walls at Bishop's Street Without uncovered two phases of 17th-century activity.[31] The earlier was a series of drainage gullies, rubbish pits, possible property boundaries and cobbled surfaces, suggesting a phase of occupation dating to the first half of the 17th-century, followed by secondary occupation during the latter part of the century. No direct structural evidence for the actual 17th-century houses was recovered, as these were almost certainly removed during a phase of activity on site dating to the period immediately before the start of the siege of 1689.

Detail from Thomas Raven's 1625 map of the city showing the original market house and the houses clustered around The Diamond

Detail from a hand coloured print etching 'Londonderry' attributed to Henry Brocas senior and dated to around 1800. The city was a busy port from the start of its foundation in the early 17th century and possibly earlier.

Life within the Walled City

The recently published *Ulster Port Books 1612-15* gives us an idea of the emerging mercantile nature of the new city and sheds light on the plantation economy.[32] The main exports from Londonderry in the early 17th-century were of an agricultural nature derived from the hinterland of the city –animal hides, wool, beef, and tallow, grain, especially oats, rye and barley, and linen yarn – as well as fish and timber. Initially, imports into the city included, understandably, building materials such as tiles, tools, nails, door locks, glass, lead, candles, coal, slack and the ubiquitous 'household goods for the use of the plantation'. But other commodities were also brought in. Items such as Malaga raisins, Genoese fustian (a thick, hard-wearing twilled cloth usually dyed in dark colours), *aqua vitae* [whisky], beer, French salt, cloth, hats, cotton, wool, hides, combs, knives, pikes, swords, muskets, gun powder and lead shot, stirrups and other horse bits, brass kettles and pans, drinking glasses, bellows, cattle, and Spanish and French wines are all listed in the *Ulster Port Books 1612-15*. When we look at the clothing items listed, it would appear that the new colonists were keen to retain their original identities by wearing the same types of contemporary clothes that would have been commonly worn in other British towns and cities.

The vast quantity and variety of artefacts uncovered during excavations within the walls gives a vivid insight into how people lived during the 17th-century and later. The material culture of the new settlement both in the range and quality of imported goods available to the citizens not

Tin glazed maiolica bowl of c.1700 date depicting the 'Virgin and Child' painted in polychrome evidently in front of the Basilica della Santa Casa in Loreto on the east coast of Italy. The vessel, probably made locally to Loreto as a souvenir for pilgrims, is inscribed CON.POL.DI.S.C[asa] (with dust of the holy house), probably indicating that it was made with 'dust of the shrine and pilgrims feet at Loreto'. The 'Holy House' of Mary, which angels had transported from Nazareth to Loreto, was a popular Roman Catholic pilgrimage destination since the 14th century. This piece may well indicate that at least one Londonderry resident undertook that pilgrimage during the early 1700s

only reflects the importance of the city but it also emphasises its significance as a port from this period onwards. For example, excavations in The Diamond in 1976 turned up coins and tokens from the 17th-century, clay pipes from the 17th–20th centuries, roof tiles – both glazed and unglazed – and a vast amount of post-Medieval pottery from England, France, Germany, Holland, Italy and Spain, as well as locally produced pottery. In 1977 more excavations were carried at a variety of locations within the walls including in the north-eastern corner of The Diamond, and large quantities of ceramics were unearthed.[33] Most of this was imported from England though some was locally made and there was a wide range of high-quality Continental products.

In 1979, at Shipquay Street, the probable 17th-century cellar area of a house at the junction of Richmond Street was excavated, and amongst the many finds was a portion of a North Devon sgraffito dish with a date inscription of 1684 incised on it. This type of English pottery is very

Earthenware container or amphora used for the storage and transportation of olive oil. During the 16th century Irish western ports enjoyed extensive trade with Spain and this continued into the early 17th century with both wine and olive oil being imported into the newly established town of Londonderry. This vessel, probably of early 17th century date, was found during excavations in the city in the 1970s.

common on plantation sites of the 17th-century in Ireland but very few have been found that can be as closely dated as this one.

Amongst the finds from excavations at Fountain Street in 1978 were a deposit of shoe leather and a small wooden wine cask. These sorts of discoveries add colour and detail to our picture of how people would have looked like in the 17th-century and the kinds of things that you would have seen in houses and cellars around the city.

Excavations at Bishop's Street Without in 1999 recovered over 5,000 artefacts of various types. These included pottery sherds of Irish, English and Continental origin, including sherds of French Saintonge Polychrome and examples of German stonewares such as Raeren, Frechen and Westerwald. Metal artefacts included a possible trigger guard and pistol pommel, as well as lead shot. Sherds of wine and window glass were also found, along with clay pipes from the early 17th-century to the late 19th centuries. Early examples of clay pipes, from perhaps the first decades of the 17th-century, may have been made by southern English pipe makers, while early to mid-17th-century pipes from the London and Bristol areas were identified along with late 17th-century Bristol pipes.

Amongst the finds recovered from an excavation inside First Derry Presbyterian Church in 2009 were oyster shells and animal bone, which give us valuable information about the diet of people in the 17th-century city; fragments of roof tile and brick fragments which are useful evidence of how the buildings would have looked like, and pieces of clay pipe of the mid- to late-17th-century which are luxury goods. The pottery found on the excavation included a fragment of Staffordshire trailed slipware of the late-17th or early 18th centuries, one fragment of possible German Westerwald stoneware, two sherds of tin-glazed earthenware, Carrickfergus Brown Ware, Staffordshire Manganese Mottled Ware and one piece of North Devon gravel-free pottery, dating to the early 17th-century.

During the 2012 excavation at St Augustine's Church, Palace Street, pottery types including sherds of North Devon Gravel Tempered and North Devon Gravel Free wares were all recovered, dating to the first half of the 17th-century, the period of the initial construction and occupation of the walled town.[34] One fragment of late-17th-century/early 18th-century Manganese Mottled pottery was found that dates to the era of the 'Great Siege' of 1689.

The immense number of post-medieval finds from excavations in the city is now in excess of 500,000 objects. These include sherds of pottery and ceramics, clay pipes, wine bottles and other glassware, gun flints, lead shot, roof tiles, coins, leather and fabric as well as many other small finds. Domestic pottery types included English, French, Dutch, German, Italian and Spanish imports as well as locally made wares. Clay pipes from the 17th–20th centuries recovered originated from England, Holland, France and various Irish towns, particularly Londonderry itself. The finds give us information about the quality of life in 17th-century Derry. Other objects relate to the thriving port that the city had become by the end of the 17th-century, as borne out by the many international imports, especially of pottery. The gunflint and lead shot remind us that the people in the city still felt that they needed to be protected from possible attack, while the debris from the houses- such as roof tiles, brick and window glass- show us what the houses within the city may looked like. All of these archaeological finds allow us to connect directly with the ordinary people of the 17th-century city (and those of later times) in a way that documents or maps cannot. In a few cases we can actually put names to the merchants who were bringing goods into the city. For example, the list of householders in the city in 1628 includes a Wilbrant Oldfert, the name suggesting that he was perhaps Dutch.[35] The Port Books for the city for 4th October 1614 list the same person (though here written as 'Wilbrand Oldfers') as having brought in 3000 'deals' (wooden boards) and 'tar' on the ship the *Peter* of Londonderry.[36] This was material needed for construction within the new city and in 1614 the city walls were still in the process of being constructed. The fact that Wilbrant Olfert was still in the city in 1628 and owned a house there shows he had chosen to make it his home. It is a nice example of continuity of settlement within the city.

Assortment of late 17th-early 18th century mallet wine bottles found during excavations in Derry-Londonderry. Although cylindrical bottles started to arrive in the later 18th century (which allowed bottles to be stored on their side in 'bins'), until 1860 all wine in the UK was purchased in barrels ('pipes'); in fact it was illegal to sell it in bottles as the industry had not figured out to make bottles a standard size. Found on excavations in Londonderry during the 1970s.

Pancake onion bottles found on excavations in Londonderry dating to the 17th century. They are made of 'black glass', the result of impurities in the glass. In fact black bottles are really amber or deep olive green and were popular at the time as they hid the sediments often found in the liquids. The 'string lip' was used to fix the string which secured the cork.

Island City. The Archaeology of Derry~Londonderry

Bristol/Staffordshire slipware. An assortment of posset pots, cups, vases and bowls of mostly late 17th century date found during excavations in Londonderry during the 1970s. The Staffordshire Burslem potteries in the late 17th century and early 18th century represent a high point in the production of slip ware or decorative lead glazed earthenware. This pottery was evidently exported to Ireland in some quantity, particularly to Derry (some other towns seem to have had a preference for North Devon rather than Staffordshire wares)

Bristol/Staffordshire slipware. A combed slipware plate of late 17th century date (top) and an assemblage of slipware possets, cups and jars, all found in excavations in the city during the 1970s. Much of the slipware being produced by the Staffordshire potteries in the second half of the 17th century was of outstanding quality, being both handsome and functional. The distinctive decoration on the mugs and vase in this picture was produced by a combination of marbling and feathering techniques. First the vessel was coated with an orange slip, then a series of white and dark red-brown slips were trailed over and run together for the variegated effect, this being often done with a quill to drag it into a feathered pattern

Island City. The Archaeology of Derry~Londonderry

Trailed English slipware of 17th century date found on archaeological excavations in Londonderry. This form of pottery, largely coming from Burslem in North Staffordshire, reached it peak during the reign of Charles II. The white slip was either trailed directly onto body of the vessel (usually pink) or onto a pink slip to create slightly embossed slip trail patterns, usually yellow, on a light brown background. Slip trailed vessels are characteristically glazed on one side only

North Devon ware 17th century bowl found in the 1970s in the city. Throughout the 17th century distinctive and usually utilitarian pottery from North Devon was exported to Ireland in increasing qualities; in 1694 for example, seventeen earthenware shipments totalling 50,400 parcels were made from Barnstaple and Bideford to Dublin, Wexford, and Waterford. The pottery included both gravel tempered ware and gravel-free pottery, often known as North Devon smooth or plain ware. It's lead glaze normally has a light brown to apple green or mottled-yellow-green glaze, often speckled with orange

North Devon Sgraffito ware dishes c1680 found on excavations in the city during the 1970s. This form of pottery (the Italian word sgraffito means to scratch or to engrave) is characterised by its incised slip decoration of brown motifs on a yellow ground. The red earthenware is coated with a white slip through which designs were incised, while the amber glaze imparts a golden yellow to the slip

Island City. The Archaeology of Derry~Londonderry

Early Qing dynasty blue and white porcelain bowl with a depiction of a dragon. The birthplace of porcelain was China, consequently this form of pottery is often known informally as 'China' or fine china'. This translucent and tough ceramic was imported from China until European potters discovered the secrets of its manufacture in the early 18th century

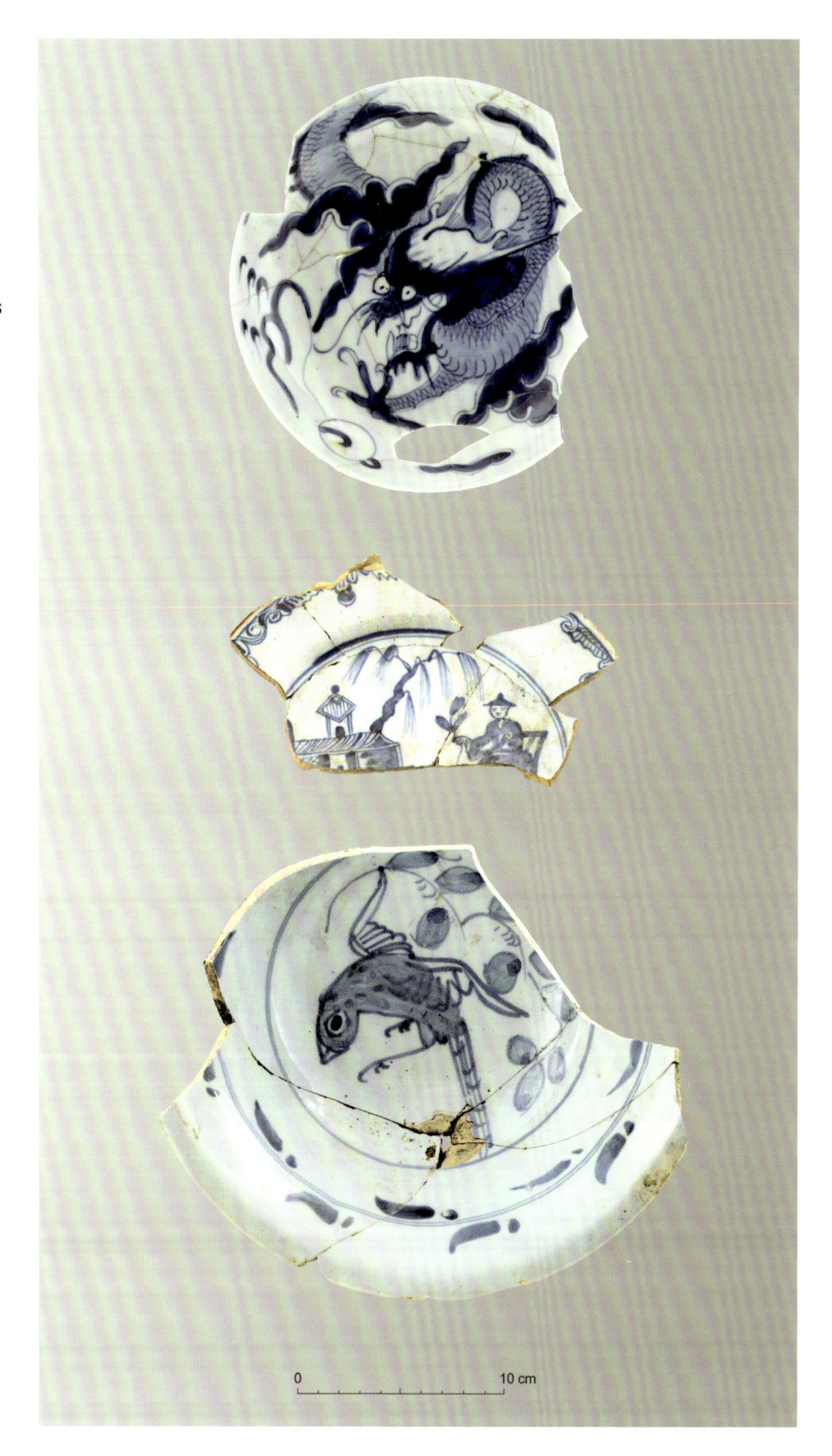

Blue and white tin glazed earthenware dish and bowl of 17th century date. European potters sought to imitate Chinese porcelain in the 16th and 17th centuries by producing earthenware with a white and blue tin-glaze. Lead glaze with tin oxide was applied to the earthenware body to produce an opaque white surface. The glaze could then be subsequently decorated with metal oxide pigments

Top left: Blackware jug of 17th century date, possibly from Buckley in North Wales. Pottery from here was produced in some quantity from the medieval to the mid-20th century, though the 17th and 18th centuries were its most productive time

Top right: Westerwald stoneware jug. Typically fine, white-fired clay with plastic body, & surface treated with salt glaze with addition of cobalt blue (and sometimes also manganese purple) painted details, these two colours being the only ones capable of withstanding the very high temperatures of stoneware kilns. The pottery originated in modern Belgium, at Raeren, but during the late 16th century moved to the Westerwald in Germany. It was very widely exported from the 17th to 19th centuries

Polychrome or multicoloured Saintonge pottery from south-western France. It is a coarse earthenware with a mottled mid-green colouring from the copper oxide added to the lead glaze finish. It was widely exported into Ireland from the late 12th century; these sherds are of 17th century date

Sherds of Werra slipware. This pottery, which has a red brown sandy fabric and a greenish yellow slip, was made in the Werra Valley of North Germany. It was exported though the port of Bremen from 1569 to 1653, though most examples date from 1590-1625

Island City. The Archaeology of Derry~Londonderry

Three imported Dutch early 17th century pipes with fleur-de-lis embossed stamps on the side of the bowls.
The shape of the pipe bowl was meant to replicate the shape of a tulip bulb. Found on excavations in the 1970s in the city

Three imported Dutch early 17th century pipes with Tudor Rose maker's stamp

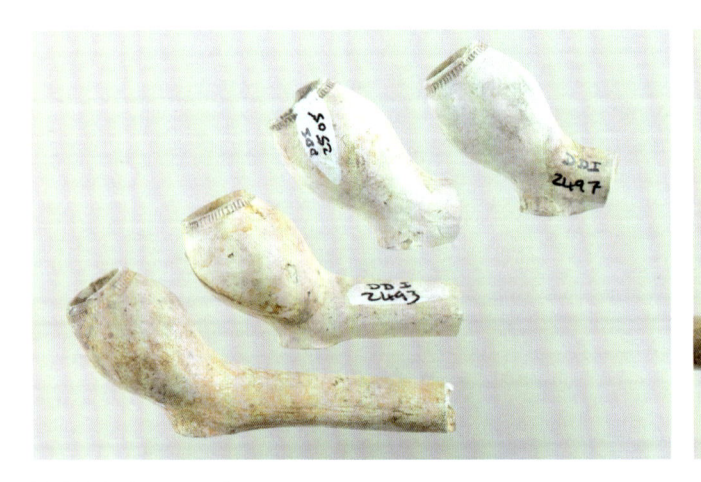

English 17th century pipes

Island City. The Archaeology of Derry~Londonderry

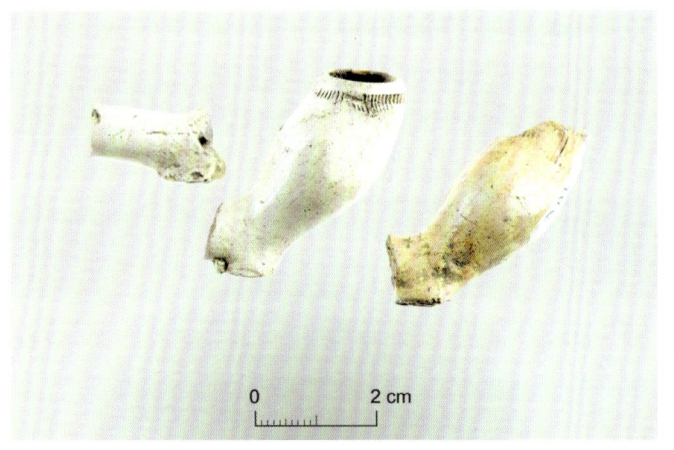

English 17th century pipes with RB stamp for the pipemaker Richard Berryman on heel of the pipe. Found on excavations in the 1970s in the city. First half of the 17th century

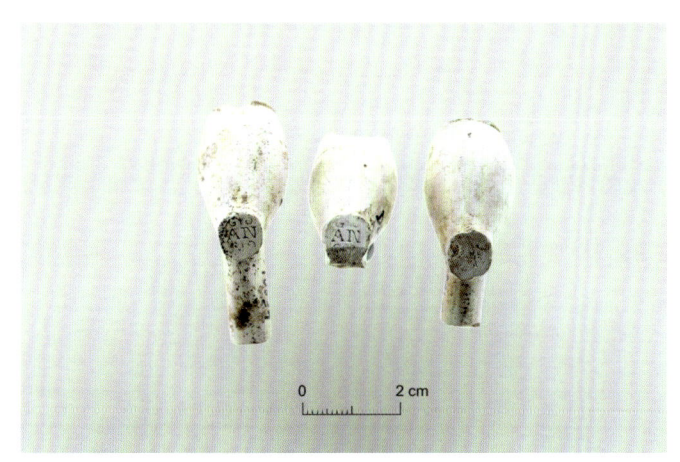

Northern English 17th century pipes

Northern English 17th century pipes

Island City. The Archaeology of Derry~Londonderry

Bishop Street Excavations of 2013: The Skeleton

Excavations in 2013 uncovered fifteen burials in the Bishop Street car park, nine of which were fully investigated exposing the skeletons, while six were later removed for analysis. Of the nine excavated, eight were found to be adults and one was a juvenile aged between four and five. All of the grave cuts, with the exception of the juvenile, respected one another. This, coupled with the absence of disarticulated human bone in the grave fills, suggests a single phase of use of the graveyard and the associated artefacts would suggest a seventeenth-century date. Eight of the nine skeletons were orientated with their head to the west with just one, on the same axis but with his head in the east. A double burial was also uncovered, this being a possible man and wife, and a pipe-smoker who had a prominent groove in one of his upper incisors caused by wear from clenching down on tobacco pipes. The burials also included a mixture of coffin and shroud interments indicated by the presence of coffin nails and shroud pins respectively. After specialist analysis by a human osteologist the skeletons will be returned to Derry and reinterred in consecrated ground.

A Louis XIII of France Double Tournois dating to 1643, which depicts Louis as a Roman emperor on one face with three fleur de lis on the opposite. These coins were produced by private contractors in large quantities at many mints throughout France and in many varieties.

Excavation of some of the burials on Bishop Street Within during the summer of 2013

Seven of the inhumation burials on Bishop Street Within during excavation. Note one is orientated with its head to the east rather than the west.

Island City. The Archaeology of Derry~Londonderry

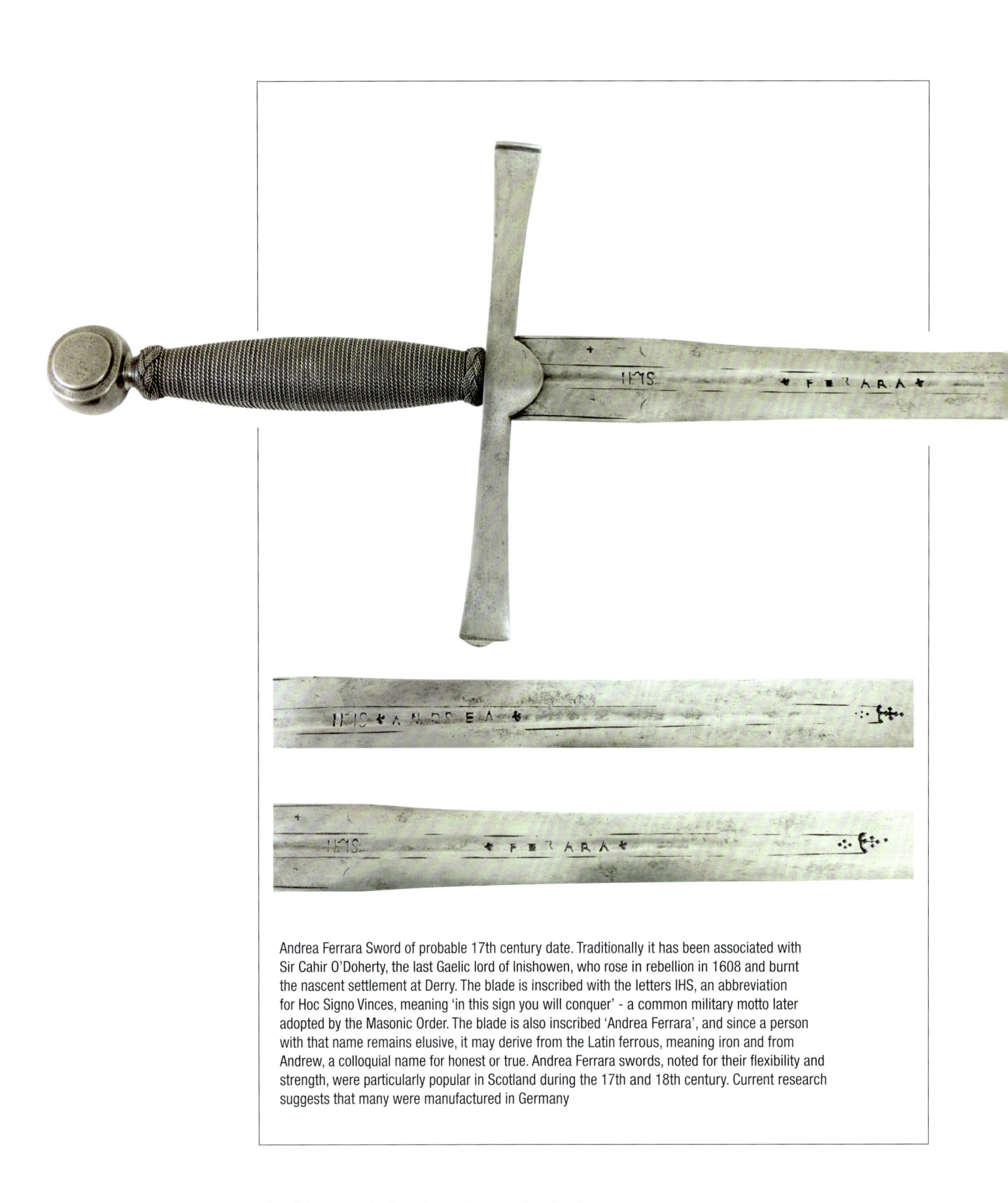

Andrea Ferrara Sword of probable 17th century date. Traditionally it has been associated with Sir Cahir O'Doherty, the last Gaelic lord of Inishowen, who rose in rebellion in 1608 and burnt the nascent settlement at Derry. The blade is inscribed with the letters IHS, an abbreviation for Hoc Signo Vinces, meaning 'in this sign you will conquer' - a common military motto later adopted by the Masonic Order. The blade is also inscribed 'Andrea Ferrara', and since a person with that name remains elusive, it may derive from the Latin ferrous, meaning iron and from Andrew, a colloquial name for honest or true. Andrea Ferrara swords, noted for their flexibility and strength, were particularly popular in Scotland during the 17th and 18th century. Current research suggests that many were manufactured in Germany

The State Sword, 1616. The Honourable The Irish Society presented the 'State Sword' with its scabbard to the City of Londonderry in 1616. The name *LON*DON*DER*RE is inscribed on the sword's pommel. The sword is now part of the city's regalia

Island City. The Archaeology of Derry~Londonderry

Drawing of the siege of Derry that took place between April to July 1689 and lasted 105 days. The illustration is from Col. John Michelburn's "Ireland Preserv'd or the Siege of Londonderry…""written by the then Governor" and first published in 1705. Mitchelburn was Joint Governor during the siege and on his death in 1721 he was buried in Old Glendermott Cemetery where Col. Adam Murray is also buried

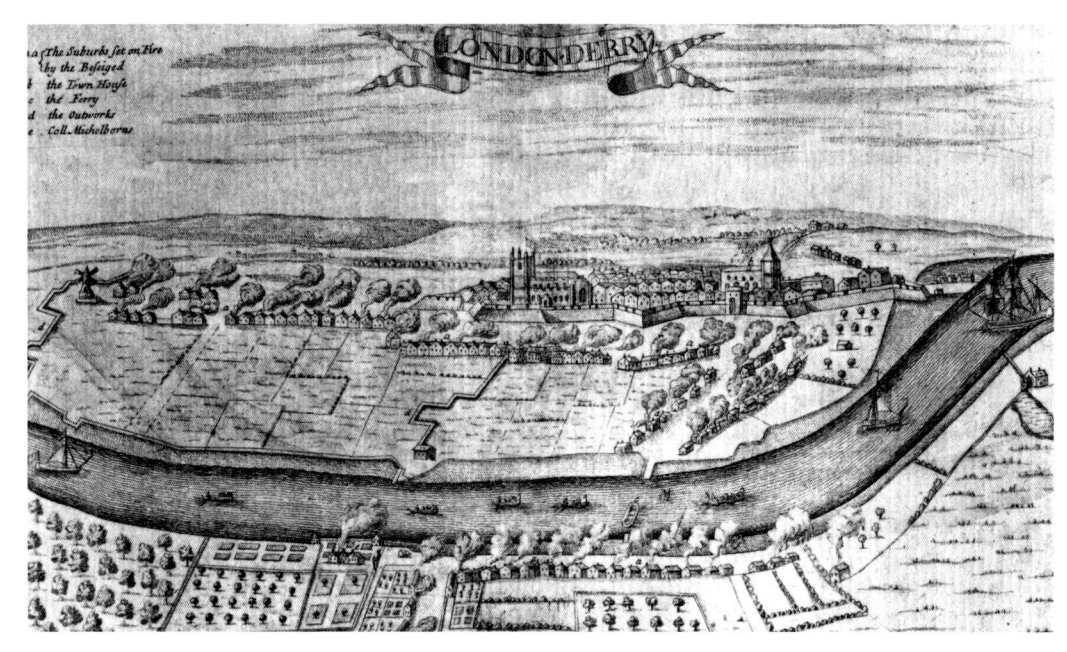

William Petty's census of 1659 records the population of the town as 586, of whom 369 were English or Scottish, the rest being Irish. In 1668, a serious fire in the city caused much damage, but we are unsure of the extent because the corporation records of the city only extend back to 1673. By the time of the 1689 siege it has been estimated that there were around 700 people, some of these probably Irish, living in and close to the City. By then there had been almost complete development within the walled area, with building having taken place along the subsidiary streets to the four main thoroughfares.

The 'Great Siege' of Londonderry

The second, and better-known siege of Derry~Londonderry lasted from April to July 1689. The events have been written about extensively elsewhere.[37] In the dispute over the English monarchy between King James II and Parliament, a group of the English nobility invited the Dutch Protestant William of Orange to be their king. James II fled to France in November 1688 when William landed in England. In Ireland, James' supporters, known as Jacobites, tried to make moves to secure the major ports and cities in advance of him coming to Ireland with an army.

When the Jacobite Earl of Antrim attempted to replace the Protestant garrison of Londonderry with a Catholic regiment on 7 December 1688, thirteen apprentice boys shut the gates of the city before his troops could gain entry. King James II started his attempted reclamation of his throne by landing at Kinsale in Co. Cork with a number of French officers on 12 March 1689. On hearing this news, the citizens of Londonderry declared for William on 24 March. The walled defences had been strengthened in advance of a possible siege and a substantial earthwork defence, or ravelin, had been created outside the walls at Bishop's Gate between Double Bastion and Church Bastion. James marched north from Cork, picking up supporters and troops on route, and arrived at the city on 18 April. It was his plan to deny ports such as Londonderry to any Williamite fleet.

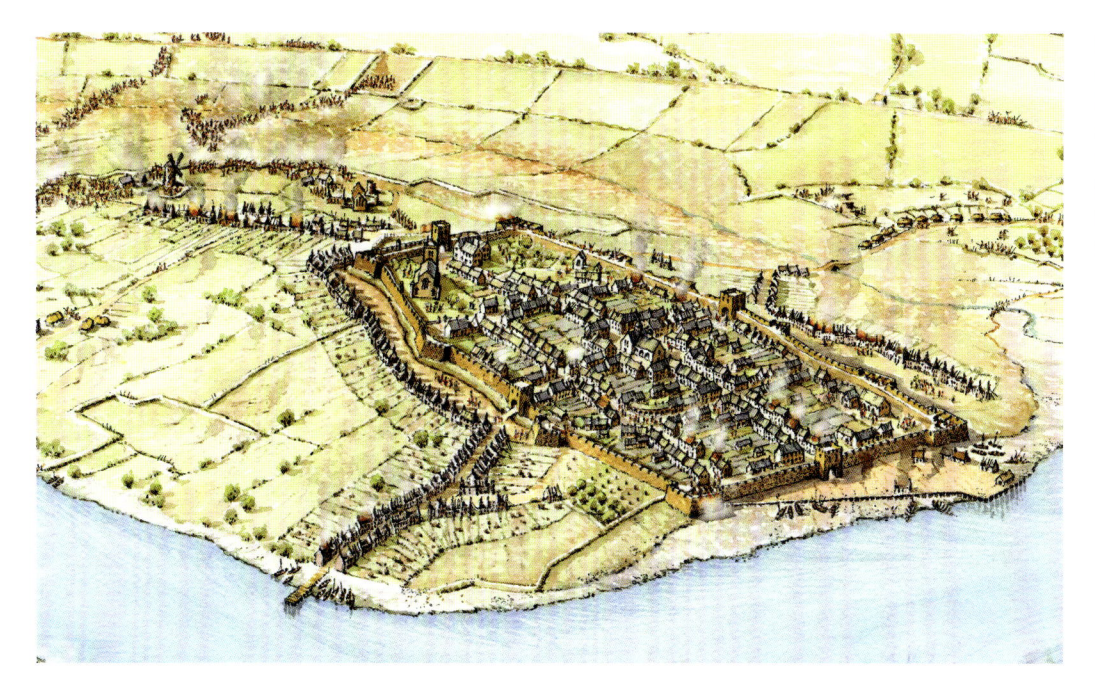

Detail of reconstruction drawing of the siege of Londonderry showing the area inside and immediately outside the city walls. For the disposition of troops further outside the city, see the fold out map in this book

As the Jacobites approached, many Protestant civilians from the surrounding areas fled to the city for safety. Given the limited space it is probable that many were forced to camp outside the walls, probably within the earthwork defences shown on maps of the siege. The extra civilians added severely to the problem of feeding the large garrison needed to defend the city, and the extra numbers meant that by the end of the siege conditions in the city were appalling. It has been estimated that fewer than the half of the people who were in the city when the siege started were alive by its end.

Like the Earl of Antrim's troops, King James was denied entry to the city. On 18 April, when he approached Bishop's Gate with a body of troops to ask for its surrender, he was fired upon from the walls. The governing council within the city later sent him a formal letter of apology but the actions of 18 April marked the start of the siege proper. James did not stay at Derry but retired south again on 20 April, leaving the conduct of the siege in the hands of his generals.

Jacobite gun emplacements were established on Creggan Hill above the Bogside, and on the east bank of the Foyle on the hills above Gobnascale, as well as at the site of what is now Ebrington Barracks. Conditions within the city grew daily worse but the defenders refused to surrender. Jacobite cannon fire inflicted comparatively little damage, but their use of mortars – the largest of which fired hollow shells of cast iron filled with up to 18lb (8kg) of gunpowder – caused great destruction and numerous casualties. A complete shell weighing some 270lb (122kg), which was fired into the city containing not powder but an offer of terms of surrender, survives in the porch of St Columb's Cathedral.[38] Fragments of shells have been found in the City, further attesting to the use of this deadly form of artillery.[39]

During April and June, there were a series of sallies from within the city on Jacobite positions and fierce fighting on two occasions at both Pennyburn Mill and around the windmill on Windmill Hill (now within Lumen Christi College grounds). Close to the modern Foyle Bridge,

Island City. The Archaeology of Derry~Londonderry

Swords of 16th and 17th date including siege swords on public display in the Chapter House of St. Columb's Cathedral. Colonel Adam Murray's sword is second from the bottom, while the sword belonging to the Rev. George Walker, Governor of Derry, is second from the top

Sword belonging to Colonel Adam Murray. He was of Scottish descent and during the 1689 siege he raised a troop of horsemen loyal to King William to help defend the city from the Jacobites. A brave soldier he was wounded during a skirmish at Windmill Hill outside the walls and did not recover until six months after the siege had been lifted. He died around 1700 and is buried in Old Glendermott Cemetery

Mortar shell weighing 270lbs, some 16-inches diameter. The shell, which is currently on a special stand in the Cathedral porch, was fired into the City during the siege and landed in the Churchyard on 10th July 1689. It contained the terms for surrender, but the reply to these terms was that the City would not surrender. The siege was to last 105 days.

the Jacobites built a boom across the river, with fortified emplacements on either bank, to stop Williamite ships from bringing supplies or military aid to the city by sea. Such a mission was attempted, but repulsed, on 11 June.

Some of the bloodiest fighting of the siege took place on 28 June when the Earl of Clancarty's troops attacked the Butcher Gate. This was repulsed after fierce fighting. By 17 July it is said that the garrison had been reduced to 5,111 men as a result of death in battle and by disease. However, only ten days later, on 28 July, a Williamite ship, the *Mountjoy*, broke through the Jacobite boom and relieved the city. Realising that they could not win, the Jacobite forces withdrew on 31 July 1689, ending the siege, which had lasted 105 days.

There was much re-building needed both in the city and repairs to the walled defences in the years after the siege ended. This redevelopment included the construction of a new market house in The Diamond and new gates along the town walls. Artefacts from the time of the siege are on display in the Chapter House of St Columb's Cathedral and the in the Museum of the Apprentice Boys Memorial Hall on Society Street. Amongst those on display in St Columb's are rare pamphlets on the 1641 and 1689 sieges, Colonel Murray and Governor Walker's swords and fragments of the Crimson Flag of Colonel John Mitchelburne.

Archaeological evidence of the 1689 siege has been uncovered at a variety of sites in and close to the city. Excavations at Bishop's Street Without in 1999 showed that the walled defences had been strengthened in advance of a possible siege and a substantial defensive earthwork and ditch known as a 'ravelin', shaped like an arrowhead, was created in front of Bishop's Gate to give extra protection to the walls between what are known now as Double Bastion and Church Bastion, as well as the Bishop's Gate and the main overland road leading up to the city. The ravelin took the

Island City. The Archaeology of Derry~Londonderry

Lead shell outer casing of a cannon ball from the siege. During the siege cannon were given stone centres and coated with lead on the outside in order to save on lead, which was in short supply during the siege. Diameter is about 15cm

Reconstruction of the constituent parts of mortar shell as used during the siege. Diameter is about 10cm

Lead shot from the city. Diameter of the largest is about 2cm

160   Island City. The Archaeology of Derry~Londonderry

Jacobite "gun money" from 1690 with the head of King James on the obverse face of the coin. "Gun money" was an issue of coinage created by the forces of James II between 1688-91, during the Williamite War, when ready finance to pay the Jacobite army was not available. The coins were minted from base metals (such as brass, copper or pewter) and the idea was that after the war the soldiers would be able to redeem the coins for silver ones. This was a Half-crown (denoted by the XXX above the crown), struck in May 1690. Although James lost the war, the coins stayed in circulation until the early 18th century before most were withdrawn from circulation. The name comes from the belief that they were made from melted down cannon but other brass objects were also used

form of a ditch oriented eastwards and fronting the destroyed earthwork before Bishop's Gate, with the remains of a sally port 2.6m wide interrupting the ditch.[40]

More evidence of the 1689 siege was also possibly uncovered during an excavation at 10–12 Artillery Street in 2006.[41] Three pits were found, one of which contained the partially articulated remains of a human skeleton possibly dating to the siege, when the dead were sometimes buried in whatever open space was available before mass reburial. It is possible that this body was overlooked at the time and, when discovered during the 18th-century re-development of the site, was hastily reburied in a small shallow pit. The burial and the other two pits were all sealed by 18th- and 19th-century garden soils.

The later of the two floors of House 1, excavated at Linenhall Street, may also be due to the effects of the siege. The floor is described as being 'made of cobbles laid on a rough platform'… 'composed of building rubble, broken bricks, broken pan tiles [roof tiles] and pieces of pottery dating roughly to the middle of the eighteenth-century set in a matrix of black soil'.[42] This 18th-century floor and the presence of building rubble on which it was set may be evidence of the re-building of houses within the city that had been damaged during the siege.

More evidence for the aftermath of the 1689 siege may have been found during an excavation inside First Derry Presbyterian Church, Magazine Street, in 2010.[43] In 1672, a Presbyterian Meeting House seems to have been constructed possibly on, or close to, the site of the later First Presbyterian Church. This church may have been suppressed, but in 1690 the First Derry Presbyterian Church was constructed on Magazine Street Upper, with the assistance of a grant from Queen Mary in recognition of the bravery displayed by the townsfolk during the siege. Several stone walls possibly related to the 1690 church were uncovered in the small trenches available for investigation. Below these were the remains of at least three individuals, whose burials must therefore predate them, in graves cut into 17th-century soils that were dated by artefacts found in them. Normal Christian burials are oriented east-west but the aberrant near south-north orientation of one of

Island City. The Archaeology of Derry~Londonderry

Above: Aerial view of Prehen House outside Derry-Londonderry. The main house was built in the 1740s, while one of the yard buildings to right of picture is late 17th century in date. The early 17th century bawn, built on lands granted to the Goldsmith's Company in 1612, lies just above the yard, hidden from view by trees. An excavation here in 2013 revealed the footprint of the flanker and a small fragment of wall with the remains of a doorway to the east

Brackfield Bawn from the air. The well preserved bawn, 18.6m square, with walls 0.8m thick and 3m high, was built by Sir Richard Doddington soon after 1611 on land granted to the Skinner's Company. It has 3.6m high bastions set diagonally at opposite corners. An excavation of the bawn carried out in 1983 uncovered the foundations of the house along the south wall and its fireplaces

Impressive earthworks consisting of a bank and ditch at Culmore, probably the work of the Jacobite garrison stationed there during the 1689 siege. An integral artillery platform would have been used by the Jacobite garrison if attacked from the landward side

the First Derry burials suggests that it may have been buried less formally than usual. This raises the possibility that it, and the others surrounding it, may not have been formal burials within a graveyard but hurried interments in a convenient location. Given the history of 17th-century city, and the associated artefacts that seem to indicate a date in the 1660s to 1680s, it seems reasonable to suggest that the individuals may have been victims of the 1689 siege.

Seventeenth-century sites in the vicinity of Londonderry

Among a number of 17th-century sites close to the city are the remains of house and bawn in the grounds of Prehen House, built in the 1740s overlooking thje River Foyle.[44] The townland was part of the plantation-period grant given to the Goldsmiths Company in 1612. Until recently all that could be seen here was a short length of curving masonry covered by a dense growth of vegetation. An archaeological evaluation and excavation carried out in March and June 2013 by Queen's University, Belfast on behalf of the Northern Ireland Environment Agency removed the vegetation and also uncovered below ground remains which joined to the upstanding walling to reveal a circular stone-built defensive flanker from the 17th-century house.[45] The remains are due to be conserved and will eventually be on show to those that stay at or visit Prehen House.

On the other side of the city at Ballynashallog, near the northwestern bank of the River Foyle, an archaeological assessment took place in March 2013 at the site of the Jacobite siege works close to the ruins of the late 18th-century house, Boom Hall.[46] The area where the evaluation took place is on land that formed part of the grant to *The Honourable The Irish Society* during the Ulster Plantation. The site takes its name from the close proximity of the house to the boom constructed across the Foyle by the Jacobite army during the siege of Derry in 1689.[47] The Jacobite siege works are shown on contemporary maps of the siege, but no definitive evidence was uncovered in the two trenches excavated. However the recovery of lead shot and a gunflint strongly suggests that they were located close to the area of 17th-century military activity. In addition, it is also possible that a rock-cut edge identified towards the south-eastern end of one of the trenches represents the back edge of one of the Jacobite entrenchments.

Further downriver lies Culmore, originally a late-medieval O'Doherty site that was captured by Sir Henry Docwra in 1600 and re-fortified by him before his occupation of the Island of Derry, was again re-fortified.[48] Between 1609 and 1629, the London Companies spent £1,100 in building and garrisoning a fort here because of its important location protecting access to and from Lough Foyle. In the 1689 siege the fort was occupied by a Jacobite garrison and hindered attempts to relieve the city by sea. The impressive earthworks that enclose Culmore Fort and cut off the peninsula may be Jacobite fortifications. The earthworks comprise a bank and ditch. The ditch has a sharp profile and is on average 7.4m wide but widens out at its northern end. The internal bank of the earthwork rises to 4m above the ditch. The angle of the ditch is contains a circular mound that is about 10m above the ditch and 4m above the interior of the earthwork. It is probably the site of an artillery platform used by the Jacobite garrison stationed here.

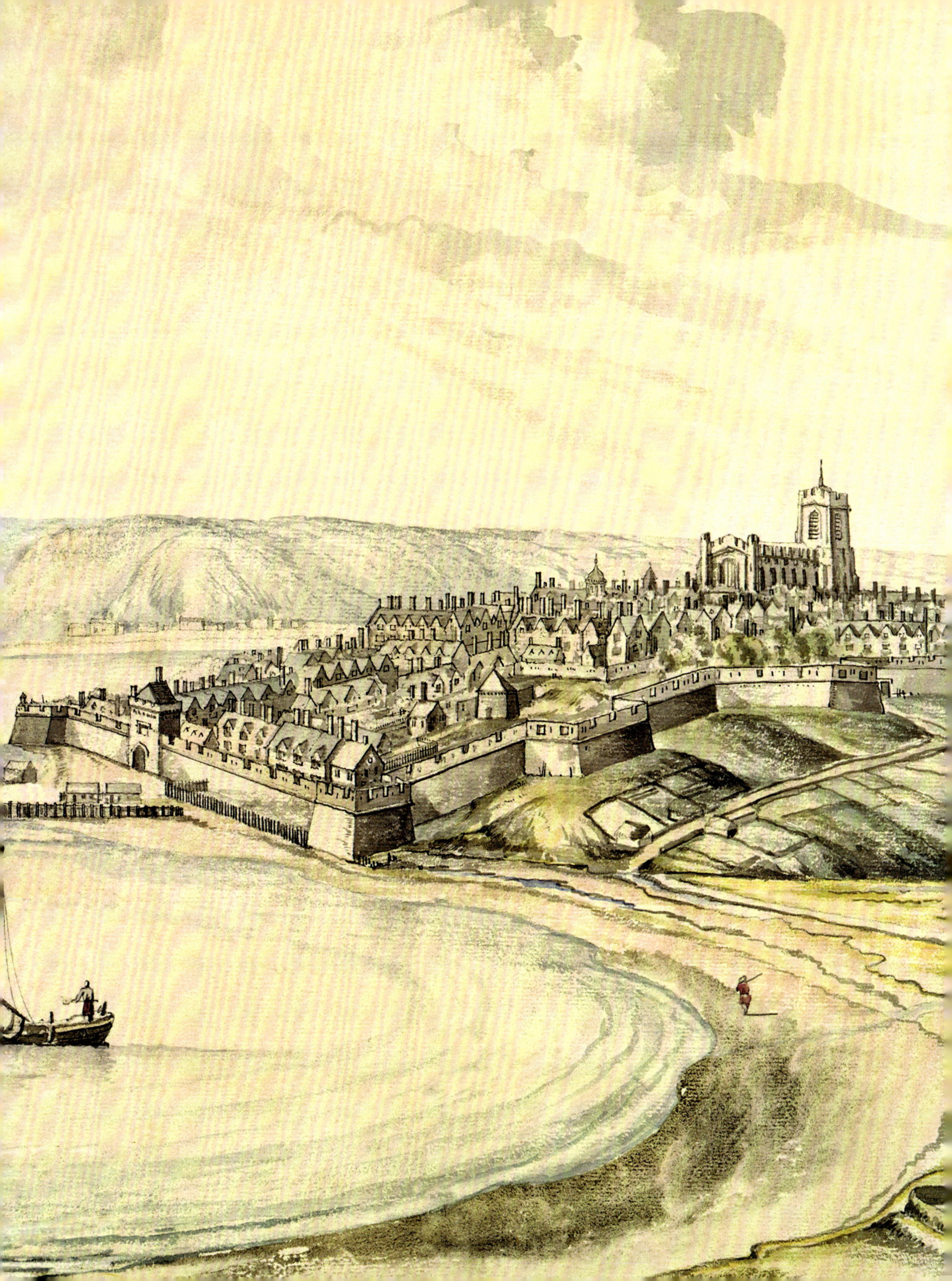

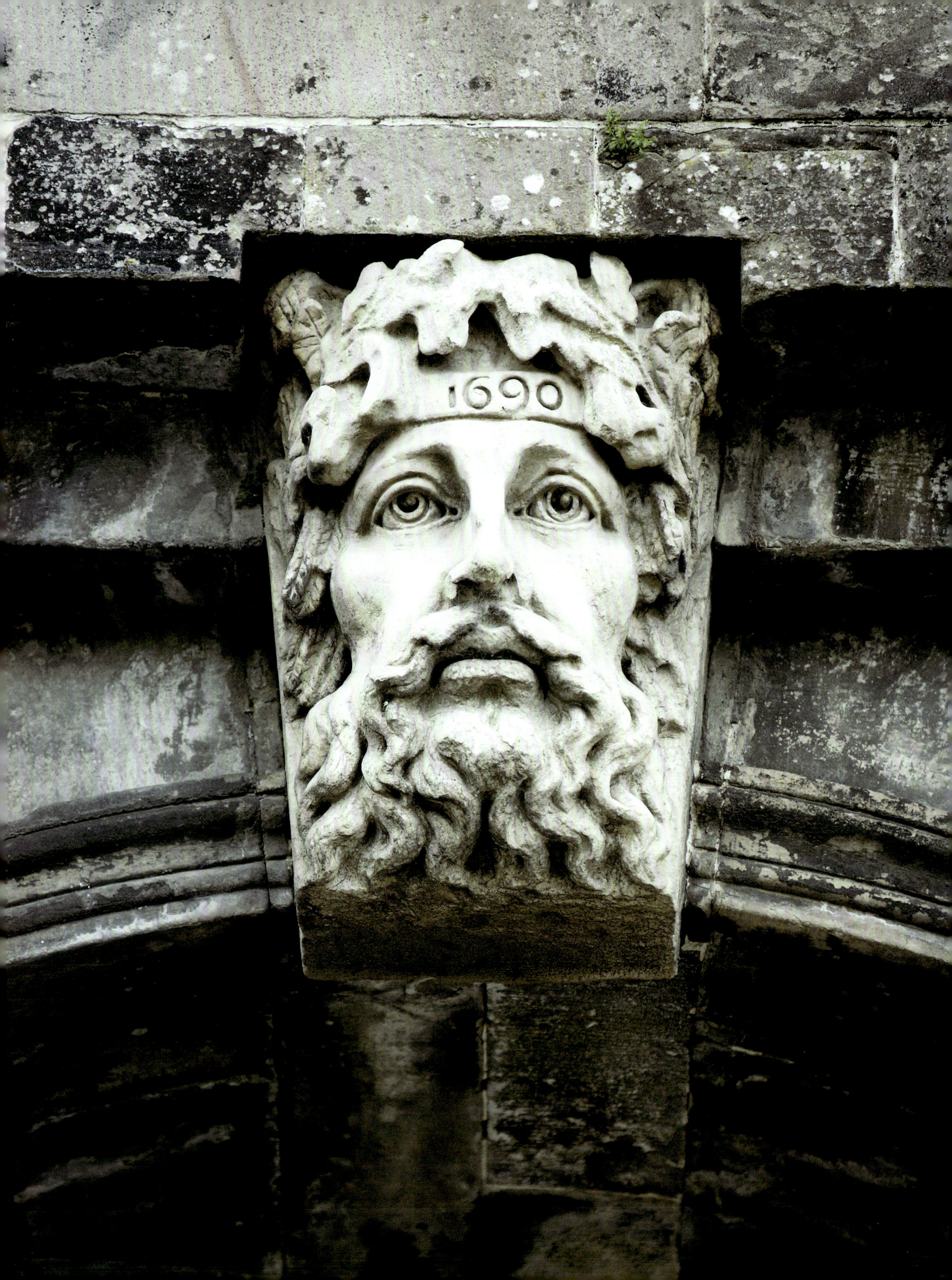
1690

Keystone on the Bishop's Gate, a neo-classical triumphant arch built in 1789 at the southern entrance into the city. The figure represents the River Boyne

Epilogue

The traumatic events of the 1689 siege were followed by a programme of rebuilding that extended well into the 18th-century. This was accompanied by a wave of emigration. Many Presbyterians, who had been loyal to King William became unhappy that the religious freedoms for which they fought for were not being granted and that they were still being discriminated against in favour of the Established Church (Church of Ireland). Many of these emigrants were to settle in North America.[1]

Robert Porter's 1799 map 'A Plan of the City and Suburbs of Londonderry with the Waterside' illustrates the city a century after the 'Great Siege'.[2] Settlement had expanded well beyond the city walls to the west on the Bogside-Creggan roads and to the south between the city walls and the riverside. The first bridge across the Foyle, which had opened less than a decade earlier, is depicted along with new housing in the waterside along the eastern bank of the River Foyle. Wharfs and quays are present along the eastern bank of the river between Ferry Quay Street and Ship Quay Place.

A variety of buildings are also shown both outside and inside the walls that give an idea of the sorts of activities taking place in the city more than 200 years ago. Buildings shown outside the walls include the old Windmill, the new Long Tower Church, 'the Casino', the Bishop's Gardens and Patterson's Orchard (by which means Colonel Robert Lundy is said to have escaped the city during the 1689 siege). Inside the walls are shown such buildings as St. Columb's Cathedral and graveyard, the Bishop's Palace, the Exchange, the Gaol, the Linen Hall, the King's Stores, the Magazine, the Custom House, various Meeting Houses and a theatre.

Above: Pearlware of late 18th century date found on excavations in Londonderry. Pearlware is often said to have been invented by Wedgwood ('pearl white') but it predates him ('China Glaze') and has mid-18th century origins. The blue painting is applied under the glaze on fired biscuit ware, and then glazed, thus sealing the design and protecting it. This was cheaper to make than pottery with on-glaze enamel decoration, which required three rather than two firings and ran the risk of the enamel chipping off during use

Creamware serving jug and teapot of later 18th century date. Creamware was first produced in England during the 1750s as a result of attempts by Staffordshire potters to imitate Chinese porcelain. Its characteristic rich yellow glaze was considered a fault at the time, but the pottery remained in popular domestic use well into the 19th century

Robert Porter's 1799 Map of Londonderry

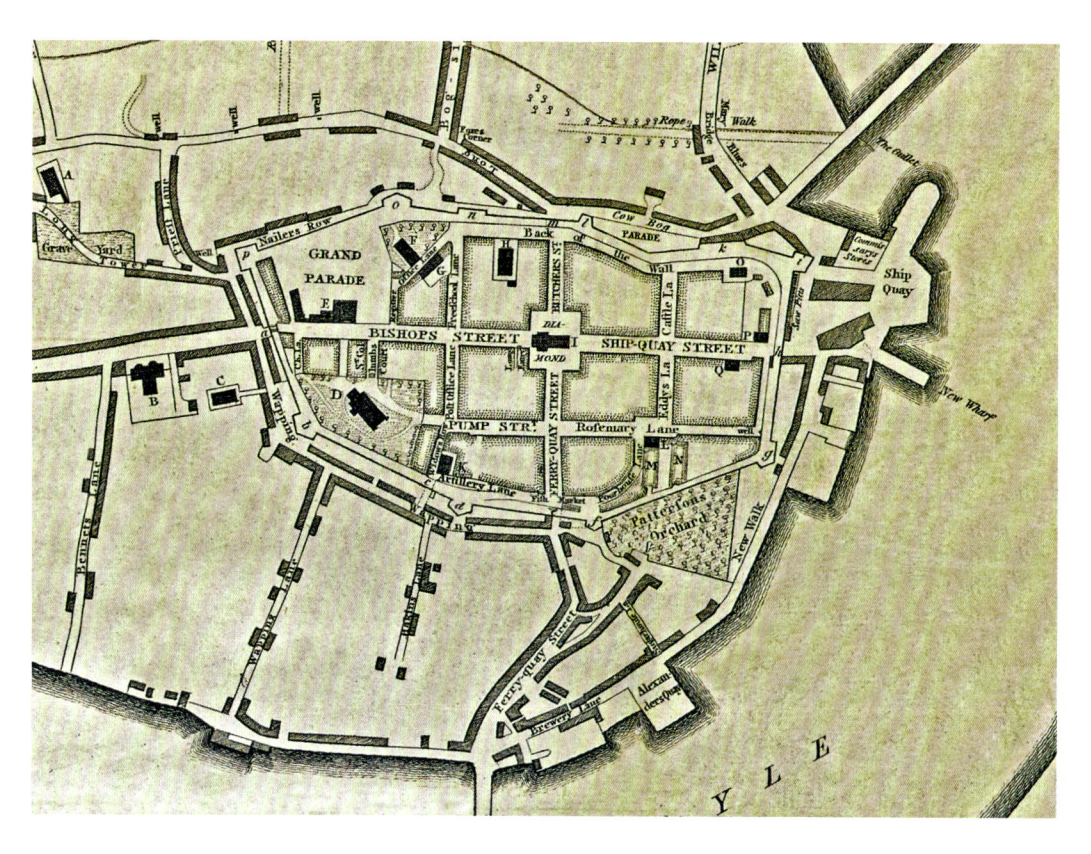

By 1800 the population was roughly 11,000. The emigration that began in the early 18th-century would have aided in the growth of Londonderry's port, though the principal contributing factor was undoubtably the rise of industry. This included shipbuilding, which was established between 1830 and 1850, and shirt manufacturing, pioneered by William Scott in 1831.[3] Shipyards included the Skipton and Henderson yard on Strand Road and the Foyle Shipyard at Pennyburn (later re-named the Londonderry Shipbuilding and Engineering Company). In the 1880s William Mc Corkell had a fleet of eight ships continuously employed in the lucrative Baltimore grain runs. Between the early 1860s and 1939, transatlantic passenger steamers that were taking emigrants to the New World lay at Moville, in the deep waters of Lough Foyle. As this was 18 miles downstream from the city, tenders took the passengers free of charge from Derry Quay (behind the Guildhall) to Moville.

The success of the shipyards and factories, along with the distilling and bacon-curing industries, confirmed the importance of the city as a centre of manufacture and a trading port worldwide. To facilitate these developments there were great improvements to the city's infrastructure.[4] In 1855 the Londonderry to Belfast railway opened, finally connecting the two biggest cities in Ulster, and in 1863 the Carlisle Bridge, a wrought-iron construction, was erected to replace the timber one that the Earl Bishop of Derry had promoted.[5] This bridge was later superseded by the Craigavon Bridge, which was opened in 1933. In 2009 and 2010, archaeological monitoring of works associated with the new Peace Bridge across the River Foyle identified episodes of 19th-century land reclamation probably associated with the construction of the new railway along

One of the most colourful figures in the history of the city and county is Frederick Augustus Hervey, 4th Earl of Bristol, who became bishop of Derry and Raphoe in February 1768. Born in 1730, he had entered the church in 1754, was appointed Chaplain to George III and in May 1767 was consecrated Bishop of Cloyne, in Co. Cork. Known popularly as the 'Earl Bishop', he was a champion of liberalism and reform, supporting Catholic emancipation and even becoming a Colonel of the Ulster Volunteers. In 1784, the Earl Bishop donated £200 to the construction of Long Tower Church, the first Catholic Church to be built on the Island since the Plantation, and he also provided the Neapolitan stone columns that still frame the altar of the church.

A lover of the arts and architecture, the Earl Bishop made several important contributions to enhancing the appearance of the City. He resided in the Bishop's Palace, built in 1761, on Bishop Street when staying in the city. There was a garden that stretched from the back of the palace to the city wall and there was also a garden beyond the wall, where St Columb's College (now Lumen Christi) is now located. Here he erected a summer palace, known as 'the Casino', which was decorated in Palladian stucco. In 1760 he heightened the tower of St Columb's Cathedral and commissioned a spire to adorn it and, in 1769, vigorously championed the first bridge, constructed of wood, across the Foyle. The bridge was not completed until 1790 but it revolutionised life in the City, as previously people had to cross the river in one of three small ferry boats that had a combined room for only 300 persons.

The Earl Bishop died in 1803 and was buried back his native Suffolk. He is perhaps better known today for his windswept demesne at Downhill, whose dramatic ruins are now in the care of the National Trust. Objects connected with Bishop Hervey, such as his desk, are on display in the Chapter House of St Columb's Cathedral.

the eastern bank of the River Foyle.[6] In 2009 as part of the intertidal and underwater assessment phase of the same project, two timber piles and two masonry blocks, of probable 19th-century date, were also recorded.[7]

By 1900 the population of Londonderry had risen to around 40,000, primarily due to the large numbers of people from Co. Donegal who settled outside the walls. But shipbuilding had gone into steep decline, and in 1922 the last ship ever to be built in the city was launched. The partition of Ireland in 1922 cut off the city from some of its natural hinterland in Co. Donegal, but the city retained much of its large textile industry. During the 1920s there were around 18,000 people employed in the industry, many thousands of whom worked in their own homes rather than the big shirt factories.

In the new century the population of Derry~Londonderry has now reached 237,000 within a 30km radius. The impressive Millennium Forum opened in 2001, the Playhouse restoration was completed in 2009, and in 2011 the latest bridge across the River Foyle, the Peace Bridge, opened. Derry~Londonderry was awarded UK City of Culture status for 2013, a fitting tribute to the 400 year history of Plantation Londonderry and the 1500 year history of Doire Colum Cille.

Stoneware beer bottles from Londonderry. Beer and ale, being carbonated, had to be kept in strong cylindrical bottles, which during the 18th and 19th century also needed to be capable of re-use. Stoneware, being sturdy and giving good protection from the detrimental effects of light, was very popular for beer, ale, cider and stout, as well as non-alcoholic beverages. Consequently, such bottles are often found in 18th and 19th century contexts on archaeological excavations. However, they had their drawbacks; in particular, they were heavy and had closure limitations. Consequently, by the end of the 19th century stoneware bottles had gone out of use

Creamware mug with fisherman and verse of late 18th century date

Island City. The Archaeology of Derry~Londonderry

Black and white creamware bowl

Plate (c1750) possibly made in Liverpool

Bibliography

Addyman, P.V. and Veron, P.O. (1966) 'A Beach Pebble industry from Dunaff Bay, Co. Donegal', *Ulster Journal of Archaeology* (3rd series) 29, pp6–15.

AFM = O' Donovan, J. ed. and trans. (1856) *The Annals of the Kingdom of Ireland from the earliest times to the year 1616*, 7 vols, Dublin (Hodges, Smith and Co., reprinted Blackrock, 1990 De Búrca Rare Books).

Allingham, H. (1894) 'The Spanish Armada: A Spanish captain's experiences in Ulster in 1588', *Ulster Journal of Archaeology* (2nd Series) Vol. 1, pp178-194.

Anderson, A.O. and Anderson, M.O. (1961) Adomnán's Life of Columba. Edinburgh. 2nd Edition, Oxford 1991.

Anon. (1833) 'The Walls of Derry', *Dublin Penny Journal* 2(58), pp41–42.

Anon. (1852) 'Visitation of the Diocese of Derry, A.D. 1397', *Ulster Journal of Archaeology* (1st series) 1, 184–197 and 232–241.

Anon. (1858) 'Saint Columba', *Ulster Journal of Archaeology* (1st series) 6, pp1–27.

Anon. (1857) 'Lough Foyle in 1601', *Ulster Journal of Archaeology* (1st series) 5, pp139–143.

Anon. (1902) 'Londonderry excursions' [in 'Proceedings'], *Journal of the Royal Society of Antiquaries of Ireland* 32, pp283–284.

Anon. (1833) 'The Walls of Derry', *Dublin Penny Journal* 2(58), pp41–42.

Anon. (1902) 'Proceedings', *Journal of the Royal Society of Antiquaries of Ireland* 32, pp279–320.

Anon. (1965) *St. Columb's Cathedral, Londonderry: Historical Guide*, Londonderry (David Irvine Ltd.).

Anon. (1992) 'Notes. Robert Lundy', *The Irish Sword* 18 (1991–1992), pp232–233.

Anon. (2001) *St. Columb's Cathedral Londonderry, Millennium Historical Guide*. A.S. Bell Publishing, Derry.

Apprentice Boys of Derry (?2009) *The Siege Heroes Trail* (Guide and Map), Derry~Londonderry (Apprentice Boys of Derry)

Archdall, M. (1876) *Monasterium Hibernicum*, 3 vols, Dublin (W.B. Kelly: originally published in 1786. new edition by P.F. Moran of the original 1786 publication, 1872–1876).

Armit, I., Murphy, E., Nelis, E. and Simpson, D. eds. (2000) Neolithic *Settlement in Ireland and Western Britain, Oxford* (Oxbow Books).

AU = Hennessy, W.M. and McCarthy, B. eds. (1901) *Annals of Ulster*, 4 vols (1887–1901), Dublin (HMSO).

Bardon, J. (2011) The Plantation of Ulster. Gill & Macmillan, Dublin.

Beckett, J.C. (1944) 'William King's Administration of the Diocese of Derry, 1691-1703', *Irish Historical Studies* 4 (14), ll164–180.

Bennett, I. (ed.) 2013 *Excavations 2010: Summary accounts of archaeological excavations in Ireland*. Wordwell, Bray.

— (2012) *Excavations 2009: Summary accounts of archaeological excavations in Ireland*. Wordwell, Bray.

— (2011) *Excavations 2008: Summary accounts of archaeological excavations in Ireland*. Wordwell, Bray.

— (2010) *Excavations 2007: Summary accounts of archaeological excavations in Ireland*. Wordwell, Bray.

— (2009) *Excavations 2006: Summary accounts of archaeological excavations in Ireland*. Wordwell, Bray.

— (2008) *Excavations 2005: Summary accounts of archaeological excavations in Ireland*. Wordwell, Bray.

— (2007) *Excavations 2004: Summary accounts of archaeological excavations in Ireland*. Wordwell, Bray.

— (2006) *Excavations 2003: Summary accounts of archaeological excavations in Ireland*. Wordwell, Bray.

— (2004) *Excavations 2002: Summary accounts of archaeological excavations in Ireland*. Wordwell, Bray.

— (2003) *Excavations 2001: Summary accounts of archaeological excavations in Ireland.* Wordwell, Bray.

— (2002) *Excavations 2000: Summary accounts of archaeological excavations in Ireland.* Wordwell, Bray.

— (2000b) *Excavations 1999: Summary accounts of archaeological excavations in Ireland.* Wordwell, Bray.

— (2000a) *Excavations 1998: Summary accounts of archaeological excavations in Ireland.* Wordwell, Bray.

— (1998) *Excavations 1997: Summary accounts of archaeological excavations in Ireland.* Wordwell, Bray.

— (1988) *Excavations 1987: Summary accounts of archaeological excavations in Ireland.* Wordwell, Bray.

— Berleth, R. (1978) *The Twilight Lords,* New York (Barnes and Noble).

Birch, S. and McElvogue, D.M. (1999) 'La Lavia, La Juliana and the Santa Maria de Vison: three Spanish Armada transports lost off Streedagh Strand, Co. Sligo: an interim report', *International Journal of Nautical Archaeology,* 28, pp265-276.

Blades, B.S. (1981) 'In the manner of England: tenant housing in the Londonderry Plantation', *Ulster Folklife* 27, pp39–56.

Bonner, B. (1982) *Derry: an outline history of the diocese*, Dublin (FNT).

— (1985) *That Audacious Traitor*, Pollaskenry, Co. Limerick. (Salesian Press Trust Ltd.).

Bourke, C. (1999) 'Northern Flames: Remembering Columba and Adomnán', *History Ireland* 7 (3), pp13–16.

— ed. (1997) *Studies in the Cult of Saint Columba*, Dublin (Four Courts Press).

Bradley, I. (2013) 'Scotland's First Minister', *History Today*, Vol. 63, Issue 7 (July 2013), pp11-15.

— (1996) *Columba, Pilgrim and Penitent,* Glasgow (Wild Goose Publications).

Bradley, J. (1995) *Walled Towns in Ireland*, Dublin (Country House).

Brannon, N.F. (1986) 'Five excavations in Ulster 1978-1984', *Ulster Journal of Archaeology* (3rd series), 49, pp89-98.

— Williams, B.B. and Williams, J.L. (1988) 'A Bronze Age Cist Burial in Shantallow Townland, County Londonderry', *Ulster Journal of Archaeology* (3rd series) 51,pp134–136.

Breathnach, E. and Cunningham, B. eds. (2007) *Writing Irish History: The Four Masters and their World*. Dublin (Wordwell).

Brindley, A.L. (2013) 'Review', *Ulster Journal of Archaeology* (3rd Series) 69, pp186–191.

Brown, D. and Clancy, T. (1999) *Spes Scotorum: Hope of the Scots. Saint Columba, Iona and Scotland.* Edinburgh (T & T Clark)

Burke, W.P. (1916) 'The Diocese of Derry in 1631', *Archivium Hibernicum*, Vol. 5 (1916), pp1-6.

Butlin, R.A. (1977) 'Irish Towns in the Sixteenth and Seventeenth Centuries', in ed. R.A. Butlin 1997, pp61-100.

Butlin, R.A. ed. (1977) *The Development of the Irish Town*, London (Croom Helm).

Bryson, J.G. (2001) *The Streets of Derry (1625-2001),* Derry~Londonderry (Guildhall Press).

Calley, D. (2013) City of Derry: An Historical Gazetteer to the Buildings of Derry. Ulster Architectural Historical Foundation, Belfast.

Camblin, G. (1951) *The Town In Ulster*, Belfast (Mullan).

Canavan, T. (2009) 'The Tower Museum Derry', *History Ireland* 17(6), pp70–71.

Canny, N. (2001) *Making Ireland British 1580–1650*, Oxford (Oxford University Press).

Carson, W.R.H. (1969) *A Bibliography of Printed Material relating to the County and County Borough of Londonderry.* High Wycombe

Centre for Archaeological Fieldwork (CAF) 2013 Data Structure Report No. 92. Five Investigations in Derry/ Londonderry. February- March 2013. Centre for Archaeological Fieldwork, School of Geography, Archaeology and Palaeoecology, Queen's University Belfast. Unpublished report submitted to the Northern Ireland Environment Agency.

Chapple, R. M. (2004) 'A cist is still a cist…the fundamental things apply: an enclosed late Bronze Age cist cemetery', *Archaeology Ireland* 18(3), pp32–35.

— (2008) 'The excavation of Early Neolithic and Early Bronze Age sites at Oakgrove, Gransha, County, Londonderry', *Ulster Journal of Archaeology,* (3rd series) 67, pp22-59.

— (2009) 'A Vase Food Vessel Burial at Shantallow, Londonderry', *Ulster Journal of Archaeology,* (3rd series) 68, pp40–46.

— (2010) *The excavation of an enclosed Middle Bronze Age cemetery at Gransha, Co. Londonderry, Northern Ireland, Oxford* (British Archaeological Reports, British Series 521).

Chart, D.A. ed. (1940) A Preliminary Survey of the Ancient Monuments of Northern Ireland. HMSO, Belfast.

Clancy, T.O. and Márkus, G. (1995) Iona: the earliest Poetry of a Celtic Monastery. (Edinburgh)

Clarke, H. B. ed. (1995) *Irish Cities. The Thomas Davis Lecture Series*, Cork (Mercier Press).

Clements, B. (2003) *Defending the North: The Fortifications of Ulster 1796–1956*, Belfast (The Universities Press).

Clinton, M. (2001) *The Souterrains of Ireland*. Dublin (Wordwell).

Coey, Alistair Architects (2006) *Derry City Walls Management Plan. Prepared for Derry City Council, Environment and Heritage Service and the Northern Ireland Board, October 2006*, Belfast (unpublished report in the archives of NIEA)..

Colby, T. (1837) *Ordnance Survey of the County of Londonderry, Memoir of the City and North-West Liberties of Londonderry, Parish of Templemore*, Dublin (HMSO, reprinted Limavady, 1990, North-West Books).

Collins, T. and Coyne, F. (2003) 'Fire and Water… Early Mesolithic cremations at Castleconnell, Co. Limerick', *Archaeology Ireland* 17 (2), pp24-27.

Cooke, S. The Maiden City and the Western Ocean. Morris and Company, Dublin.

Crooks, W.T. (2001) *Living stones: A Historical Survey of the Churches of the dioceses of Derry and Raphoe*, Belfast (Styletype Printing).

Cullen, L.M. (1981) *The emergence of modern Ireland 1600-1900*. New York (Holmes and Meier)

Cunningham, B. (2007) *O'Donnell Histories: Donegal and the Annals of the Four Masters*, (Rathmullan and District Historical Society).

Curl, J.S. (1986) *The Londonderry Plantation 1609–1914*, Chichester (Phillimore).

— (2000) *The Honourable The Irish Society and the Plantation of Ulster 1608-2000*, Chichester (Phillimore).

Daly, E. (1980) 'Bishops of Rathlury and Derry', *Derriana, The Journal of the Derry Diocesan Historical Society* 3, pp3–8.

Davies, O. (1941) 'Trial Excavation at Lough Enagh', *Ulster Journal of Archaeology,* (3rd series) 4(1), pp88–101.

— (1948) 'Stone Head at Ashbrook House, near Derry', *Journal of the Royal Society of Antiquaries of Ireland 78(2),* 177 and Plate XXXVI: pp1-2.

— and Swan, H.P. (1939) 'The Castles of Inishowen', *Ulster Journal of Archaeology* (3rd series) 2(2), pp178–208.

Dawson, Rev. A. (1854) 'Biographical Notice of George Walker, Governor of Derry during the Siege in 1688', *Ulster Journal of Archaeology* (1st series), 2, pp129–135 and pp261–277.

Day, A., McWilliams, P., English, E. and Dobson, N. (eds.) (1996) *Ordnance Survey Memoirs of Ireland. Vol. 34. Parishes of Londonderry XIII 1831-1838: Clondermot and the Waterside*, Belfast (Institute of Irish Studies, The Queen's University of Belfast).

Delaney, T.G. ed. (1977) Excavations 1975-76. Summary accounts of Archaeological work in Ireland.

Department of the Environment for Northern Ireland (DOENI) 1926. (Second impression with revisions) 1987. *Historic monuments of Northern Ireland: An Introduction and Guide.* HMSO, Belfast.

Derry City Council Heritage and Museum Service (ndg) *Derry and the Northwest 1846: The paintings of John Noah Gosset.*

Devlin, C. (2013) *The making of Medieval Derry.* Veritas Publications, Dublin.

— (1999) 'The Rise and Fall of a Dynasty [in] Medieval West Tyrone as Reported in the Annals', *Clogher Record* 16 (3), pp71–85.

— (2000a) 'The formation of the diocese' in eds. H.A. Jefferies and C. Devlin 2000, pp85–113.

— (2000b) 'Some episcopal lives' in eds. H.A. Jefferies and C. Devlin 2000, pp114–139.

(See also Ó Doibhlin, C.)

Dillon, C. and Jefferies, H.A. eds. (2000) *Tyrone History and Society*, Dublin (Geography Publications).

Doherty, R. (1990a) 'The Londonderry Regiment', *The Irish Sword* 17(69), pp288–289.

— (1990b) 'The Siege of Derry', *Templemore* 3, 42–57 (reprinted in *Ulster Local Studies: Journal of the Federation For Ulster Local Studies* 12(2), 1990).

— (1995) *Key to Victory: The Maiden City in the Second World War,* Antrim (Greystone).

— (1998) *The Williamite War in Ireland 1688-1691,* Dublin (Four Courts Press).

— (2008) *The Siege of Derry 1689: the Military History,* Stroud (The History Press).

— and Webster, T. (2012) *Derry-Londonderry. A Walk Around The Walls,* Derry (Yes Publications).

Doherty, Rev. W. (1902) 'Derry Columbkille', *Journal of the Royal Society of Antiquaries of Ireland* (5th series) 32 (3), pp257–260.

Donnelly, C. J. (1998) "Sectionally constructed tower houses: A review of the evidence from County Limerick", *Journal of the Royal Society of Antiquaries of Ireland* 128, pp26-34. (volume published in 2002).

— (1999) "A typological study of the tower houses of County Limerick", *Journal of the Royal Society of Antiquaries of Ireland* 129, 19-39. (volume published in 2003).

— (2001a) "Tower houses and Late Medieval secular settlement in County Limerick", in P. Duffy, D. Edwards and E. FitzPatrick (eds.), *Gaelic Ireland: Land, Lordship and Settlement c. 1250-1650.* Dublin (Four Courts Press), pp315-328.

— (2001b) "Decline and Adaptation: The Medieval Irish tower house in Early Modern   County Limerick", in G. Malm (ed.), *Archaeology and Architecture, BAR International Series* 930. Oxford (Archaeopres*).*

— (2004) "Passage or Barrier? Communication between bawn and tower house in Late   Medieval Ireland – the evidence from County Limerick", *Chateau Gaillard* 21, pp57-64

— (2007) "Thomas J. Westropp and his study of the Medieval tower houses of Counties Clare and Limerick", in C. Manning (ed.), *From Ringforts to Fortified Houses: Studies on castles and other monuments in honour of David Sweetman.* Bray *(*Wordwell Ltd) pp131-142.

— (2009) "Architecture and Conflict: Limerick's Tower Houses *c*1400 to *c*1650", in L. Irwin, G. Ó Tuathaigh, and M. Potter (eds.) *Limerick: History and Society.* Dublin (Geography Publications), pp71-89.

— (2011) "The Tower Houses of County Limerick", in R. Stalley (ed.) *Limerick and South-West Ireland: Medieval Art and Architecture,* The British Archaeological Association Conference Transactions 34, Maney Publishing, Wakefield, pp189-201.

C. Donnelly, P. Logue, J. O'Neill and J. O'Neill, (2007) "Timber castles and towers in Sixteenth-century Ireland: Some evidence from Ulster", *Archaeology Ireland* 21.2, pp22-25.

Downham, G. and Reynell, W.A. (1897) 'The Estate of the Diocese of Derry', *Ulster Journal of Archaeology,* (2nd series), Vol. 3 (April, 1897), pp187-192.

Duffy, P.J., Edwards, D. and Fitzpatrick, E. (2001) *Gaelic Ireland: Land, Lordship and Settlement c.1250-c.1650*, Dublin (Four Courts Press).

Duffy, T. (1984) 'Urban Living Conditions and Public Health in Derry 1815-1885', *Derriana: Journal of Derry Diocesan History Association.*

— (1983) 'Social and Economic Conditions in Derry 1820-1850', *Retrospect: Journal of the Irish History Students Association* 2 (1983).

Dumville, D.D. (1999) 'Derry, Iona, England and the Governance of the Columban Church', in ed. G. O'Brien 1999, pp91–114.

Durnin, P. (2001) *The Workhouse and the Famine in Derry*, Derry~Londonderry (Guildhall Press).

Dwyer, P. ed. (1893) T*he Siege of Londonderry in 1689 as set forth in the literary remains of Colonel the Rev. George Walker, D.D.*, London (Elliott Stock).

Edwards, D. ed. (2004) *Regions and Rulers in Ireland 1100-1650*, Dublin (Four Courts Press).

Edwards, N. (1990) *The Archaeology of Early Medieval Ireland*. London (Batsford).

Edwards, R.J. and Brooks, A.J. (2008) 'The Island of Ireland: Drowning the Myth of an Irish Land-Bridge?' in Davenport, J.J., Sleeman, D.P and Woodman, P.C. (eds.) *Mind the Gap: Postglacial Colonisation of Ireland. Special Supplement to The Irish Naturalists' Journal*, 2008, pp19 -34.

Eogan, G. (1984) *Excavations at Knowth (1)*. Royal Irish Academy, Dublin.

Fallon, N. (1978) *The Armada in Ireland*. London (Stanford Maritime).

Falls, C. (1950) *Elizabeth's Irish Wars*, London (Methuen and Co.).

Fanning, H. (1978) 'The Dominicans of Derry', *Derriana, The Journal of the Derry Diocesan Historical Society* 1, pp53–56.

Faulkner, A. (1988) 'Some Aspects of the Siege of Derry', *Donegal Annual* 40, pp78-83.

— (1982) 'Franciscans of Inishowen and Derry', *Donegal Annual* 34, pp3-17.

— (1980) 'Donegal writers and Derry of the Oaks', *Donegal Annual* Vol. XIII (4), pp502–507.

Ferguson, W.S. (2005) *Maps and views of Derry 1600-1914: a catalogue,* Dublin (Royal Irish Academy Irish Historic Towns Atlas).

— Rowan, A.J. and Tracey, J.J. (1970) *List of Historic Buildings, Groups of Buildings, Areas of Architectural Importance, In and Near The City of Derry*, Belfast (Ulster Architectural Heritage Society).

Finlay, I. (1979) *Columba*, London (Victor Gollancz).

FitzPatrick, E. (2004) *Royal Inauguration in Gaelic Ireland, c.1100-1600*, Dublin (Four Courts Press).

Flanagan, L. (1974-75) *Girona*. Belfast (Ulster Museum).

— (1988) *Ireland's Armada Legacy*. Dublin (Gill and MacMillan).

Frasier, T.G. (2001) 'The Siege: Myth and Reality' in ed. W.P Kelly 2001, pp11–17.

— (1999) 'The Siege: Its History and Legacy, 1688-89' in ed. G. O'Brien, G. 1999, pp378–403.

Fredengren, C. (2002) *Crannogs*. Bray (Wordwell).

Geoghegan, A. G. (1863) 'A Notice of the Early Settlement, in A.D. 1596, of the City of Derry by the English, to Its Burning by Sir Cahir O' Doherty in A.D. 1608', *Journal of the Kilkenny and South-East of Ireland Archaeological Society* 4 (2), pp386–404.

— (1864) 'A Notice of the Early Settlement, in A.D. 1596, of the City of Derry by the English, to Its Burning by Sir Cahir O' Doherty in A.D. 1608', *Journal of the Kilkenny and South-East of Ireland Archaeological Society* 5 (1), pp153–172.

Gibson, A. and Sheridan, A. eds. (2004) *From Sickles To Circles, Britain and Ireland at the Time of Stonehenge*, Stroud (Tempus Books).

Gillespie, F. (1995) 'Gaelic Families of County Donegal' in Nolan, W., Ronayne, L. and Dunlevy, M., eds. (1995): *Donegal History and Society. Interdisciplinary Essays on the History of an Irish County*, Dublin (Geography Publications), pp759-838.

Gillespie, R. (1984) 'The Origin and Development of an Ulster Urban Network, 1600-41', *Irish Historical Studies* 24.

— (1985) *Colonial Ulster. The Settlement of East Ulster 1600-1641*, Cork (Cork University Press).

— (1994) 'Historical revisits: T.W. Moody, *The Londonderry Plantation, 1609-41* (1939)', *Irish Historical Studies* XXIX (113), pp109–113.

Ginn, V. (2013) 'As Time Goes By': A Reappraisal of a Bronze Age site', *Archaeology Ireland* 27 (2), pp34-36

Gormley, E. (1978) 'Essex and the River Foyle, *Derriana, The Journal of the Derry Diocesan Historical Society* 1, pp76–80.

Gormley, K., Magee, T., Malley, A. and Webster, T. (1980) *"Blackened with Hunger". A Walking Tour of Derry Under Siege 1689*, Derry~Londonderry (Foyle Tourism Association in conjunction with the North West Archaeological and Historical Society).

Gowen, M. (1980) '17th-century artillery forts in Ulster', *Clogher Record* 10 (2), pp239–257.

Gray, T. (1975) *No Surrender! The Siege of Londonderry 1689*, London (Macdonald and Jane's).

Grindon, A.J. and Davison, A. (2013). 'Irish Cepaea nemoralis land snails have a cryptic Franco-Iberian origin that is most easily explained by the movements of Mesolithic humans', *PLOS ONE.* 8(6), e65792

Gwynn, A. and Hadcock, R.N. (1970) *Medieval religious houses: Ireland: with an appendix to early sites*, London (Longmans: reprinted 1988).

Hall, V. (2011) *The Making of Ireland's Landscape Since the Ice Age.* Cork (The Collins Press).

Hamlin, A.E. (1976) 'The Archaeology of Early Christianity in the North of Ireland'. PhD thesis.

Harbison, P. (1991) *Pilgrimage in Ireland: The Monuments and the People.* London (Barrie and Jenkins).

Harkness, D. and O'Dowd, M. eds. (1981) *The Town In Ireland*, Belfast (Historical Studies XIII, Appletree Press).

Hayes-McCoy, G.A. (1964) *Ulster and Other Irish Maps, c.1600.* Dublin (Stationery Office and Irish Manuscripts Commission).

Hennessy, W.M. and Mac Carthy, B. eds. (1887-1901*) Annala Uladh: Annals of Ulster, otherwise Annála Senait, annals of Senat: a chronicle of Irish affairs 431-1131, 1155-1541*. Dublin. Facsimile reprint with introduction by Nollaig O Muraíle (4 vols, Dublin, 1998)

Herbert, M. (1988) Iona, *Kells and Derry: the history and hagiography of the monastic familia of Columba*, Oxford (reprinted Dublin 1996).

Hill, G. (1877) *An Historical Account of the Plantation in Ulster at the Commencement of the Seventeenth-century,* Belfast (McCaw, Stevenson & Orr): reprinted 2002, Books Ulster, Bangor).

Hore, H.F. (1857) 'Lough Foyle in 1601', *Ulster Journal of Archaeology*, (1st series) 5, pp139–143.

Horning, A. (2007) 'Ireland and North America in the Seventeenth-century' in Horning, A., Ó Baoill, R., Donnelly, C. and Logue, P. (eds.) (2007) *The Post-Medieval Archaeology of Ireland 1550-1850*, Bray (Irish Post-Medieval Archaeology Group Proceedings 1, Wordwell Books), pp51-70.

Horning, A., Ó Baoill, R., Donnelly, C. and Logue, P. (eds.) (2007) *The Post-Medieval Archaeology of Ireland 1550-1850*, Bray (Irish Post-Medieval Archaeology Group Proceedings 1, Wordwell Books).

Hume, J. (2002) *Derry Beyond the Walls: Social and Economic Aspects of the Growth of Derry 1825-1850*, Belfast (Ulster Historical Foundation).

Hunt, J. (1974) *Irish Medieval Figure Sculpture 1200–1600*, 2 vols, Dublin and London (Irish University Press and Sotheby Parke Bernet Publications)

Hunter, R.J. (1981) 'Ulster Plantation Towns 1609-41', in eds. D. Harkness, D. and M. O'Dowd 1981, *The Town in Ireland*. Belfast: Appletree Press, 55-80.

— (1995) 'The End of O' Donnell Power', in eds. W. Nolan *et al.* 1995, pp229-266.

— (2012) *The Ulster Port books, 1612–15*. Belfast (Ulster Historical Foundation).

Jackson, K. (1964) *The Oldest Tradition: a Window on the Iron Age*. Cambridge (Cambridge University Press).

James, F.G. (1954) 'Derry in the Time of George 1: selections from Bishop Nicolson's Letters, 1718-1722', *Ulster Journal of Archaeology* (3rd series) 17, pp173–186.

Jeffries, H.A. (1999) 'Derry Diocese on the eve of the Plantation', in ed. G. O'Brien 1999, 175–204.

— (2000) 'George Montgomery, first Protestant bishop of Derry, Raphoe and Clogher (1605-1610)', in eds. H.A. Jefferies and C. Devlin 2000, pp140–166.

— and Devlin, C. eds. (2000) *History of the Diocese of Derry from Earliest Times*, Dublin (Four Courts Press).

Jope, E.M. and Jope, H.M. (1952) 'Four recently discovered Bronze Age burial groups', *Ulster Journal of Archaeology* (3rd series), Vol. 15 (1952), pp61–70.

Kelly, F. (1988) *Early Irish Law. Early Irish Law Series, Volume III.* Dublin (Dublin Institute for Advanced Studies).

— (1997) *Early Irish Farming. Early Irish Law Series, Volume IV.* Dublin (Dublin Institute for Advanced Studies).

Kelly, W.P. (2001) 'The Forgotten Siege of Derry, March-August, 1649' in ed. W.P. Kelly 2001, pp31–52.

— (2003) *Docwra's Derry: A Narration of Events in North-west Ulster 1600-1604*, Belfast (Ulster Historical Foundation).

— (2009) 'The Guildhall: Derry's Museum in Glass', *History Ireland* 17(6), pp66–69.

— (2011) *The Legacy of the Plantation in Derry and Donegal*, Letterkenny, (Donegal County Museum).

— ed. (2001) *The Sieges of Derry*. Dublin (Four Courts Press).

Kerr, T. (ed.), with contributions from Bell, J., Kyle, A., Meek, M., and Sloan, B. 2008: *The Archaeology of Early Christian Ireland* (Ann Elizabeth Hamlin) BAR British Series 460.

Kerrigan, P.M. (1980-82) 'Seventeenth-century fortifications, forts and garrisons in Ireland: a preliminary list', *Irish Sword* XIV (1980-82), pp3-24, pp135-156.

— (1995) *Castles and Fortifications in Ireland 1485-1945*. Cork (Collins Press).

Killanin, Ld. and Duignan, M.V. (1967), *Shell Guide to Ireland* London (Ebury Press)

Lac(e)y, B. (1979) 'The Archaeology of the British Colonisation in Ulster and America: A Comparative Approach', *The Irish-American Review* 1, pp1–5.

— (1980) *Implication Survey: Derry City*, Belfast (unpublished summary of archaeological excavations in Derry City, 1976-80 in the archives of NIEA).

— (1981) 'Two seventeenth-century houses in Linenhall St, Londonderry', *Ulster Folklife* 27, pp57–62.

— (1983) *Archaeological Survey of County Donegal*, Lifford (Donegal County Council).

— (1984) 'The Grianán of Aileach', *Donegal Annual* 36, pp5–24.

— (1988) 'The Development of Derry, 600-1600', in eds. G. Mac Niocaill and P.F. Wallace 1988, pp378-396.

— (1988) *Historic Derry*, Dublin (The Irish Heritage Series No.) 61, Eason and Sons, Ltd.).

— (1989) *The Siege of Derry*, Dublin (The Irish Heritage Series: No. 65, Eason & Sons, Ltd.)

— (1990a) *Siege City: The Story of Derry and Londonderry*, Belfast (Blackstaff Press).

— (1990b) ''Siege' Archaeology in Derry?', *Archaeology Ireland* 4(2), pp57–60.

— (1991) 'The archaeology of the Ulster plantation', in Ryan, M. ed. *The Illustrated Archaeology of Ireland*. Dublin: Country House, pp201-05.

— (1995) 'Prehistoric and Early Historic Settlement in Donegal', in eds. W. Nolan *et al.* 1995, pp1–24.

— (1997a) *Colum Cille and the Columban Tradition*, Dublin (Four Courts Press).

— (1997b) 'A lost Columban *turas* in Derry', *Donegal Annual* 49 (1), pp39–41.

— (1998) *The Life of Colum Cille by Manus O' Donnell*, Dublin (Four Courts Press).

— (1998) 'Columba, founder of the monastery of Derry?- 'Mihi manet Incertus', *Journal of the Royal Society of Antiquaries of Ireland,* Vol 128, pp35–47.

— (1999a) *Discover Derry*, Dublin (O'Brien Press).

— (1999b) 'County Derry in the Early Historic Period' in ed. G. O' Brien 1999, pp115–148.

— (2000) 'Colum Cille and the Diocese of Derry' in eds. H.A. Jefferies and C. Devlin 2000, pp17–29.

— (2001) 'The Grianán of Aileach: A Note on Its Identification', *Journal of the Royal Society of Antiquaries of Ireland* 131, pp145–149.

— (2004) 'Constructing Colum Cille', *Irish Arts Review* 21(3), pp120–123.

— (2006b) *Cenél Conaill and the Donegal Kingdoms AD 500-800*, Dublin (Four Courts Press).

— (2006a) 'Derry, the Cenél Conaill and Cenél nEógain', in ed. M. Meek 2006, pp65-69.

— (2009) 'Archaeology and War in an Irish Town', *History Ireland* 17 (6), pp60–61.

— (2010a) 'Colum Cille's first steps as a baby', in Davies, M., MacConville, U. and Cooney, G. (eds.), A Grand Gallimaufry: collected in honour of Nick Maxwell. Wordwell Books, Bray, pp67-68.

— (2010b) 'Mitchelburne's 'holy' well in Derry: its Catholic 'saint' a Protestant 'hero'', in Davies, M., MacConville, U. and Cooney, G. (eds.), A Grand Gallimaufry: collected in honour of Nick Maxwell. Wordwell Books, Bray, pp143-145.

— (2013a) *Saint Columba: His Life and Legacy*. Dublin (The Columba Press).

— (2013b) *Medieval and Monastic Derry, Sixth century to 1600*, Dublin (Four Courts Press).

Leask, H.G (1951) *Irish Castles*. Dundalk (Dundalgan Press).

Leslie, J.B. (1937) *Derry Clergy and Parishes*, Enniskillen (J.B. Leslie).

Lewis, S. (1837) *A Topographical Dictionary of Ireland,* 2 vols, London (Samuel Lewis and Co., reprinted Belfast 2004, Friar's Bush Press).

Loeber, R. (1991) *The Geography and Practice of English Colonisation in Ireland from 1534 to 1609*, Athlone (The Group for the Study of Irish Historic Settlement and Temple Printing).

Logan, F.W. (1938) 'Bellarmine jug from Derry', *Ulster Journal of Archaeology* (3rd series) 1 (1938), p216.

Logue, P. (2003) 'Excavations at Thornhill, Co. Londonderry', in eds. I. Armit *et al.* 2003, pp149–155.

— (2007) The Archaeology of Post-Medieval Derry and Londonderry, 1550-1800', in eds. A. Horning *et al.* 2007, pp131–150.

— and McHugh (2013) *The Lost Settlement of Dunnalong*. Derry (Derry City Council and Museum Service).

— and O' Neill, J. (2006) 'Excavations at Bishop's Street Without: 17th-century conflict archaeology in Derry City', *Journal of Conflict Archaeology* 2, pp49–75.

Londonderry Sentinel (1936) *A Particular of the Howses and Famylyes in London Derry May 15th, 1628*, Londonderry (reproduction of the earliest list of the householders in the newly walled town).

Lucas, A.T. (1967) 'The Plundering and Burning of Churches in Ireland, 7th to 16th-century', in ed. E. Rynne 1967, pp172–229.

— (1989) *Cattle in Ancient Ireland*. Kilkenny (Boethius Press)

Lynch, A. (1988) ' Poulnabrone: A Stone in Time...', *Archaeology Ireland* 2(3), pp105–107.

Lynn, C. (2003) *Navan Fort: Archaeology and Myth*, Bray (Wordwell).

— (2011) *Deer Park Farms: The Excavation of a Raised Rath in the Glenarm Valley, Co. Antrim. Northern Ireland Archaeological Monographs, No. 9*. Belfast (TSO for the Northern Ireland Environment Agency).

Macrory, P. (1980) *The Siege of Derry*, London (Hodder and Stoughton).

MacAirt, S. and Mac Niocaill, G. eds. (1983) *The Annals of Ulster (To A.D. 1131),* Dublin (Dublin Institute For Advanced Studies).

MacNiocaill, G. and Wallace, P.F. eds. (1988) Keimelia: Studies in Medieval Archaeology and History in Memory of Tom Delaney, Galway (University Press).

McCarthy, D.P. (1998) 'The Chronology of the Irish Annals', *Proceedings of the Royal Irish Academy*, Section C: volume 98C, Number 6, pp203-255.

McConway, C. and Donnelly, E. (2006). 'Daggers at dawn', Archaeology Ireland 20 (2), p5.

McCormick, F. (1995) 'Cows, ringforts and the origins of early Christian Ireland', *Emania* 13 (1995), pp 33-37.

— (2008) 'The Decline of the Cow: agricultural and Settlement Change in early Medieval Ireland', *Peritia* 20 (2008), pp210-225.

McCourt, D. and Evans, E.E. (1968) 'A Late Seventeenth-Century Farmhouse at Shantallow, near Londonderry', *Ulster Folklife* 14, pp14–23.

— (1971) 'A Late Seventeenth-Century Farmhouse at Shantallow, near Londonderry- Part II', *Ulster Folklife* 17, pp37–41.

MacDonald, A.D.S. (1984) 'Aspects of the Monastery and Monastic life in Adomnán's Life of Columba', *Peritia* 3, pp271–302.

— (1985) 'Iona's Style of Government Among the Picts and Scots: The Toponymic Evidence of Adonmnán's Life of Columba' *Peritia* 4, pp174–186.

McElvogue, D. M. (2002) 'A description and appraisal of ordnance from three Spanish Armada transports c 1588', *Journal of the Ordnance Society* 14. pp31-50

McGettigan, D. (2005) *Red Hugh O' Donnell and the Nine Years War*, Dublin (Four Courts Press).

McGonigle, M.(2012) Large Early Neolithic Houses Found on the A2, Co. Derry', *Archaeology Ireland* Vol. 26. No. 4, Issue 102, pp13-16.

McGovern, M. (1997) 'Myths and Marches: History, Class and the Siege of Derry 1689', *History Ireland* 5(4), 6–8.

McGrath, M. (1921) 'St. Columba of Iona', *The Irish Monthly* 49 (577), pp279–283.

McGurk, J. (1997) *The Elizabethan Conquest of Ireland*, Manchester (Manchester University Press).

— (2006) *Sir Henry Docwra 1564-1631: Derry's Second Founder*, Dublin (Four Courts Press).

McKeefry, Rev. J. (1902) 'Shane Crossagh, the County Derry "Rapparee", *Journal of the Royal Society of Antiquaries of Ireland*, (5th series) 32(3), pp232–238.

— and Milligan, S.F. (1902) 'Londonderry excursions: Enagh and Clooney', *Journal of the Royal Society of Antiquaries of Ireland* (5th series) 32(3), pp282–289.

McKenny, K. (2005) *The Laggan Army in Ireland 1640-1685: The Landed Interests, Political Ideologies and Military Campaigns of the North-West Ulster Settlers*, Dublin (Four Courts Press).

McLaren, D. (2011) *Plantation Architecture and Landscape in Derry and Donegal,* Letterkenny (Donegal County Museum).

McLoughlin, P. (1833) 'Burt Castle, County Donegal', *The Dublin Penny Journal* 2 (64), pp92–93.

McNaught, B. (1998) 'Early Mesolithic Site Discovered in Donegal', *Donegal Annual* 50, pp64-65.

McNeill, T.E. (1975) 'Ulster Mottes: A Checklist'. *Ulster Journal of Archaeology*, (3rd series) 38, pp49–56.

— (1997) *Castles in Ireland: Feudal Power in a Gaelic World*. Routledge, London.

— (1980) *Anglo-Norman Ulster. The History and Archaeology of an Irish Barony, 1177-1400*. Edinburgh (John Donald).

— (2001) 'The Archaeology of Gaelic Lordships East and West of the Foyle' in Duffy, P.J., Edwards, D. and Fitzpatrick, E., eds. *Gaelic Ireland: Land, Lordship and Settlement c.1250-c.1650*, Dublin (Four Courts Press), pp346-356.

Mac Niocaill, G. (1975) *The Medieval Irish Annals. Medieval Irish History Series, No. 3* Dublin (Dublin Historical Association).

Mac Niocaill, G. and Wallace, P.F. eds. (1988) *Keimelia: Studies in Medieval Archaeology and History in Memory of Tom Delaney*, Galway (Galway University Press).

McSparron, C. (2003a) 'The Excavation of a Neolithic House and Other Structures at Enagh, County Derry', *Ulster Journal of Archaeology* (3rd series), 62, pp1–15.

— (2003b) 'The excavation of a Neolithic house in Enagh Townland, Co. Derry' in eds. I. Armit *et al.* (2003), pp172–175.

— (2008) 'Have you no homes to go to: calling time on the early Irish Neolithic', *Archaeology Ireland*, Autumn 2008, Volume 22 No. 3, pp18-21.

— (2013) Excavations at St. Augustine's Church, Londonderry. CAF Data Structure Report No. 90. http://www.qub.ac.uk/schools/CentreforArchaeologicalFieldworkCAF/PDFFileStore/Filetoupload,370176,en.pdf

Maguire, W.A. ed. (1990c) *Kings In Conflict: The Revolutionary War in Ireland and its Aftermath 1689-1750*, Belfast (The Blackstaff Press).

Malley, A. (2006) *A History of Ebrington Barracks Londonderry*, Belfast (unpublished manuscript in the archives of NIEA).

Mallory, J.P. (1994) 'The Other Twin: Haughey's Fort' in Mallory, J.P. and Stockman, G. (eds.) *Ulidia: Proceedings of the First International Conference on the Ulster Cycle of Tales, Belfast* (December Publications), pp187-192.

Marks, P. (1999) *A Physical and literary assessment of the site of Elagh Castle, County Londonderry*. Unpublished undergraduate dissertation, Department of Archaeology, Queen's University Belfast.

Martin, F.X. (1968) 'Derry in 1590', *Clogher Record* 6 (3), pp597–605.

Marsdon, J. (1991) *The Illustrated Columcille*. London.

Meek, M. ed. (2006) *The Modern Traveller to Our Past: Festschrift in Honour of Ann Hamlin*, Downpatrick (DPK).

Miller, R. (1898) 'An Officer's Experience in '98. A Sketch of the Life of Rowley miller during the Twenty-five Years He Was Actively Employed in the Derry Militia', *Ulster Journal of Archaeology* (2nd series) 4(4), pp228-231.

Milligan, C.D. (1946) *The Relief of Derry: Browning and the Boom - Its Making and Its Breaking*. Londonderry (Londonderry Sentinel)

— (1948 and 1950) *The Walls of Derry: Their Building, Defending and Preserving*, 2 vols, 1948–1950, Derry~Londonderry (W & G Baird, reprinted in one volume by Ulster Society Publications, Lurgan, 1996).

Mitchell, B. (1989) *On the Banks of the Foyle: Historic photographs of Victorian and Edwardian Derry,* Belfast (Friar's Bush Press).

— (1990) *Derry: A City Invincible*, Eglinton (Grocer's Hall Press).

— (1992) *The Making of Derry. An Economic History*, Derry~Londonderry (Genealogy Centre).

Moody, T.W. (1939) *The Londonderry Plantation 1609-41*, Belfast (Mullan).

— and Simms, J.G. eds. (1983) *The Bishopric of Derry and the Irish Society of London, 1602–1705*, 2 vols, Dublin (Irish Manuscripts Commission).

Moore, D.G. (2004) 'Hostilities in Early Neolithic Ireland: Trouble with the New Neighbours - The Evidence from Ballyharry, County Antrim', in eds. A. Gibson and A. Sheridan, 2004, pp142-154.

Moore, F., McMahon, P. and Moore, D. (2010) *The Grianán of Aileach, Co, Donegal: Archaeology Ireland Heritage Guide No. 48*. Dublin (Wordwell).

Morgan, H. (1993) *Tyrone's Rebellion. The Outbreak of the Nine years War in Tudor Ireland*, Dublin (Gill and Macmillan).

Mullin, T.H. (1986) *Ulster's Historic City, Derry/Londonderry*, Coleraine (Coleraine Bookshop).

Munn, A.M. (1925) *Notes on the Place-Names of the Parishes and Townlands of the Co. of Londonderry*, Cookstown.

Nolan, W. and Simms, A. eds. (1998) *Irish Towns. A Guide to Sources*, Dublin (Geography Publications).

— Ronayne, L., and Dunlevy, M. eds. (1995) *Donegal History and Society: Interdisciplinary Essays on the History of an Irish County*, Dublin (Geography Publications).

Northern Ireland Environment Agency (NIEA) (1977) *LondonDerry. Guide to City Walls. Guide Card*, 2nd impression, Belfast (Northern Ireland Department of the Environment, Historic Monuments and Buildings Branch, first published 1970).

— (2007) *Derry City Walls Conservation Plan*, Belfast (NIEA).

— (2009) *A Guide to the Historic Monuments of Northern Ireland in State Care*. TSO, Belfast.

— (2011) *Derry City Walls Gazetteer*, Belfast (NIEA).

— (2013a) *Derry~Londonderry: A guide to the historic city walls*, Belfast (NIEA).

— (2013b) *Derry~Londonderry: A history and tour of the city walls*, Belfast (NIEA).

Ní Loingsigh, M. (1994) 'An Assessment of the Castles and landownership in Late Medieval North Donegal', *Ulster Journal of Archaeology*, (3rd series) 57, pp145–158.

Neill, K. (1999) 'Microliths, Megaliths, Beakers and Bronze – The Prehistoric Archaeology of County Londonderry 7000-400 BC', in ed. G. O'Brien 1999, pp29-68.

Nolan, W., Ronayne, L. and Dunlevy, M. (eds.) (1995): *Donegal History and Society. Interdisciplinary Essays on the History of an Irish County*, Dublin (Geography Publications).

Ó hAnnracháin, E. (2006) 'Derry Veterans in the Hôtel Royal des Invalides', *Seanchas Ard Mhacha: Journal of the Armagh Diocesan Historical Society* 21(1), pp55–74.

Ó Baoill, R. (2011) *Hidden History Below Our Feet: The Archaeological Story of Belfast*, Belfast (Tandem for the Northern Ireland Environment Agency and Belfast City Council).

— (2008) *Carrickfergus. The Story of the Castle and Walled Town*, Belfast (TSO Ireland for the Northern Ireland Environment Agency).

2006 Ó Baoill, R. and Logue, P. "Excavations at Gordon Street and Waring Street, Belfast", *Ulster Journal of Archaeology* 64, pp106-139.

O'Brien, G. ed. (1999) *Derry and Londonderry History and Society: Interdisciplinary Essays on the History of an Irish County*, Dublin (Geography Publications).

Ó Carragáin, T. (2010) *Churches in Early Medieval Ireland*, New Haven and London (Yale University Press).

Ó Catháin, S. trans. and annotated (1985) *Uair an Chloig Cois Teallaigh/ An Hour by the Hearth. Stories told by Pádraig Eoghain Phádraig Mac an Luain*, Dublin (Comhairle Bhéadloideas Éireann, University College).

Ó Ciardha, É. (ndg ?2010) *A Guide to the Plantation of Ulster In Derry and Donegal*, Letterkenny (Donegal County Museum).

Ó Doibhlin, C. (1978) 'The Clerics of Derry', *Derriana, The Journal of the Derry Diocesan Historical , Society* 1, pp18–52.

— (1980) 'Derry Clergy List of 1631', *Derriana, The Journal of the Derry Diocesan Historical Society* 3, pp8–13.

— (2004) 'Revisiting Reform: Armagh and Derry in the Twelfth-century', *Seanchas Ard Mhacha: Journal of the Armagh Diocesan Historical Society* 20(1), pp1–18.

(See also Devlin, C.)

Ó Doibhlin, D. (1979) 'Hearth Money Rolls (1663) : City and County of Derry', *Derriana, The Journal of the Derry Diocesan Historical Society* 2, pp41–91.

— (2000) 'Penal days' in eds. H.A. Jefferies & C. Devlin 2000, pp167–186.

Ó Domhnaill, S. (1943) 'Sir Niall Garbh O'Donnell and the rebellion of Sir Cahir O' Doherty', *Irish Historical Studies* 3 (1942–1943), pp34–38.

O' Kelleher, A. and Schoepperle, G. (1918) *Betha Colaim Chille: Life of Columcille*. Reprinted Dublin 1994.

Ó Muraíle, N. (1997) 'The Columban Onomastic Legacy' in C. Bourke (ed.) Studies in the Cult of Saint Columba'. Four Courts Press, Dublin, pp193-246.

Ó Néill, J. (2004) CAF Data Structure Report 038: *Excavations at Ballyarnet, County Londonderry.* (Licence No. AE/04/64; SMR No. LDY 14A:026). Unpublished but available on the CAF website: http://www.qub.ac.uk/schools/CentreforArchaeologicalFieldworkCAF/Reports/DataStructureReport

Ó Néill, J., Plunkett, G. and Whitehouse, N. (2009) 'The archaeological and palaeoecological investigation of a Middle Bronze Age settlement at Ballyarnet Lake, County Derry'. *Ulster J. Archaeol.* 66 (2007), 39-49. Published in 2009.

Ó Néill, J., Schulting, R., Whitehouse, N., Adams, K. and Kerr, T. (2002) CAF Data Structure Report 005: *Ballyarnet, County Londonderry.* (Licence No. AE/02/71: SMR No. LDY 14A:026). Unpublished but available on the CAF website: http://www.qub.ac.uk/schools/CentreforArchaeologicalFieldworkCAF/Reports/DataStructureReport

Ó Néill, J., Logue, R. and Schulting, R. (2002) CAF Data Structure Report 010: *Ballynashallog, County Londonderry.* (Licence No. AE/02/54; SMR No. LDY 14A:010 and LDY14A:011). Unpublished but available on the CAF website: http://www.qub.ac.uk/schools/CentreforArchaeologicalFieldworkCAF/Reports/DataStructureReport

Ó Nuallain, S. (1983) 'Irish portal tombs: topography, siting and distribution', *Journal of the Royal Society of Antiquaries of Ireland* 113, pp75–105.

O' Sullivan, A. (1998) *The Archaeology of Lake Settlement in Ireland. Discovery Programme Monographs 4.* Dublin (Discovery Programme/ Royal Irish Academy)

Parlin, H. (1925) 'Dates of Columba's Birth, Exile and Death', *Journal of the County Louth Archaeological Society* 6(1), 3.

Patterson, N. (1994) *Cattle-Lords and Clansmen: The Social Structure of Early Ireland.* Indiana (University of Notre Dame Press).

Perceval-Maxwell, M. (1973) *The Scottish migration to Ulster in the reign of James 1 London* (Routledge and Kegan Paul).

Phillips MSS = Chart, D.A. ed. (1928) *Londonderry and the London companies, 1609-1629: being a survey and other documents submitted to King Charles I by Sir Thomas Phillips*, Belfast (HMSO).

Price, S. (2011) *The Earl Bishop*, Portstewart (Great Sea Publications).

PSAMNI = Chart, D.A. ed. (1940) *A Preliminary Survey of the Ancient Monuments of Northern Ireland*, HMSO (HMSO).

Raftery, B. (1994) *Pagan Celtic Ireland: The Enigma of the Irish Iron Age*, London (Thames and Hudson).

Rankin, P. (1972) *Irish Building Ventures of the Earl Bishop of Derry, 1730-1803*, Belfast (Ulster Architectural Heritage Society).

Reeves, W. (1850) *Acts of Archbishop Colton in his Metropolitan Visitation of the Diocese of Derry A.D. 1397*, Dublin (Irish Archaeological Society).

— (1857) *The Life of St Columba, Founder of Hy, written by Adamnan*, Dublin (University Press for the Irish Archaeological and Celtic Society).

Ritchie, A. (1997) *Iona*. B.T. Batsford Ltd/ Historic Scotland, London.

Ridella, R.G. (2004) 'Dorino II Gioardi: A 16th-century Genoese gunfounder', *Journal of the Ordnance Society* Vol. 16, pp27-41.

Robinson, P.S. (1984) *The Plantation of Ulster: British Settlement in an Irish Landscape 1600–1670*, Dublin (Gill and Macmillan).

Roulston, W. (2000) 'The Ulster Plantation in the manor of Dunnalong. 1610-70', in eds. C. Dillon and H.A. Jefferies 2000, pp267-289.

Rowan, A. (1979) *The Buildings of Ireland. North-West Ulster. The Counties of Londonderry, Donegal, Fermanagh and Tyrone*, London (Penguin Books).

Ryan, J. (1963) 'St Columba of Derry and Iona', *Studies: An Irish Quarterly Review* 52 (205), pp37–51.

Ryan, M.F. ed. (1991) *The Illustrated Archaeology of Ireland*, Dublin (Country House).

Rynne, E. ed. (1967) *North Munster Studies: Essays in Commemoration of Monsignor Michael Moloney*, Limerick (Thomond Archaeological Society).

Sampson, G.V. (1802) *Statistical Survey of the County of Londonderry*, Dublin.

Scott, B.G., Brown, R.R., Leacock, A.G. and Salter, C.J. (2008) *The Great Guns Like Thunder: The Cannon From The City of Derry*, Derry~Londonderry (Guildhall Press).

— (2009) 'Cannon in the Maiden City: symbol and document', *History Ireland* 17(6), pp57–59.

— (2011) 'Plans and economies: defending the Plantation city of Londonderry', *Journal of Irish Archaeology* 20, 141–154.

— (forthcoming) 'Some relics from the Londonderry magazine and from the 1689 siege', in T. Reeves-Smyth and P. Logue (eds) *Beyond the Horizon of Memory. Essays in Honour of Chris Lynn*

Sharpe, R. trans. (1995) *Adomnán of Iona: life St Columba*, London (Penguin Books). Reprinted 2005.

Sigerson, G. (1874) 'Discovery of Fish-Remains in the Alluvial Clay of the River Foyle, with Observations on the Existence and Disappearance of an Upper Lough Foyle, and on the Former Insulation of Derry and of Inishowen', *Proceedings of the Royal Irish Academy* 1A (1870–1874), pp212–224.

Simington, R.C. (1937) *The Civil Survey, AD 1654-1656. Volume 3: Counties of Donegal, Londonderry and Tyrone*. Dublin (Irish Manuscripts Commission, The Stationery Office).

Simms, J.G. (1964) 'The Siege of Derry', *The Irish Sword* 6 (1963–1964), pp221–233.

Simms, K. (1987) *From Kings to Warlords: The Changing Political Structure of Gaelic Ireland in the Later Middle Ages*, Woodbridge (The Boydell Press).

— (1999) 'Tír Eoghain 'North of the Mountain', in ed. G. O'Brien 1999, pp149–174.

— (2009) *Medieval Gaelic Sources*. Maynooth Research Guides for Local Irish History: Number 14. Dublin (Four Courts Press).

Smyth, Jessica (2006) 'The Role of the House in Early Neolithic Ireland', *European Journal of Archaeology* Vol. 9 (2-3), pp229-257.

— (2011) 'The house and group identity in the Irish Neolithic', *Proceedings of the Royal Irish Academy*, Vol.111C (2010), pp1-31.

Smyth, Jim (2001) 'Siege, Myth and History: Derry 1688-1988' in ed. W. Kelly 2001, 18-30.

Stout, M. (1997) *The Irish Ringfort. Irish Settlement Studies, No. 5*. Dublin (Four Courts Press)

Sweetman, D. (1999) *The Medieval Castles of Ireland*. Cork (The Collins Press).

Thomas, A. (1992) *The Walled Towns of Ireland*, 2 vols, Dublin (Irish Academic Press).

— (1995) 'Derry – a spectacular maiden', in ed. H.B. Clarke, H. B. (ed.), Irish Cities. The Thomas Davis Lecture Series. Mercier Press, Cork, pp69-81.

— (1999) 'Londonderry and Coleraine: Walled Towns or Epitome' in ed. G. O'Brien 1999, pp259-278.

— (2005) *Derry/Londonderry. Irish Historic Towns Atlas, No. 15*, Dublin (Royal Irish Academy).

Thomas, C. (2000) 'Family Formation in a Colonial City: Londonderry, 1650-1750', *Proceedings of the Royal Irish Academy* 100C, pp87–111.

Tierney, A. (2003) 'A note on the identification of Aileach', *Journal of the Royal Society of Antiquaries of Ireland*, Vol. 133 (2003), pp182-186.

Walker, B. (2001) 'Remembering the Siege of Derry; the Rise of popular religious and Political tradition 1689-1989', in ed. W.P. Kelly 2001, pp123–144.

Walsh, J.R. (2000) 'The early Church' in eds. H.A. Jefferies and C. Devlin 2000, pp30–48.

— (2001) *Noble Story. A Short History of the Diocese of Derry*, Strasbourg (Editions du Signe).

Walsh, P. ed. and trans. (1957) *Beatha Aodha Ruaidh Uí Dhomhnaill (The Life of Aodh Ruadh O Domhnaill), Transcribed from the Book of Lughaidh Ó Clérigh*, 2 vols, 1948 and 1957, Dublin (Irish Tests Society 42 and 45).

Warner, R.B. and Cahill, M. (2011) 'Analysing ancient Irish gold: an assessment of the Hartmann database', *The Journal of Irish Archaeology* XX, pp45–52.

Went, A.E.J. (1968) 'Spears and Gaffs for Salmon used in the Foyle System', *Ulster Folklife* 14, pp34–38.

Wills, E. (?2001) *The Walled City: The Story on the Streets*, Derry~Londonderry (Derry City Council).

Woodman, P. (1985) *Excavations at Mount Sandel, 1973–1977*, Belfast (Northern Ireland Archaeological Monographs 2, Northern Ireland Environment Agency).

Young, J.R. (2001) 'The Scottish Response to the Siege of Londonderry, 1689-90' in ed. W. Kelly 2001, pp53–74.

Notes

Introduction

1 (Lacy 1990a, 1–5; Thomas 2005, 1)

The Prehistoric Period

1 (Hall 2011; Edwards and Brooks 2008)
2 (Woodman 1985)
3 (Collins & Coyne 2003)
4 (Grindon, A.J. and Davison, A. 2013)
5 (McSparron 2003a, 7)
6 (Davies 1941, 100)
7 (McNaught 1998)
8 (Addyman and Veron 1966)
9 (McNaught 1998, 65)
10 (SMR 14A:022)
11 (SMR 022:037)
12 (Schulting and Ó Néill in Bennett 2004, Entry No. 377, 99)
13 (SMR 14A:010 and 14A:011)
14 (SMR 14A:030)
15 (SMR 15A:005; Gahan in Bennett 2004, Entry No. 378, 99)
16 (SMR 14A:033; Halpin in Bennett 2004, Entry No. 385, 100)
17 (SMR 14A:029)
18 (Hurl in Bennett 1997. Entry No. 58, 14)
19 (SMR 14A:020; McSparron in Bennett 2000. Entry No. 97, 25-26)
20 (Davies 1941a; O.S. Field Report No. 96)
21 (Smyth 2010, 4–5; 2006)
22 (McSparron 2008; Smyth 2010)
23 (McSparron 2008, 19)
24 (SMR 14A:023; Logue 2003)
25 (SMR 014:009-014:011)
26 (McSparron 2003a and b)
27 (*ibid*, 2003a, 2)
28 (*ibid*. 4)
29 (SMR 014:066; Bowen in Bennett 2006. Entry No. 362, 80–81)
30 (*ibid*. 80)
31 (McGonigle in Bennett 2012. Entry No. 197, 50-52; McGonigle 2012)
32 (SMR 022:036)
33 (SMR 022: 005; O.S. Field Notes No.156; Day *et al*. 1996, 44)
34 (SMR 015:028)
35 (SMR 14A:019; O.S. Field Report No.112; Ó Nuallain 1983, 80 and 93)
36 (SMR 014:007)
37 (SMR 022:006; O.S. Field Report No.157)
38 (SMR 14A:023; Logue 2003)
39 (Eogan 1984, 211–244)
40 (Warner and Cahill 2011)
41 (Pers. Comm. Philip Macdonald)
42 (Mallory 1994; Lynn 2003, 65-79)
43 (SMR 14A: 026; Ó Néill *et al* 2009; Ó Néill in Bennett 2007. Entry No. 346, 71–72; Ó Néill and Schulting in Bennett 2004. Entry No. 376, 98–99 ; Ó Néill 2004; Ó Néill *et al* 2002).
44 (Chapple 2004, 2008 and 2010)
45 (SMR 014:013)
46 (Brindley 2013; Ginn 2013)
47 (Davies 1941a, 91; O.S. Field Report No. 96)
48 (SMR 022:037)
49 (Farrimond in Bennett 2009. Entry No. 402, 87-88)
50 (SMR 14:012, SMR 14:065; McSparron 2003a and b)
51 (SMR 14A:029)
52 (SMR 014:078; Gahan in Bennett 2004. Entry No. 392, 106)
53 (McGonigle in Bennett 2012. Entry No. 197, 50–52; McGonigle 2012)
54 (SMR 14A: 033; Halpin in Bennett 2004, Entry No. 385, 100)
55 (McClorey in Bennett 2012. Entry No. 183, 47)
56 (SMR 14A:028)
57 (McConway in Bennett 2006. Entry No. 374, 83)
58 (SMR 014A:025, SMR 014A:031 and SMR 014A:032)
59 (Donnelly in Bennett 2009. Entry No. 403, 88; McConway and Donnelly 2006)
60 (Brannon *et al*. 1988; Brannon in Bennett 1989. Entry No. 43, 26–27)
61 (SMR 014:019; Jope and Jope 1952, 70)
62 (SMR 014:079; McCooey in Bennett 2007. Entry No. 349, 72)
63 (Lacy 1983, 64–65)
64 (SMR 022:035)
65 (SMR 013:002; O.S. Field Report No.62; *PSAMNI* 193)
66 (SMR 014:024; *Derry Journal* 24 April 1956)
67 (Donnelly in Bennett 2009. Entry No. 403, 88; McConway and Donnelly 2006)
68 (Chapple 2009)
69 (McGonigle in Bennett 2012. Entry No. 197, 50–52; McGonigle 2012)
70 (SMR 015:016; O.S. Field Report No.111)
71 (SMR 014:006; O.S. Field Report No.100; Scheduled Monument)
72 (SMR 014:036)
73 (SMR 014:060)
74 (SMR 022:014; *PSAMNI* 198)
75 (SMR 022:007)
76 (Jackson 1964; Raftery 1994, 13*ff*)
77 (Bowen in Bennett 2006. Entry No. 362, 80-81)

The Early Christian Period

1 (Lucas 1989; Patterson 1994; Kelly 1988, 1997)
2 (McCormick 2008)
3 (Lacy 1995, 1996, 2006a and b)
4 (Lacey 1990a, 18–19)
5 (Edwards 1990)
6 (Colby 1837, Vol. 1, 217–232; Lacey 1984 and 2001; Lacey *et al*. 1983, 111–112, and Plate 3 and Fig 54; Tierney 2003, Moore *et al*, 2010)
7 (Lacey 2001, 148; 2006, 109-11)
8 (Stout 1997)
9 (McCormick 1995)
10 (Lynn 2011)
11 (McCormick 2008, 220-222)
12 (SMR 022:008)
13 (SMR 14A:024)
14 (SMR 022:012; O.S. Field Report No. 151; Devlin in Bennett 2012. Entry No. 191, 49)
15 (SMR 022: 27)
16 (SMR 14A: 027)
17 (SMR 014: 001)
18 (SMR 014:005- though this also may be a Medieval motte – see McNeill 1975, 54, no.118)
19 (SMR 014: 052)
20 (Clinton 2001)
21 (McCormick 28, 221-222)
22 (SMR 014:012)
23 (SMR 14A:038)
24 (SMR 014:038/ 040 and SMR 014A: 007)
25 (SMR 014:071)
26 (SMR 014:061)
27 (SMR 022:033)
28 (SMR 022:034)
29 (O' Sullivan 1998, 2000; Fredengren 2002)
30 (SMR 15A:002; O.S. Field Report No. 123)
31 (SMR 014:009 and 010; Davies 1941a, 88; O.S. Field Report No. 97: SMR 014:011)
32 (SMR 14A: 006)
33 (Ó Carragáin 2010)
34 (SMR 013: 001; Colby 1837, 234; Leslie 1937, 238; O.S. Field Notes 22-23, No. 63)
35 (SMR 014: 002; Scheduled; Anon. 1902, 283–284; O.S. Field Report No. 90; *PSAMNI* 194; Reeves 1850, 31–32)
36 (CAF 2013, 38-52)
37 (SMR 022:010; Lewis 1837, I, 662; Munn 1925, 98; O.S. Field Reports No. 153-154)
38 (SMR 014: 016; Gwynn and Hadcock 1970, 374)
39 (SMR 014:015)
40 (SMR 014:017; Davies 1941b, 141; Hamlin 1976, 560)
41 (Colby 1837, 233-234)
42 (SMR 014:026–028)
43 (SMR 022:032)
44 (SMR 022:011; Lewis 1837, I, 662; O.S. Field Report No. 155)
45 (SMR 022:010)
46 (SMR 014:014)
47 (Lacey 2010b; Day *et al* 1996, 43)
48 (ARM 032:006)
49 (see Lacey 1983, 240-298)

The Medieval Period

1 (Harbison 1991, 52-54 and 177)
2 (SMR 014:025; Colby 1837, 24–25; Archdall 1876, Vol. 1, 165–171; Anon. 1902, 286–289; Gwynn and Hadcock 1970, 67–68; Kerr (ed.) 2008, 563–565; Lacy 1990, 24–28, 36–40 and 50–52)
3 (Ó Carragáin 2010, 268)
4 (see Colby 1837, 21–24 and 26–35 for lists of annalistic and documentary references to clergy in Derry from the 12th–early 17th centuries)
5 (Bryson 2001, 143)
6 (SMR 014: 030; Archdall 1876, 171; Colby 1837, 25; Gwynn and Hadcock 1970, 316)
7 (Lacy 1990a, 53)
8 (SMR 014:031; Colby 1837, 25; Archdall 1876, Vol. 1, 171; Gwynn and Hadcock 1970, 224; Fanning 1978; Lacy 1990a, 52–53)

9. (Lacy 1990a, 53)
10. (SMR 014:062; Colby 1837, 26; Archdall 1876, vol. 1, 171; Gwynn and Hadcock 1970, 278)
11. (McNeill 1980, 31; Lacey 1990a, 49)
12. (Hunt 1974, I, 78 and II, Plate 168)
13. (Hunt 1974, 1, 80 and II, Plate 170)
14. (the SMR 014:018 says shoe size 7)
15. (Colby 1837, 233-235)
16. (PSAMNI 193; Fitzpatrick 2004, 236 and Fig. 27)
17. (SMR 014:032; Phillips MSS 1622; Colby 1837, 98–99; Moody 1938, 187; Davies and Swann 1939, 202; Milligan 1948, I, 7–8; Lacy 1990a, 61–62)
18. (Lacy 1999a, 19)
19. (Logue 2007; Logue and O' Neill 2007. See Chapter Three for a fuller account of the excavation)
20. (Anon. 1850; Reeves 1857; Doherty 1902; O' Kelleher and Schoepperle 1918; McGrath 1921; Parlin 1925; Anderson and Anderson 1961; Ryan 1963; Finlay 1979; Macdonald 1985; Herbert 1988; Marsden 1991; Clancy and Márkus 1995; Sharpe (ed.) 1995; Ritchie 1997; Dumville 1999; Bourke 1999, 1997 (ed.); Brown and Clancy, 1999; Jefferies and Devlin (eds) 2000; Bradley 2013 and 1999; Lacey 2013, 2010a, 2004, 2000, 1998 (ed.), 1997)
21. (Lacey 2013, 8)
22. (Ritchie 1997)
23. (Sharpe 1995)
24. (1980, 1)
25. (Lacey (ed.) 1998, 46-47)
26. (Lacey 1997)
27. (Ibid, 40-41)
28. (ibid. 41)
29. (Ó Catháin 1985, 1–12)
30. (Lacy 1997b)
31. (Anon. 1852; Reeves 1850, 188–189)
32. (Lacy 1980, 6)
33. (SMR 14A:003; Colby 1837, 234-236; Davies and Swan 1939, 178 and 202-204; PSAMNI 195; Evans Field Notebook VI, 14; O.S. Field Report No. 104; Marks 1999)
34. (McNeill 1997, 163)
35. (Colby 1837, 234)
36. (CAF 2013, 64-87 and McSparron, pers. comm).
37. (SMR 014:009; Scott forthcoming; Brannon 1987; McNeill 2001, esp. 346–348; O.S. Field Notes 34)
38. (SMR 014:010- discussed in Chapter 1)
39. (Scott et al. 2013)
40. (Scott forthcoming)
41. (SMR 014:015; Reeves 1850, 28-29 and 1857, 19; Anon. 1902, 282–283; O.S. Field Report No. 93; Sampson 1814, 224-225)
42. (Davies 1948)
43. (Falls 1950, Berleth 1978; Morgan 1993; McGurk 1997)
44. (Kelly 2003, 43; McGurk 2006, 61-66)
45. (Kelly 2003, 43-44; McGurk 2006, 61-62)
46. (O' Donovan, 1856, Vol. 6, 2189-2193)
47. (CSPI November 1600 – July 1601, 92-95)
48. (National Archives SP 63/207, Pt. VI, No. 84[90])
49. (Trinity College Dublin, MS 1209, No. 14)
50. (Davies and Swan 1939, 178-208; Lacy et al. 1983, 370–371)
51. (Lacy 1990a, figs on 73 and 78)
52. (SMR 14A:001; O.S. Field Report No.103; Colby 1837, 36 and 236-240; Davies and Swan 1939, 201–202; PSAMNI 194–195)
53. (SMR Tyr 001: 002; Colby 1837, 236; Logue and McHugh 2013)
54. (SMR Tyr 001: 002; Colby 1837, 236; Logue and McHugh 2013)

The Glengalliagh Bell – An Armada legacy?

1. Swann 1949, 12
2. Ridella 2004, 27–41 & McElvogue 2002, 31-50

The Plantation City of Londonderry

1. (Moody 1939; Perceval-Maxwell 1973; Robinson 1984; Bardon 2011)
2. (McGurk 2006, 231-235)
3. (Milligan 1948, 24-27; Curl 1986, 60-62)
4. (ibid, 38)
5. (Ó Baoill 2007)
6. (Colby 1837, 98–100; Hill 1877, 386 and 573–574; Moody 1939, 79-80, 150,160, 171-2, 186, 196 and 254; Chart (ed.) 1940, 193 and Pl. 44; Milligan 1948 and 1950; Rowan 1979, 364–404; D.O.E.N.I. 1977 and 1983, 131; Brannon 1986; Lacey 1990, 92-6; Mitchell 1992, 14; Thomas 1992, 2, 154–162; Scott et al. 2008; NIEA 2007, 2009, 111-112 and 2011; Calley 2013, 92-109).
7. (Milligan 1948, 32-33)
8. (Milligan 1948, 33)
9. (Scott 2011, 146)
10. (Scott et al. 2008)
11. (SMR 014:035; Gilmore in Bennett 2000. Entry No. 96, 24-25. See also Colby 1837, Vol. 1, 42; Derry Journal, 4 April 1980; Milligan 1948, Vol. 1, 124–125; Moody 1939, 254; Roddy 1968)
12. (SMR 014:039; Logue in Bennett 2000b. Entry No. 128, 38)
13. (Horning 2007, 57; Cullen 1981, 65)
14. (For detailed accounts of maps of the city see Camblin 1951 and Ferguson 2005)
15. (Trinity College Dublin, MS 864)
16. (text reproduced in Hill 1877, 573–574)
17. (SMR 014:034; Colby 1837, 102-108; Anon. 1902, 32, 287–288; Moody 1939, 276-277; Anon. 1965 and 2001; Lacy 1990a, 99–101; Curl 2006, 142-149; Calley 2013, 343-353)
18. According to Curl [1986, 399] the Cathedral had 'a western tower crowned by a wooden spire clad with lead…The spire appears to have been demolished before the celebrated siege [of 1698] and the lead was used to make bullets'. See also Calley (2013, 344) who references Dr William King- Anglican Bishop from 1691-1703- as the source of this information. No spire is visible on Thomas Phillips' 1685 perspective of the town [British Library, Maps, K Top 54 33.a]). Perhaps the original spire was removed during the use of the Cathedral as a citadel in the l650s.
19. (Lacey 1990a, 106–109; Kelly 2001)
20. (Scott et al 2008, 77-79)
21. (*ibid* 77)
22. (Farrimond in Bennett 2009. Entry No. 416, 90–91)
23. (Lacey 1981)
24. (*Ibid*, 57)
25. (Dunlop in Bennett 2008. Entry No. 301, 66-67)
26. (Blades 1981, especially fig 6)
27. (Curl 1986, 182-184 and figs 82 and 83)
28. (Ó Baoill 2011; Ó Baoill and Logue 2006)
29. (Lacy in Manning and Hurl 1988 Entry No. 20: section on Richmond Street Area, 71)
30. (SMR 014:034; Brannon in Bennett 2000. Entry No. 95, 24)
31. (SMR 014:064/ 014: 039; Logue in Bennett 2000b. Entry No. 129, 38; Logue and O' Neill 2006)
32. (Hunter 2012)
33. (Lacey in Manning and Hurl 1987/88; Entry No. 20; section on The Diamond, 70)
34. (AE/12/145; McSparron 2013. See Chapter Four and Calley 2013, 301-303 for more information on the church)
35. (Londonderry Sentinel 1936, 22)
36. (Hunter 2012, 16)
37. (Milligan1946, 1948- 1950; Gray 1975; Macrory 1980; Lacy 1989 and 2009; Doherty 1990b, 1998 and 2008; Simms 1999; Kelly 2001; Gormley *et al.* 1980)
38. (Scott et al 2008, 93)
39. (Scott forthcoming)
40. (Logue 2007, 140-142; Logue and O' Neill 2007)
41. (Jamieson in Bennett 2009. Entry No. 410, 89)
42. (Lacey 1981, 60-61)
43. (McSparron in Bennett 2013. Entry No. 159, 44-45)
44. (SMR 014:083)
45. (CAF 2013, 52–63)
46. (CAF 2013, 88-106)
47. (SMR 014:068)
48. (SMR 14A:001)

Epilogue

1. Lacy 1990a, 147–149).
2. (Thomas 2005, Map 17)
3. (Duffy 1983; Hume 2002)
4. (Calley 2013, 64-69)
5. (Calley, *loc.cit*)
6. (Farrimond in Bennett 2012. Entry No. 182, 47; Farrimond in Bennett 2013. Entry No. 160, 45-46)
7. (Bangerter in Bennett 2012. Entry No. 184, 47)

Illustration Credits

The publishers should like to thank the following people and institutions for permission to use their material in this book:

Frontispiece: image of St Columba (Oxford Bodleian Library, University of Oxford, Ms Rawl.B.514 fol iii, verso); Page x: Londonderry Aerial View (Cambridge University Collection of Aerial Photography, Department of Geography, Downing Place); page xvi: View of Londonderry by Henry Brocas (National Library of Ireland, ET D18); Page 2: 'Map of Ulster' pt of 'A true description of the North part of Ireland compiled by Mr Griffin Crocket' (Trinity College, Dublin, MS 1209, 081-Hardiman Atlas, No. 14); Page 6: map produced for the book by the Central Archaeological Fieldwork unit, QUB; Page 21: reconstruction of Thornhill by James Patience; Page 38: map produced for the book by the Central Archaeological Fieldwork unit, QUB; Page 40: page from the Cathach or the Psalter of St Columba (Royal Irish Academy, 12R 33,, Fol 21R); Page 59: Map of 'The Island and the Fort of the Derry', c1600 (National Archives, SP 63/207, Pt. VI, No. 84-90); Page 60: detail from 'A true description of the North part of Ireland compiled by Mr Griffin Crocket' (Trinity College, Dublin, MS 1209, 081-Hardiman Atlas, No. 14); detail from Nicholas Pynnar's 'London-Derry' (Trinity College, Dublin, MS 864); detail from Thomas Raven's 'Plat of the Cittie of London Derrie' 1622 (Lambert Palace Library); Page 72: detail from 'A true description of the North part of Ireland compiled by Mr Griffin Crocket' (Trinity College, Dublin, MS 1209, 081-Hardiman Atlas, No. 14); Page 77: detail from 'The Derry' (Trinity College, Dublin, Ms 2656, 16); Page 88: 'The Iland and forte of the derry' (National Archives, SP 63/207, Pt. VI, No. 84-90); Page 92: detail from 'Loch Swilly and the River Foyle' by Robert Ashby, 1601' (National Archives, MFP 1335-336-1); Page 93: Culmore Fort (Worshipful Company of Drapers of the City of London); Page 94: Doonalong, Tyrone, Ireland (National Archives, SP63-207 Pt-6 (84ii); Page 95 detail from 'A true description of the North part of Ireland compiled by Mr Griffin Crocket' (Trinity College, Dublin, MS 1209, 081-Hardiman Atlas, No. 14); Page 96: detail from 'Loch Swilly and the River Foyle' by Robert Ashby, 1601' (National Archives, MFP 1335-336-1); Page 98: detail from 'A true description of the North part of Ireland compiled by Mr Griffin Crocket' (Trinity College, Dublin, MS 1209, 081-Hardiman Atlas, No. 14); Page 99: Proposal for layout of Derry 1611 (Trinity College, Dublin (Mss 1209-24); Page 102: 'View of Londonderry' by Willem Van Der Hagen, circa 1718-21 is lost painting having disappeared from the Guildhall in Londonderry some years ago; Page 109: photograph of Market Street from the Bigger and McDonald Collection, Derry Central Library; Page 119: photograph of the Grand Parade and Walker Testimonial from the Bigger and McDonald Collection, Derry Central Library; Page 124: Plan of the City of Londonderry by Thomas Raven, 1622 (Lambeth Palace Library); Map of Londonderry made for Pynnar's survey of 1618-19 (Trinity College, Dublin, Ms 1209, No 22); Page 126: Plan of Londonderry, 1625 from 'Ordnance Survey of the County of Londonderry', published in 1835, based on an original in TCD Library; Page 134: map produced for the book by the Central Archaeological Fieldwork unit, QUB; Pages 136-137: 'A perspective drawing by Thomas Phillips from 1685' (British Library, Maps, K Top 54 33.a); Page 138: engraving courtesy of Terence Reeves-Smyth; Page 140: detail of 'View of Londonderry' by Henry Brocas Senior (National Library of Ireland, ET D18); Page 153: detail from 'A perspective drawing by Thomas Phillips from 1685' (British Library, Maps, K Top 54 33.a); Page 158: 'Londonderry before the siege' a plate from 'Ireland Preserv'd or the Siege of Londonderry...written by the Governor' published 1705. The three pull out paintings, plus the watercolour of the early church at Derry (pages 54-55) were specially undertaken for this book by Philip Armstrong (Paint the Past). The colour aerial photographs were taken for this book in 2013 by Gail Pollock, NIEA, whilst all other colour photographs in the book, plus the Dungiven tomb on page 56, were taken by Tony Corey, NIEA.

Appendix

List of licensed archaeological excavations carried out in Derry~Londonderry and its environs, 1976-2011.

1. Junction of Henrietta Street & Long Tower Street (1976). C435157. B. Lacey/U.U.
2. Long Tower Street (1976). C435157. B. Lacey/U.U.
3. NE quadrant of The Diamond (1976). C 435157. B. Lacey/U.U.
4. Fountain Street area (1976). C435157. B. Lacey/U.U.
5. Long Tower Street (1976). C435157. B. Lacey/U.U.
6. NE corner of The Diamond (1977). C435167. B. Lacey/U.U.
7. SW corner of The Diamond (1977). C435167. B. Lacey/U.U.
8. NE corner of The Diamond (1978). C435167. B. Lacey/U.U.
9. Fountain Street (1977; 1979). C435167. B. Lacey/U.U.
10. Abbey Street/ William Street (1977; 1979) C435167. B. Lacey/U.U.
11. Fulton Place/ Long Tower area (1977; 1979) C435167. B. Lacey/U.U.
12. No. 1 Magazine Street (1977; 1979). C435167. B. Lacey/U.U.
13. Richmond Street area (1977; 1979). C435167. B. Lacey/U.U.
14. Castle Street (1978). C435167. B. Lacey/U.U.
15. Nailor's Row (1978). C435167. B. Lacey/U.U.
16. Nos. 33-35 Shipquay (1978). C435167. B. Lacey/U.U.
17. Magazine Street (1978). C435167. B. Lacey/U.U.
18. Shipquay Street/ Richmond Street (1979). C435167. B. Lacey/U.U.
19. Linenhall Street (1980). C435167. B. Lacey/U.U.
20. Derry~Londonderry Walls. Water Bastion. (1983). C435166. N.F. Brannon/NIEA.
21. Straid (1985). C596058. N.F. Brannon/NIEA.
22. 'Creggan Rath' (1987). C425168. J. Hadfield.
23. No. 32 Bishop's Street Within (1988). C434165. N.F. Brannon/NIEA.
24. Shantallow (1988). C452 207. N.F. Brannon/NIEA
25. Ballyarnet Lake, Shantallow (1996). C447215. D.P. Hurl/NIEA.
26. Shantallow (1996). C447 215. D.P. Hurl/NIEA.
27. Site of Millennium Theatre (1998) C436167. N.F. Brannon/NIEA.
28. Millennium Complex, East Wall. C436137. S. Gilmore/NAC Ltd.
29. Shantallow (1998). C44542150. C. McSparron/NAC Ltd.
30. Lough Enagh (1998). C. McSparron/NAC Ltd.
31. Bishop's Street Without (1999). C43211645. P. Logue/AEU: NIEA.
32. Site of Millennium Theatre (1999). C43631674. P. Logue/AEU: NIEA.
33. Thornhill, Ballynashallog and Ballynagard (2000). C45942130. P. Logue/AEU: NIEA.
34. 26-28 Bishop's Street Within (2000). C McConway/ADS Ltd.
35. Fountain Estate. C433164. A. Gahan/ADS Ltd.
36. 23 Bishop's Street Within (2001). C434166. A. Gahan/ADS Ltd.
37. 26-28 Bishop's Street (2001). C434165. C. McConway/ADS Ltd.
38. 8 Castle Street (2001). C434167. A. Gahan/ADS Ltd.
39. The Diamond (2001). 23435 416653. S. Gilmore/NAC Ltd.
40. Fountain Estate (2001) C433165. A. Gahan/ADS Ltd.
41. Woodside Road (2001). C434154. C. McConway/ADS Ltd.
42. Ballyarnet (2001). C434154. C. McConway/ADS Ltd.
43. Ballynashallog (2002). C4594 2130. R. Schulting and J. O'Neill/CAF: QUB.
44. Campsie (2002). C486198. A. Gahan/ADS Ltd.
45. Cam (2002). C466172. R. Halpin/ADS Ltd.

46. Caw (2002). C2460 4183. P. Bowen/ADS.
47. Oakgrove Integrated College, Gransha (2002). C4607 1993. R. Chapple/NAC Ltd.
48. St Columb's Hall, Orchard Street (2002). C436167. C. McConway/ADS Ltd.
49. Maydown Industrial Estate (2002). C483206. A. Gahan/ADS Ltd.
50. Coolkeeragh (2002). C4751 2117. E. Halpin/ADS Ltd.
51. Shantallow (2002). C447215. R. Schulting and J. O'Neill/CAF: QUB.
52. Campsey Industrial Estate, Upper Campsie (2003). C508214. P. Bowen/ADS.
53. Caw (2003). C2460 4180. P. Bowen/ADS.
54. Culmore Water Treatment Plant, Culmore (2003) 24770 42325. C. MacManus/ADS Ltd.
55. Lenamore Road, Ballyarnet (2003). L. Heaney/NAC Ltd.
56. Rear of St Columb's Hall, Orchard Street (2003). C. McConway/ADS Ltd.
57. The Manse, 130 Racecourse Road (2003). C. Dunlop/NAC Ltd.
58. St Patrick's School, Shantallow (2003). S. Gilmore/NAC Ltd.
59. Shipquay Street (2003). S. Gilmore/NAC Ltd.
60. Woodside Road (2003) C4330 1510. C. McConway/ADS Ltd.
61. Ballyarnet (2004). 24470 42190. J. O'Neill/QUB.
62. Shantallow (2004) C4245 1970. P. McCooley/NAC Ltd.
63. Blackthorn Manor phase II, Rosdowney Road (2004) C466173. C. Farrimond/ADS Ltd.
64. Oakgrove Integrated College, Gransha (2004). C4607 1993. R. Chapple/NAC Ltd.
65. Prehen House, grounds of (2005). 24207 41433. C. Breen & D. Rhodes/Univ. of Ulster
66. Synod Hall, London Street (2005). 4345 1650. E. Donnelly/ADS Ltd.
67. Rialto Theatre (2005) 24357 41664. C. Dunlop/NAC Ltd.
68. Ebrington Barracks (2005). C. Long/Gahan & Long Ltd.
69. Galliagh Road Upper, Galliagh (2006). C4300 2150. J. Kovacik and W. Baillie/ ADS Ltd.
70. Ballynagalliah/ proposed Skeoge Link Rd (2006). C. Farrimond/FarrimondMacManus Ltd
71. Ballyoan/Carn/Lisneal (2006). C4635 1820 & C4610 1500. E. Donnelly/ADS Ltd.
72. Artillery Street (2006). C4350 1650. B. Jamieson/ADS Ltd.
73. Bellevue Av/ Maureen Av (2006). 4320 1615. C. Farrimond/Farrimond MacManus Ltd.
74. Buncrana Road Whitehouse Road (2006). 24114.42013. M. Keery.
75. Crescent Link (2006) C463165. D. Sneddon/GUARD
76. Ebrington Barracks (2006). C. Long/Gahan & Long Ltd.
77. Lisneal College, Waterside (2006) 2465 4166. C. Farrimond/Farrimond MacManus Ltd.
78. Siege Heroes Monument/St Columb's Cathedral (2006). Farrimond MacManus Ltd.
79. A2 Dualling, Maydown to the Airport (2006) C52202085/51902090. J..McKee/ADS Ltd.
80. Glengalliagh Distributor Road, Ballynagalliagh (2007). 2425 42111. W. Bailie/ADS Ltd.
81. Campsie Industrial Estate (2007). 25566 42095. C. MacManus/FarrimondMacManus Ltd.
83. Derry~Londonderry City, Public Realm. 2434 4169. C.Farrimond/FarrimondMacManus .
84. Peace Bridge, Clooney (2009). C24334 42674. C. MacManus/FarrimondMacManus Ltd.
85. Haw Road, Coolkeeragh (2009). 247485 421175. V. McClorey/ADS Ltd.
86. Peace Bridge Supports (2009). 2439 4169. Rex Bangerter/Archaeological Diving Co. Ltd.
87. Waterloo Street (2009). 243344 416748. C.Farrimond/FarrimondMacManus Ltd.
88. A2 Maydown to airport scheme. C481200/C544213. M.McGonigle, John Cronin & Ass.
89. Kittybane (2009). C41610 12920. L. Devlin, Gahan & Long Ltd.
90. First Derry Presbyterian Church (2010). C4334016660. C.McSparron/CAF: QUB.
91. Peace Bridge (2010). 243344 417648. C. Farrimond/Farrimond MacManus Ltd.
92. Culmore Road (2010). 246715 42307. C. Farrimond/Farrimond MacManus Ltd.
93. Brunswick Superbowl, Pennyburn (2010) 2434 4185.C.MacManus/FarrimondMacManus.
94. Longfield More (2010) J 25386579/J42184383. R. Logue/CAF: QUB.
95. Lisneal (2011). 246162 416424. K. Ward/ADS Ltd.

Index of People and Places

Adomnán, St. 62, 73
Aileach 39, 41–44, 47, 49, 70, 77–81, 89
Aileach Mór 43
Altnagelvin 49
Anglesey (Wales) 35
Annals of the Four Masters 39, 58, 62, 86
Annals of Ulster 39, 58, 59, 62, 76, 81
Antrim (County) 10, 11, 20, 21, 26, 44, 102,
Antrim, Earl of 109, 156, 157
Apprentice Boys of Derry 110, 120, 121, 131, 156, 159,
Ard-Macha/Armagh 37, 40, 60
Ard-sratha /Ardstraw (Co. Tyrone) 59
Ashbrook House 81
Atlantic Ocean 1, 3, 8, 66
Augustine, St. 39, 58, 62, 66, 74, 76, 99, 120, 123, 124, 142
Avish 32

Baker, Captain John 103
Balloughry 46
Ballyarnett 11, 26, 27, 28, 29
Ballyarnett Lake 12, 27
Ballyharry (Co. Antrim) 24
Ballymagrorty 30, 32, 49
Ballynagalliagh 46
Ballynagard 11, 29
Ballynashallog 11, 163
Ballyoan 5, 29, 30, 32, 33
Bann (River) 6, 59
Belfast 32, 94, 138, 139, 163, 169
Bellarmino, Cardinal Roberto 85
Belmont House 65, 70
Belmont School 70
Bennett, Isabel *vi*, 3
Benson, Peter *xi*, 77, 103
Bernard, Dr. Walter 41
Bishop of Raphoe 63
The Bogside 116, 120, 157, 167
Book of Durrow 52
Boom Hall 163
Boyne (River) 34, 114
Brecan, St. 48, 59
Bristol 66, 142, 144, 145
Brockley 10
Buncrana 31
Richard de Burgo (de Burgh), The Red Earl of Ulster 57, 63
Burt 2, 9, 87, 90
Burt Castle, Co. Donegal 90, 91

Caechscuile 39
Cairnes, David 105

Calgach 1, 34, 39, 60
Campsey Lower 47
Campsey Upper 11, 16, 31
Cannice (Cainnech), St. 49, 59
Canons Regular 58, 62, 76
Carndonagh 37, 48, 51, 52, 97
Carrakeel 47
Carrickfergus (Co. Antrim) 59, 102, 109, 142
Cathach, The 40, 73
Caw 16, 34
Cecil, Sir Robert 87
Cenél Conaill 38, 41, 59, 63, 73, 76
Cenél nEógain 38, 39, 41, 43, 62, 63, 76
Centre for Archaeological Fieldwork (CAF), Queen's University Belfast *vi*, *xiii*, 48, 94
Centre for Maritime Archaeology at the University of Ulster, The 94
Charles I, King 129
Charles II, King 130, 146
Chichester, Sir Arthur 77
Chichester, Thomas 90
Christ Church Cathedral, Dublin 88
Cistercians 52
City of Derry Airport 16, 31
City of London 2, 101, 111, 120, 132
Clampernow 30
Clancarty, Earl of 121, 159
Cloghole 13, 14, 16, 17
Clonard (County Meath) 54, 73
Clondermot 2, 81
Clooney Church 48, 51
Cocket, Griffin 2, 60, 61, 72, 88, 95, 98
Colby, Thomas 49, 70
Coleraine 6, 59, 62, 101, 102
Cologne-Frechen (Germany) 85
Colm Cille, St./ Colum Cille, St./ Columba, St. *xi*, 1, 3, 32, 39, 40, 49, 52, 54, 57, 58, 59, 62, 70–74, 76
Colton, John (Archbishop of Armagh) 76
Coolkeeragh 11, 29
Coote, Sir Charles 130
Cork 121, 138, 156, 170
Coshquin 46
Courcy, John de 59
Creevagh Upper 30
Creggan 117, 167
Creggan Hill 116, 157
Cú Chulainn 34
Cúl Dreimmne (Co. Sligo), Battle of 73
Culmore 46, 86, 93, 164
Culmore Fort 77, 89, 90, 92, 93, 103, 163, 164
Culmore Point 86, 92, 93
Currynierin 11, 28, 81
Cushendall (Co. Antrim) 10

Dáire Calgach 34
Daire Coluim Cille 39
Dál Araidi (Dal Riada) 39
Davies, Oliver 81
Dearg-Bruach church (Gransha) 27
Deer Parks Farms (Co. Antrim) 44
The Derrie 2, 63, 99
'island' (of Derry) 1, 35, 48, 49, 63, 86
Island of Derry 35, 57, 66, 71, 74, 77, 90, 92, 164

Derry~Londonderry: Architecture and places
- The Apprentice Boys Memorial Hall 121, 159
- The Augustinian Abbey 39
- The *Caiseal-an-urlair* 58
- Cemetery of St Martin 62
- The Chapter House (St. Columb's Cathedral) vi, 129, 159, 170
- The Convent of St. Mary 62
- Craigavon Bridge 51, 169
- The Custom House 127, 167
- The Corporation Hall 107, 127
- The Dominican Priory 63, 87
- *Dubh Regles* Church (*Duibreiclés Coluim Cille*) 39, 58, 59, 63, 74, 76, 86, 105, 123, 124
- First Derry Presbyterian Church 142, 161
- Foyle Bridge 157
- The Franciscan Friary 63
- The Guildhall 105, 169
- The Long Tower 39, 49, 58, 63, 74, 76, 87
- Long Tower Church 49, 74, 76, 167, 170
- Long Tower Primary School 76
- Lumen Christi College 137, 157, 170
- Corn and Butter Market 121
- The Millennium Complex 108, 122, 17
- The Millennium Theatre 122, 139
- O'Doherty tower house 87, 88, 124
- The Peace Bridge 105, 169, 171
- Pennyburn Mill 157
- *Port na Long* (The Ship Quay) 74, 105
- Presbyterian Meeting House 161
- Rialto Theatre 138
- The Richmond Centre 126
- 'The Righthand-wise Turn'/ *An t-Iomodh Deisiul* 74
- St. Columb's Wells/ St Colm's Wells 59
- The 'Siege Heroes' Mound 131, 135
- The *Tempull Mór* church 58, 59, 63, 74, 76, 82, 87
- Tower Museum 30, 63, 65, 70, 71, 72, 75, 105, 123, 124
- The War Memorial 105, 106, 107, 109, 121
- The Walker memorial pillar 118, 119, 120
- The Well of St. Adomnán 62
- The Windmill 123, 124, 137, 157, 167
- Windmill Hill 114, 157
- YMCA gym 122

Derry~Londonderry: Gates
- Bishop's Gate (*Bishopps Gate*, 1622) 114, 117, 123, 139, 156, 157, 159
- Butcher's Gate (*no name, 1622; referred to as New Gate elsewhere*) 109, 116, 121, 123
- Castle Gate 105, 121
- City Gate 121
- East Wall 122
- Ferryquay Gate (*Ferry Gate*, 1622) 109, 110, 111, 123
- Magazine Gate 71, 105, 121
- New Gate 105, 111, 114, 121, 123
- Shipquay Gate (*Water Gate*,1622) 105, 106, 108, 123, 124, 126, 137

Derry~Londonderry: Streets and Roads
- Abbey Street 63
- Artillery Street 161
- Bank Place 122
- Bishop's Street Within (*Queene's Street*, 1622) 114, 117, 123
- Bishop's Street Without 71, 114, 126, 139, 142, 159
- Bridge Street 109
- Butcher Street (*Shambles Street*, 1622) 123
- Charlotte Street 76
- The Diamond 105, 106, 107, 109, 121, 123, 124, 126, 139, 140, 141, 159
- Fahan Street 62
- Ferryquay Street (*Gracious Street*, 1622) 123, 124, 126
- Fountain Street 123, 126, 142
- Fox's Corner 62
- Foyle Street 108, 121, 122, 123
- Lecky Road 49, 62
- London Street 127
- Linenhall Street 122, 126, 135, 138, 139, 161
- Long Tower Street 58, 74, 76, 77, 126
- Magazine Street 74, 76, 139, 161
- Magazine Street Upper 161
- Newmarket Street 108, 109, 122
- Orchard Street 108
- Palace Street 142
- Richmond Street 139, 141
- Rossville Street 62, 63
- Shipquay Square/ Guildhall Square 105
- Shipquay Street (*Silver Street*, 1622) 123, 124, 139, 141
- Society Street 58, 121, 159
- William Street 63

Derry~Londonderry: Walls
- Artillery Bastion (*Lord Deputy's Bulwark*, 1622; *Ferry Bastion* 1689) 109, 111
- Church Bastion (*King James' Bulwark*, 1622; *Church Bastion*, 1689) 111–116, 156, 159
- Coward's Bastion (*Lord Chichester's Bulwark*, 1622; *Coward's Bastion*, 1689) 121

- Double Bastion (*Prince Charles' Bulwark, 1622; Double Bastion, 1689*) 103, 116–118, 120, 156, 159
- Gunner's Bastion (*Mayor of Londonderry's Bulwark, 1622; Gunner's Bastion, 1689*) 121
- Hangman's Bastion 121
- New Gate Bastion (*London Bulwark, 1622; New Gate Bastion, 1689*) 108–110
- Royal Bastion (*Lord Docwra's Bulwark, 1622; Royal Bastion, 1689*) 119–121
- Water Bastion (*Governor of the Plantation's Bulwark, 1622; Water Bastion, 1689*) 103, 108, 121, 123
- Grand Parade 117–120
- The 'Platform' 121
- The Ravelin 159
- Terreplein 105
- The Turas (Columban pilgrimage route) 74

Derry City Council Heritage and Museum Service *xiii*, 94
Devon, North 139, 141, 142, 144, 147
Doddington, Capt. Sir Edward 103
Doire 1, 35, 54, 58, 59, 62, 73
Doire Calgach/ Doire Calgaigh 1, 39, 60
Doire Colmcille 1, 54, 59, 60, 73, 171
Docwra, Sir Henry 3, 57, 59, 63, 72, 77, 78, 80, 86-92, 94, 95, 97, 99, 102, 105, 120, 121, 164
Dominicans 63
Donagh Cross (aka St. Patrick's Cross) 51
Donegal (County) *xi*, 2, 3, 9, 21, 26, 27, 30, 37, 38, 40, 41, 48, 50, 51, 54, 57, 62, 63, 71, 76, 82, 83, 86, 91, 101, 103, 169, 171
Down (County) 21, 54, 73
Downhill 21, 170
Druim Cett (Limavady), Synod of 73
Dunaff Head (Donegal) 9
Dunnalong 77, 89, 94, 95
Dunnalong Fort 91, 95, 96
Dungiven 28, 44, 45, 58, 70
Durrow (Co. Offaly) 52, 73

Earl-Bishop of Derry (Frederick Augustus Hervey) 129, 138, 170
Ebrington Barracks 48, 157
Edenappa (Co. Armagh) 51
Edenreagh Beg 17
Edward II, King 63
Eglinton 59
Elagh (Aileach) Castle *xiii*, 41, 77–81, 86, 89, 97
Elagh More 17, 43, 77
Elizabeth I, Queen 63, 81
Emain Macha (Navan Fort) 34
Enagh 15, 16, 46, 59
Enagh Church/Domnach Dola 49, 81
Enagh (Lough) 8, 9, 12, 15, 28, 29, 32, 47, 80
Enagh East (Lough) 12, 47, 81, 82
Enagh West (Lough) 29, 81

Erne (River) 34

Fahan 51
Faughanvale 59
Febail (Lough Foyle) 39, 40
Fincairn 46
Finnian, St. 40, 54, 71, 73
Fitton, Rotsel 59, 81
Floudd, Captain Ellis 77
Foyle (Estuary) 1, 9, 21
Foyle (Lough) 1, 7, 8, 9, 21, 39, 41, 46, 63, 87, 90, 93, 96, 108, 164, 169
Foyle (River) 1, 2, 7, 8, 13, 15, 19, 26, 27, 29, 30, 34, 35, 38, 39, 51, 59, 70, 74, 76, 77, 80, 86, 91, 92, 93, 99 105, 108,114, 121, 138, 157, 163, 167, 169, 170, 171
Foyle Civic Trust 94
France 8, 66, 71, 141, 142, 149, 156
Franciscans 63
Frechen (Germany) 85, 142

Galloway (Scotland) 62
Garonne, River (France) 8
Gartan 54, 71
Glenderowen 17, 46
Glengalliagh Bell 97
Glengalliagh Hall 97
Gobnascale 29, 51, 157
Gordon, Rev. James 109
Gortgranagh 17
Gortica 17, 32
Gortinure 46
Gransha 27, 30, 59
Green Island (Lough Enagh East) 47, 80, 82
Greenan Mountain 41, 43
Greencastle (Donegal) 9
Greencastle (a.k.a. Northburgh) 57, 63
Grianán of Aileach, The 41–43, 44, 47, 49, 70, 79, 81, 89

The Hamilton Family 97
Haughey's Fort (Co. Armagh) 26
Henry, Françoise 52
Holland 141, 142
Holywell Hill 30
The Honourable The Irish Society 101, 102, 131, 132, 155, 163
Hunt, John 58, 65, 70

Inch 2, 9, 77
Inishowen 8, 9, 38, 51, 62, 86, 97
Iona/Hy (Scotland) 54, 73
Islandmagee 24
Italy 141

James 1, King 2, 101

James II, King 111, 120, 156, 157, 161
Johnson, Thomas 105
La Juliana (ship) 97

Kells (Co. Meath) 58
Killea 48
Kilnasaggart (Co. Armagh) 51
Kincora (Co. Clare) 43
King, Bishop 129
Kinsale (Co. Cork) 156
Kinnegoe Bay 97
Kittybane 46
Knockdhu (Co. Antrim) 26
Knowth (Co. Meath) 19

Lacey, Brian *vi*, 3, 43, 73, 74
Letterkenny 71
Limavady 73
Limerick (County) 8
Lisdillon 17
Lisglass 32, 51
Lismore or The Trench 32
London 2, 101, 103, 111, 120, 127, 132, 142
London Companies – The Mercers, Drapers, Salters, Vintners, Grocers, Haberdashers, Ironmongers, Merchant Taylors, Goldsmiths, Skinners, Fishmongers and Clothworkers 91, 93, 101, 102, 111, 164
London Salters Company 111
Longfield More 31
Lundy, Robert 108, 160, 167

Mac Ainmire, Áed 73
Mac Cathmhaoil / McCamayll, Dr. William 76
Mac Cerbail, Díarmait 73
Mac Ciárain, Fiachrach 39
Mac Lochlainn 38, 43, 71, 76
Mac Lochlainn, Aedh 62
MacLochlainn, Ardgal 59
Mac Lochlainn, Diarmait 62
Mac Lochlainn, Donal (King of Aileach) 43
Mac Lochlainn, Mael-Sechlainn 62
Mac Lochlainn, Muircertach 58, 62
Mac Randal, Rory 62
MacUchtry, Thomas 62
McNeill, T.E. 77
Maghera 62
Managh Beg 46
'The Marigold Stone' (Carndonagh) 52, 53
Martin-camp (France) 71
Mary, Queen 161
Maydown 16, 29, 31
Mitchelburne, Colonel John 61, 159
Monuments and Buildings Record (MBR) 3
Mount Sandel 6, 7, 9, 59
Movilla (Co. Down) 73

The Mountjoy (ship) 159
Muff 2, 27, 30
Murray, Adam 105, 158, 160

Neville, Captain Thomas 105
New Buildings 46, 49
Nine Years' War (1594-1603) 57, 59, 82
Northern Ireland Environment Agency (NIEA) *xiii*, 3, 21, 30, 32, 94, 122, 163
Niall Noígíallach (Niall of the Nine Hostages) 38

O'Brien, Murtough (king of Munster) 41, 43
Ua/ O'Brolcháin, Flaithbertach 54, 58
Ua/ O'Brolcháin, Mael Coluim 58
O'Cahan/ Ua Cathain 62
O'Deery 76
O'Doherty, Sir Cahir 57, 90, 91, 121
O'/ Ua Dochartaich, Echmarcach 59
O'Doherty, Sir John 77, 90, 91
O'Donnell 38, 57, 63, 70, 82, 121
O'Donnell, Calvagh 70
O'Donnell, (Red) Hugh 82, 86
O'Donnell, Manus 70, 73
O'Donnell, Nechtan 77
O'/ Ua Maeldoraidh, Flaithbertach 59
O'Neill/ Uí Néill 38, 62, 70, 82, 86, 91, 94
Uí Néill/ O'Neill, Northern 38, 41, 43, 79
O'Neill, Conaill 38
O'Neill, Conall Gulban, son of Niall 38
O'Neill, Eoghan Roe 130
O'Neill, Hugh 82
O'Neill, Niall 62
O'Neill, Owen, son of Niall 38
O'Neill, Shane 82
Oakgrove Integrated College, Gransha 27
Oldfert, Wilbrant (Wilbrand Oldfers) 143

Panton, Captain 102
Paulett, Sir George 88
The Peter (ship) 143
Petty, William 143
Phillips, Sir Thomas 105, 137
Poulnabrone (County Clare) 21
Prehen 29
Prehen House *xiii*, 162, 163
Public Record Office Northern Ireland (PRONI) 126
Pynnar, Nicholas 60, 61, 123, 124, 126
Pyrenees 8

Queen's University Belfast 48, 94, 163

Raeren (Germany) 142, 149
Randolph, Colonel Edward 61, 82
Raphoe 54, 63, 170
Rathlin Island 10

Raven, Captain Thomas 61, 72, 93, 99, 103, 105,124, 126, 139
'Roaring Meg' (cannon) 116
de Rosen, Marshal Conrad 116
Rossnagalliagh 49
Rough Island (Enagh Lough East) 8, 12, 28, 29, 47, 80, 82

St. Augustine's Church of Ireland church 99
St. Columb's/ St. Brecan's Church 48, 59
St. Columb's Cathedral vi, 62, 63, 97, 103, 111, 114, 117, 127–129, 130, 131, 137, 138, 157, 159, 167, 170
St. Columb's Park 48
St. Columb's Stone 49, 70
St. Comgal's Church 49
St Mary's Abbey, Dungiven 70
St. Patrick 70
St. (San) Severo, Bishop of Barcelona 97
Saintonge (France) 66, 71, 142, 149
Scotland 54, 71, 73, 154
Scriptorium at Derry 39
Shantallow 11, 29, 30,31, 46, 64, 65, 70
Skeoge 28
Smithes, George 102
Spain 8, 82, 141
Spanish Armada 97
Springham, Mathias 102
Staffordshire 142, 144, 145, 146
Strabane (Co. Tyrone) 62
Stradreagh Beg 12
Streedagh Strand (Co. Sligo) 97
Swilly (Lough) *xi*, 9, 41, 43, 77, 87, 89, 92, 96

Tailtiu/ Teltown (Co. Meath) 73
Templemore (parish) 2, 58, 76
Termonbacca 46
Thornhill *xi*, 11, 13, 15, 16, 18–25, 27
Thornhill College 19
Tievebulliagh 10
Tindal, Nicolas 76
Tír Conaill 38, 70
Toome/ Tuaim (Co. Antrim) 59
La Trinidad Valencera (ship) 97
Tully 31
Tyrone (County) 21, 38, 41, 59, 62, 82, 86, 91, 101
Tyrone/Tir-Eogain 38, 59, 62

Ulster Coarse Ware pottery 71
Urrismenagh (Donegal) 9

Vaughan, Sir John 127
The Vikings 37, 39, 40, 41

Wales 35, 149
Walker, Rev. George 109, 120, 121, 158, 159
Waring Street (Belfast) 139, 139
Waterman House, Belfast (NIEA) 3
Westerwald (Germany) 142, 149
Whitehorse Hotel 16
Whitehouse 30
William of Orange, King 156, 167
Woodside Road 29

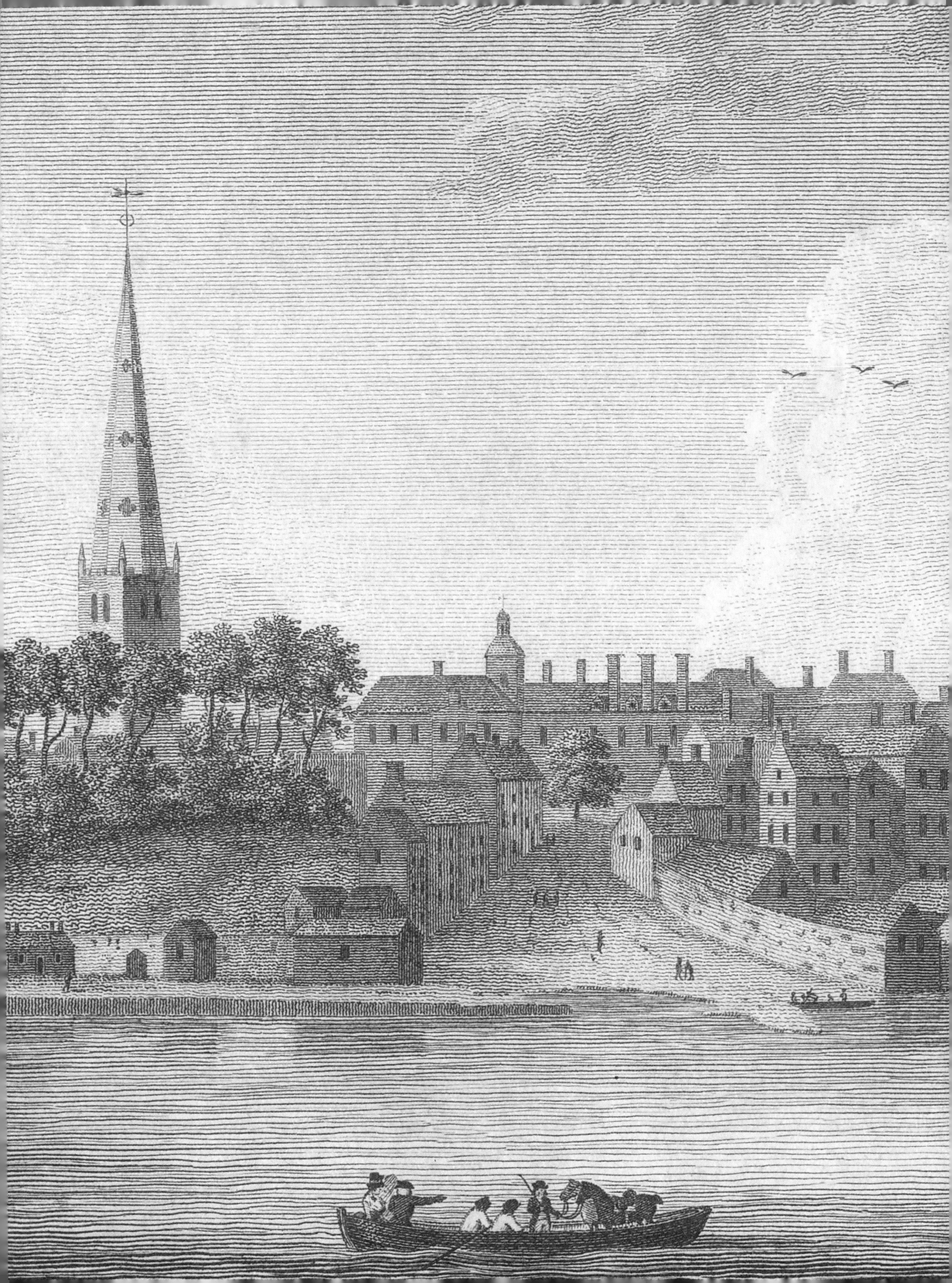